Mister Rogers and Philosophy

Popular Culture and Philosophy®   Series Editor: George A. Reisch

For full details of all Popular Culture and Philosophy® books, visit www.opencourtbooks.com.

Popular Culture and Philosophy®

Mister Rogers and Philosophy

Wondering through the Neighborhood

Edited by
ERIC J. MOHR AND
HOLLY K. MOHR

OPEN COURT
Chicago

Volume 128 in the series, Popular Culture and Philosophy ®, edited by George A. Reisch

To find out more about Open Court books, visit our website at www.opencourtbooks.com.

Open Court Publishing Company is a division of Carus Publishing Company, dba Cricket Media.

Copyright © 2020 by Carus Publishing Company, dba Cricket Media

First printing 2020

Mister Rogers and Philosophy: Wondering through the Neighborhood

ISBN: 978-0-8126-9477-2
Library of Congress Control Number: 2019946627

This book is also available as an e-book (ISBN 978-0-9481-9).

Contents

Welcome to the Neighborhood

HOLLY K. MOHR

The summer between my junior and senior years of high school, I received a giant envelope in the mail. Inside were excerpts from Plato's *Republic* and a copy of the *Apology*, readings for my college prep summer program. As I dove into Plato's writings, I realized I'd been philosophizing since at least elementary school, when I used to write down my questions and insights about life in a journal after bedtime. I'd crouch near my bedroom closet, turning on its small light, cracking the door just enough to write clearly.

Re-watching *Mister Rogers' Neighborhood* as an adult, I realize Fred Rogers would not have been at all surprised about my childhood "philosophy journal." Wondering, as Fred reminds us in episode after episode, is something children do best. And the capacity to wonder (to seek meaning, to stay curious) is exactly what philosophy is about.

Mister Rogers looks straight at the camera, talking directly to his child viewer. He takes children seriously, teaching them (and all the rest of us) that they matter, that they have something real to contribute. Mister Rogers teaches us that a child is a full person, not some inferior being simply waiting to become an adult.

In today's competitive culture, we often speak as though only adults with certain occupations can really derive or contribute meaning to life. We create hierarchies for ourselves and others, deeming some work "creative" and others mundane. But for Mister Rogers, we *all* matter. Mister Rogers visits with factory workers, farmers, teachers, children with disabilities, as well as those in the creative arts, showing delight and respect in all these encounters. His visits show us that wonder is readily available and it can be operative in every work and life situation. Our lives and our imaginations really need not remain so limited.

Where does Mister Rogers return after visiting people from all these walks of life? To the Neighborhood, of course! Because as Mister Rogers also shows us, we find and make meaning *together*, in community. Wonder is not an exclusively solitary experiment—it affects how we live and exist with one another. This is the paradox both of philosophy and of *Mister Rogers' Neighborhood*: while I am unique and unrepeatable (and so are you), we make sense of life (even when it's scary) and live most creatively when we share ourselves with each other.

It just so happens to be a beautiful day in the neighborhood. Won't you be my neighbor?

Thanks

Many thanks to all those who helped with the production of this book.

We owe a debt of gratitude especially to the other authors of this volume for their thoughtful contributions and for seeing their work through, and to David Ramsay Steele and George Reisch at Open Court for their work on, and support of, this project.

Also, a special thanks to Roberta Schomburg and Dana Winters at the Fred Rogers Center for their support and collaboration, and to Matthew Shiels and Fred Rogers Productions for permission to use copyrighted material, including song lyrics.

And finally, to our children, Juliana, Andrew, and Sage, for their monumental research help by watching episodes upon episodes of Mister Rogers' Neighborhood with us. Thank you, Juliana, for your indexing assistance.

I

Did You Know It's All Right to Wonder?

1
The Wonderful Feeling of Being Alive

JACOB GRAHAM

The joyful and unwavering light in Fred Rogers's eyes reminds us to open our own, to explore, to ponder, to enjoy ourselves and our world. The spring in Mister Rogers's step as he leads his television neighbors to a zoo, a farm, a grocery store, or even his kitchen, bespeaks an excitement about the world and the nexus of ordinary things and people that make it up.

He helps us to see that the ordinary world is extraordinary, if we open ourselves to it and look at it as his eyes do. Mister Rogers opens a door for us and leads us gently behind the scenes of everyday life and back again. He asks the right questions—the sorts of questions a child might ask—and does not succumb to the prejudice that ordinary things are obvious or unworthy of attention. The education of *Mister Rogers' Neighborhood* is one rooted in wonder, a feeling that Plato (428–348 B.C.E.) said was the beginning of philosophy. Fred Rogers invites children to live and linger in that feeling, which is already familiar to them, and invites adults to remember it.

So, I invite you, book-chapter neighbor, to explore this feeling of wonder with me. Let's ponder this feeling that drives us to ask about ourselves and who we are. Let's dwell awhile with this feeling that has us asking how and why our world is the way that it is, but also allows us to see it for what it is. With Mister Rogers as our guide, let's learn to make something new of ourselves and our world. At its root, *philosophy* means "love of wisdom." If philosophy is a love of wisdom, and wonder is the beginning of it, then let's be beginners together, unafraid to stop, look, and listen to the ordinary world.

Behind the Scenes, on the Scene

In an episode during the week's theme of "work," Mister Rogers takes us behind the scenes of his studio (episode 1530). This happens just after the opening song of the show. Mister Rogers reminds us that he's been talking a lot about work and wants to show us where he works. The camera pans away from the cozy little house into the expansive workshop floor of the studio, with all the big cameras, coworkers milling, and my personal favorite, Johnny Costa's jazz trio, who played every single note of the show live.

We're able to see that it is a *studio*, and he names it as such, with gravity and grace. With this word, we're transported into a new world—the world that allows the world of *Mister Rogers' Neighborhood* to be. Mister Rogers is often called courageous and radical for his commentary on the most serious and difficult areas of life (divorce, race, war, disabilities), and rightfully so. When I was watching this episode with my daughter, I thought that he was equally courageous to allow children to go behind the scenes, if only for a few moments. Mister Rogers is unafraid to show us the ordinary world in its surfaces and also the people and the machinery that underpin those surfaces.

My great grandmother lived with my family while I was growing up and had a significant hand in raising me. With her, I never felt that I was being treated as just a child. I was always taken seriously. It's the same with Mister Rogers. He is not trying to trick his television neighbors. He feels no need to maintain any illusion that, say, his studio house is a real house, or that the Neighborhood of Make-Believe is anything other than make-believe.

He can shift seamlessly between these worlds while recognizing, and allowing his audience to recognize, what he is doing. Likewise, Mister Rogers then comfortably and seamlessly moves back to his cozy studio house after showing us the studio. He tells us that it takes a lot of people to make a television program. Then, he recognizes the fact that children also do their own work, and we are taken to see some of the different types of work that children do.

After seeing some of the things that children do for their work—playing the piano, feeding a pet, setting the table, painting—Mister Rogers tells us that some of the work children do seems like play. Unabashedly, he tells us that "playing and understanding things is a big part of children's work" (we'll come back to this thought). As if this weren't taking the child seriously enough, he continues by talking about what he did as a child. He liked to play with puppets. He then pulls out some puppets from his bag, instantly recognizable as some of the most important figures in Make-Believe: Queen Sarah, X the Owl, Daniel Striped Tiger, and King Friday. For all of these but Daniel, whom Mister Rogers says is sometimes too shy to talk, he does the voices as he shows the puppets. The viewer can see the man behind the curtain.

There is much that is philosophical about Fred Rogers, but what we see here is the essential attitude of the philosopher at play. The philosopher is ready to open him or herself to the world to see it for what it is. The questions the philosopher asks are guided by the love of seeing things as they are, understanding them for what they are, which sometimes requires sweeping away illusion, but sometimes inviting it in, fully recognizing what it is. If it is a studio, let it be a studio. If it is make-believe, let it be make-believe. The feeling that drives these investigations into, and appreciations of, the world, whose goal is ultimately to see and understand it as it is, is wonder. Without it, the world is a colorless stage of business and busyness wherein we forget what is real.

At the Root of Loving Wisdom

Plato's neighborhood was ancient Athens. Plato wrote dialogues, much like plays, in which Socrates (469–399 B.C.E.) is almost always allotted a starring role. That he wrote dialogues rather than, say, treatises, is important. This way, Plato could imitate the flux and flow of real, living conversation, the way Mister Rogers moves fluidly from one topic to the next, while still maintaining an overarching theme.

Knowledge is the theme of Plato's dialogue, *Theaetetus*. In it, Socrates and Theaetetus are wanting to understand what knowledge is and is not. What makes knowledge, knowledge? Early in their discussion, Theaetetus reports feeling giddy or dizzy in the excitement of his wonder. Socrates replies that this feeling is "very characteristic of a philosopher: philosophy has no other starting-point." Wonder is the beginning of philosophy.

It is important for us to notice, first, that Plato calls wonder a feeling (the Greek word is *pathe*). It is not, first and foremost, a cognitive disposition like curiosity or inquisitiveness. It is a feeling, a mood, a lens through which we may view ourselves and our world. After that, Plato is tightlipped about the nature of wonder, so it'll be up to us to work through it together. If it is a feeling, and if, like Theaetetus, it can leave us giddy or dizzy over what we're wondering about, then we'll need to explore that feeling and see what we can do with it.

While wonder is not most properly a cognitive disposition, it may lead to one. It may drive us to ask questions about our world, much like the ones we hear in *Mister Rogers' Neighborhood*: what are our feelings and where do feelings come from?; how do electric cars work?; how are pretzels made? If, however, wonder is a feeling that can generate such questions and, thus, is distinct from them, what sort of a feeling is it and how might it arise? Let's turn to Mister Rogers for some clues.

"It's such a good feeling to know you're alive." That line of Mister Rogers's song is sufficient unto itself, although it plays its role among other lines in the closing song. When we ask questions out of mere curiosity, it is possible that we ask them just to ask them or out of a bare desire just to know. This is fine. It is part of who we are. Wonder, though, overtakes us, and we ask questions out of a raw and beautiful confrontation with the being of ourselves and the world. In wonder, we come up against the world and ourselves to encounter the strangeness and excitement of it all. What is familiar becomes new.

This good feeling of knowing we're alive just is the feeling of wonder and, as many feelings do, it has a tendency not only to perpetuate itself, but to urge us into action, to make a snappy, new day. But it doesn't urge us into busyness and noise. It urges us, rather, to slow down, despite our giddiness; for, this giddiness isn't the sort to bring disquiet and noise, but rather calm and equanimity. In wonder, there is the giddily quiet fascination that we even *are* at all.

Slowing Down and Listening

In what Socrates says is a "digression" in his conversation with Theaetetus, a digression that goes on for several pages (Plato's hint that it's actually important business), he lays out what he thinks are some of the distinctive characteristics of a philosopher. In what is on course to become a rather long conversation, Socrates pauses to mention that they've found themselves in yet another, bigger—perhaps too big—discussion. Another person who enters the discussion, called Theodorus, nevertheless encourages Socrates to carry on because "we've got plenty of time." Socrates responds that having plenty of time, as opposed to moving too quickly through life and being a busybody, is characteristic of the philosopher. Thus, the digression begins.

The ancient Athenians were litigious. Have a problem? Then learn to speak smoothly and suavely enough to resolve it in court. Socrates drives a wedge between the characteristics of a philosopher and the characteristics of those who spend their time in court.

> Philosophers always have . . . plenty of time; they carry on their discussions in peace and with time to spare . . . It doesn't matter at all whether they talk for a long time or a short one, provided only that they hit on that which is. (lines 172d3–11)

Contrary to busybodies who spend their time in court, those who are "hurried on by the clock," philosophers are slow. They must be slow if they are to be thorough and careful with the most important questions of life, the ones about just what the nature of something is.

Socrates says that the philosopher "has been brought up in freedom and leisure," and may not be accustomed to everyday tasks; someone like Fred Rogers, perhaps, who grew up with leisure and was unable to use a screwdriver, as one commenter says in the documentary, *Won't You Be My Neighbor?* The ancient Greek word for "leisure" was *skole*, whence we get our word "school." We must have time and space to explore and learn. We must have time and space to wonder and enter into the sort of reflection that hits on that which is.

Also in the documentary, Margy Whitmer, who was a producer of *Mister Rogers' Neighborhood*, paraphrasing the words of a former director, said, "If you take all the elements that make good television and do the exact opposite, you have *Mister Rogers' Neighborhood*. Low production values. Simple set. Unlikely star. Yet, it worked, because he was saying something really important."

It's no secret that Fred Rogers was not the run-of-the-mill television star. His will was strong, the documentary tells us, and what he willed was an entirely new space in television. It was a space in which viewers were encouraged to take their time and be slow, sometimes even in silence. As Max King said, "Fred used time totally differently" in his show. His slow pace went hand-in-hand with silence, which David Newell called Fred's "delight." These basic elements of slowness and silence are necessary to explore, to think, to strive to understand.

Notice where we have now situated philosophy, with Plato's and Mister Rogers's help. Philosophy is the *love* of wisdom and it begins in a *feeling* that we call wonder. This feeling comes about in the recognition of our own being, of the world's being, and our being part and parcel of it. For that feeling to proliferate and drive genuine questioning, it needs its proper pace and space. To wonder, we need to be slow and dwell in the quiet space of listening.

In a hurried and harried world, one cannot wonder. We need space and the free play of reflection to ask questions and to feel giddy or excited about them. Earlier, we heard Mister Rogers tell us that children have work, too, even though it's different from grown-up work. Play and understanding things is a child's work. I would like to suggest that it is also a grown-up's work.

The play of children, you might have noticed, can sometimes be quite serious. Is the play of thinking and figuring things out not the same? Adults need time and space to play in, reflect upon, and understand the world and ourselves. We need time to wonder. We should be able not only to cover new ground, but to cover what appears to be the same ground—space to look at ourselves and the world, to breathe a sigh, and say, "all of this *is*." Like Johnny Costa's trio, improvising over the same tunes for years and years, we need space and quiet to make the same tunes new, to let them be heard as new. We need space to start over and do it all again, to make a snappy, new day, and to be good beginners.

In Plato's *Theaetetus*, Socrates more than once says that they'll need to start over from the beginning with their conversation. They need to resume the feeling of wonder. Is this not what Mister Rogers does for us? As he says, the opening song holds an invitation open for us to be his neighbor. This means that we are to join him in our pursuit of play and understanding. The closing song reminds us that we are alive, that we are free and ready to wonder, and indicates the beginning and starting again that is required for us to wonder again ("I'll be back, when the day is new . . ."). This wonder allows us to ask questions. But the very nature of a question is that it wants a response. For that, we need to be quiet and listen, and also to take care to let the world be what it is. What we seek with our hows, whys, and our whats is a better understanding of ourselves and our world—to let it be seen and heard more clearly for what it is, not to cover it back up with more noise.

The (Extra)Ordinary

Plato's student, Aristotle (384–322 B.C.E.), agreed with his teacher that philosophy begins in wonder. In his *Metaphysics*, a work about the nature of being or reality, Aristotle says that philosophy begins in wonder, wondering first about obvious difficulties and then about "greater matters," such as astronomical phenomena. The goal of this wonder is to escape from ignorance and simply to know, for no other end or purpose than to know. If you have a burning question, then you are wondering, and this wondering will be quelled when your questions are answered, and there is peace in your knowledge.

As the *Metaphysics* draws to a close, however, Aristotle's version of wonder becomes richer. As he discusses his conception of God, or the ultimate reality that always just is, he says that our contemplation of God leads us to wonder at God's state of pure being and thinking. Since human beings strive for this sort of divinity—for Aristotle, this means to employ our highest capacity of thought and contemplation—but fall short of it, we wonder at God's being. This sort of wonder is no mere curiosity. What might have begun with burning curiosity ends in a still-burning flame that cannot be quenched, so long as we are contemplating the truth.

This is wonder at its pinnacle. This sort of wonder leaves us speechless. Yet, I think that we need not reach such lofty heights of contemplation to get there. As Fred Rogers reminds us, the world in which we are enmeshed is wonderful. It is through the eyes of wonder that we can recognize each person, each thing, each place, as unique and special. Mister Rogers takes this unicity to be axiomatic—it is self-evident.

The universe is a multiplicity of unicity: there will never be another you or another me, and it is our charge to recognize and nurture this. This unicity is radical and wonderful. When we come up against it, in truth, then we are again left speechless. This is the silence that lets be. A real love of wisdom begins in the wonder at the very being of the world and ends with letting it be what it is, and we come out better for it, because now we recognize that being in a new way.

Just as Mister Rogers revealed the studio to us, the underpinning to his show's reality, what gets revealed in philosophical reflection doesn't become some obvious fact. Rather, what was there all along but was once concealed is now revealed, and we see it for what it is. This good feeling of knowing we're alive, knowing that we're growing inside, also therefore grows. We can become once again who we are: just you, just me. And I like us just the way we are.

2
Mesmeric Mister Rogers

MARLENE CLARK

Decades ago, I was the mother of a young son who, while utterly adorable and very smart, seemed on the border of, if not fully into, hyperactivity.

He ran everywhere and went from one pursuit to another with a gusto that was exhausting for everyone but him. He never napped, and he didn't sleep much more than five or six hours a night, if that.

Exasperated and nearly worn out, his father and I brought him to an expert for a "diagnosis," but she concluded that while he was one very active little boy, he was not technically hyperactive. So we bumped along, coping daily—if we turned our backs for more than a few minutes—with near-disastrous climbs, tumbles down stairs, refrigerator raids, walls decorated with ingenious finger paintings in various media that were definitely *not* finger paint, and countless other forms of mischief and mayhem, the memories of which have now fortunately dimmed.

His father and I did have two half-hours of total peace every day, though: Mister Rogers in the morning, and again in the late afternoon. Twice a day, at the sound of tinkling chimes, followed by the notes of a piano, my son would stop in his tracks and run as fast as his toddler legs would take him to the television, shouting "Rogers! Rogers!" all the way. He would then plop his little self on the carpet right in front of the small screen, his head up, eyes riveted, his mouth slightly agape, and remain in that posture, completely engrossed, for thirty minutes without interruption. Clearly, my son was mesmerized.

*   *   *   *   *

He was mesmerized because Fred Rogers, to the end of his days, was a mesmerist, and he didn't mesmerize just children. Adults too fell under his spell, much to the benefit of us all.

"Mesmerism" comes by its name thanks to one Franz Friedrich Anton Mesmer, an Austrian physician, who first dabbled in the mesmeric arts in 1774. According to philosopher of science Edward John Nygren, Mesmer believed "the human body contains a magnetic fluid or ether . . . he called the magnetic force produced by this fluid 'animal magnetism' and he believed it could be used to treat illness, particularly nervous disorders." Learned societies in Vienna and Paris readily debunked his claims, and Dr. Mesmer himself soon after disappears from the record.

But his idea, from the first wildly popular with the public, quickly picked up steam in both Europe and the United States, where mesmeric performers continued to ply their trade for decades. In front of packed houses, by dint of "animal magnetism," they "cured" all sorts of ailments and elicited from their unwitting subjects just the response they earlier promised astounded—and gratified—audiences.

Eventually, scientists exposed these men as performers of nothing more than elaborate shams. But the theory of mesmerism did not die with Franz Mesmer. Rather, according to Nygren, as the eighteenth century passed into the nineteenth, and as the memory of mesmerism's connection to chicanery faded, mesmerisim instead became associated with hypnosis, particularly in the psychoanalytical treatment of patients with "nervous disorders," including Freud and Breuer's studies on hysteria.

As Freud soon discovered, however, hypnosis per se is not a necessary condition of psychoanalytic treatment. Nevertheless, the idea of a degree of mesmerism, built upon the "animal magnetism" (what we would today call "transference") inherent in the personal bond between analyst and analysand, stubbornly clung to the psychoanalytic community for some time.

Nowadays the phrase "animal magnetism" brings to mind *big* screen idols such as Brad Pitt, Benicio del Toro, Bradley Cooper, Mahershala Ali, and Ben Affleck. It's largely a male phenomenon, connected to a visceral, perhaps primitive (in the Freudian sense) sex appeal that magnetically pulls in audience members, both male and female, guaranteeing "box office." And film, as philosophers such as Walter Benjamin and Guy Debord have noted, could be said to exert a soothing effect on our amped up, present-day culture, allowing audience members to participate in fantastic sexual or violent behavior by proxy, in effect "treating" world-wide "nervous disorders."

But we would be remiss if we did not include in this regard another animal magnet of the *small* screen: Fred Rogers.

*   *   *   *   *

Fred Rogers? He of the dorky around-the-ears 1950s haircut; the neatly-knotted necktie (with tie clip), or worse yet, daffy little bow-tie; the zip-up sweaters hand knitted by, of course, Mom; the slightly sunken chest; the pants pulled up just a little too high on the waist; the sensible shoes and sneakers?

Yes, *that* Fred Rogers. Please, bear with me. For despite, maybe because of, his appearance, he somehow managed to exemplify a blend of magnetic attraction with a more benign form of hypnotic appeal, which he used to noble effect: explaining the ways of the big wide world to little children and mitigating their fears.

In his words, from the documentary movie, *Won't You Be My Neighbor?* (2018), he wanted in his half-hour visits to cultivate a "real relationship with the child," and he built that connection by concentrating on what for children were the "difficult modulations of life." To put it more colloquially, he focused on those things that tend to give kids the heebie-jeebies.

From how to open and close an umbrella (episode 1648) to the operation of the zipper (episode 1517)—utilitarian items adults use daily without giving a second thought—Fred Rogers understood that these simple machines were often beyond a youngster's ken, baffling and thwarting in turn. As he explains in the movie, he "remembered being six, seven, eight years old," and the steep learning curve we need to climb to understand the function and mechanics of each. He took his time. He repeated himself. Open, close. Zip, unzip. Eye contact. Smile. See? Not so hard; nothing to get upset about.

As to life's bigger, more philosophical problems: Yes, sunglasses do change an adult's appearance. And that can be concerning (episode 1409). Yes, sometimes children need to go to daycare. There are good reasons why; you are not alone (episode 1519). Yes, there are good dreams and bad dreams. And we wake up from both (episode 1519). And yes, everything grows together, because we're all one piece (episode 1650).

In this vein, Fred Rogers reminds us in the movie of an episode when a stuffed toy that made frequent appearances, Thatcher, unfortunately loses an ear. Why yes, that happens to toys sometimes, he explained to his audience in his slow, carefully enunciated way. But *our* ears don't fall off; *our* legs don't fall off. Adults in the room may have to stifle giggles overhearing a grown man speaking of a toy that way, drawing parallels as he does between toy and human anatomy. But to children, who identify with toys so closely they often become alter egos, the fear is very real. Will *I* fall apart like that? Will *I* wake up tomorrow morning to find one of *my* ears on the pillow? *Perhaps I should not sleep tonight.*

Fred Rogers's reminiscence brought to mind another example I happened to overhear long ago, when I uncharacteristically lingered during my precious "quiet time." It turns out to be episode 1588, one within the weekly theme on "Nighttime." The episode begins with Mister Rogers showing his new toy scuba diver and donning a scuba mask and snorkel. (Fred Rogers spent a good deal of time on appearance changes, something children likely find hard to fathom.) He takes the toy scuba diver into the bathroom to show the audience how it works. He fills the bathtub with water, and places several toys in the tub, including a toy rocking chair. He then turns the toy scuba diver on, and away it goes, while the audience sees a short movie about underwater sea life.

*　　*　　*　　*　　*

When we return from the movie, Mister Rogers gets down to brass tacks. Sitting on the edge of the tub, he carefully explains that when he lets the water out, it will go away, down the drain, right here, but the toys will not; they are too big. Similarly, when *you* are in the bathtub, *you* can never go down the drain; you too are too big. And, for added emphasis, he sings one of his standards, "You Can Never Go Down the Drain."

That would be enough if the episode ended right there. But it doesn't. As is typical, during the mid-portion of the episode, we go to the Neighborhood of Make-Believe, a dream-like world, for reinforcement. There, we find Neighbor Aber, dressed in scuba gear, which, predictably, due to his change in appearance, scares the bejesus out of Henrietta Pussycat. Mr. Aber explains the reason for his change. He is going scuba diving with Betty Templeton later that day. Henrietta Pussycat sighs with relief. As Mr. Aber makes his way to Betty Templeton's house, Lady Elaine mistakes him for a visitor from outer space. And in Southwood, Betty Templeton startles Carrie Dell when she sees Betty Templeton in her scuba gear.

Carrie Dell calms down after Betty Templeton explains the change. Meanwhile, Corney finishes a gift, an underwater rocking chair, for Betty Templeton.

Finally, back in the neighborhood, Mr. McFeely visits with full firefighter gear, which Mister Rogers quickly dons. Another change in appearance, but now his viewers understand the harmless, and purposeful, ways that those changes come about. Still in his gear, Mister Rogers plays the piano softly, and defines the word "soporific" to his, at this point, fully mesmerized young viewers. *Maybe I can sleep tonight.*

*   *   *   *   *

Won't You Be My Neighbor? shows us one of the most important—and ultimately, productive—examples of Mister Rogers making his magic with adults as well as children. On May 1st, 1969, Fred Rogers appeared before the Senate Subcommittee on Communications.

Lyndon Johnson, as part of his Great Society initiative, had budgeted $20 million for Public Television, then in its infancy. But soon after, Richard Nixon was elected, and he needed the money for the Vietnam War. Nixon's animus toward television was already well known, as he railed against stations he felt did not give him the favorable coverage he felt he deserved. What better line item to slash to recoup some much needed cash, with the added benefit of harming a medium he despised? He cut the PBS budget in half, to $10 million. A hearing for PBS to make its case for the full appropriation was scheduled.

For two long days, the mounting impatience of the Chair of the subcommittee, Senator John O. Pastore of Rhode Island, simmers, before coming to a full boil for all to see—on television. One gentleman after another reads prepared remarks, and Pastore is having none of it. He is bored, and he is angry. "All right," he snarls dismissively, "who's the next witness?" Things are not looking good for PBS.

After a prepared statement is read to introduce Fred Rogers and explain his importance to children's programing, Pastore practically barks, "All right, Rogers, you got the floor." He hoists himself up in his seat, and settles back in, his right arm positioned in a way to suggest a hand on a hip—ready for a fight. His lips are set, indicating a skeptical, somewhat angry resistance to having to sit still for yet another reading.

Fred Rogers flips the script, by explaining why he's decided not to read his prepared ten-minute "philosophical" remarks, and instead "trust" Pastore to read them later. To that, Pastore, dripping sarcasm, rebuts, "Would it make ya happy if ya read it?" "I'd just like to talk about it, if it's all right," Rogers responds, and continues as calmly as possible under the circumstances, obviously, at this point, contentious.

As Fred Rogers begins to explain the importance of children to him, Pastore's face quickly softens. "Feelings," Rogers explains he tells children (and Pastore), "are mentionable and manageable." Pastore changes his posture in his chair, leans forward, and his eyes meet those of Rogers with full attention. Reading his viewer, as usual, with a fully empathic understanding few others can manage, Rogers then asks if he can quote a "very important" song he wrote for children about "that good feeling of control," and after Pastore answers with a soft, "Yes," begins to speak the words:

> What do you do with the mad that you feel?
> When you feel so mad you could bite?
> When the whole wide world seems oh so wrong,
> And nothing you do seems very right?
> It's great to be able to stop,
> When you've planned a thing that's wrong.
> And be able to do something else instead,
> And think this song:
> I can stop when I want to;
> I can stop when I wish;
> I can stop! stop! stop! anytime.
> Know that there's something deep inside
> That helps us become what we can.

Pastore, his hand resting on his cheek (propping up his head), his eyes drowsily trained on his witness, his jaw relaxed, is at this point fully mesmerized. He's no doubt enveloped in that "good feeling of control" now, the power of hypnotic suggestion having worked its magical miracle once again, bending his moral arc towards justice. Calmed, he follows the advice of his witness's very important song. He reaches deep inside and becomes what he [fully] can; he stops the wrong and does indeed do something else instead. "I think it's wonderful. I think it's wonderful," he practically purrs. "Looks like you just earned the $20 million dollars." *I can sleep well tonight.*

*   *   *   *   *

I recently met my now-adult son for dinner. As a conversation starter, I told him I was about to write an essay on his old friend, Mister Rogers. I was prepared to tell him some anecdotes about his undying devotion to the crew: Daniel, Mr. McFeely, Betty Okonak Templeton, Henrietta Pussycat, Lady Elaine, Queen Sarah, and King Friday XIII, Thatcher, Lady Aberlin, Officer Clemmons, Handyman Negri, Bob Dog—to name only some of many—and the way Fred Rogers quite possibly was responsible for saving his parents' sanity. But before I could explain my theory as to how he did so, my son interrupted me:

> I just went to see that film about him! The theater was packed, mostly people around my age. Ten minutes into the film, I looked around the theater. Sure enough, everyone sitting there had their heads tilted up, their eyes glued to the screen, their mouths open, like this [he demonstrated the look of the entranced, then laughed]. I knew he had the effect on me, but I guess he does on everyone. What is it about that man?

Mister Rogers, I proceeded to explain to him, is a mesmerist.

3
Wonder and Philosophy as a Way Home

NATHAN MUELLER AND LEILANI MUELLER

Mister Rogers welcomes us into his cozy living room. With an affable smile, he comes through the door, takes off his jacket, hangs up his hat, switches his going-about town shoes for house shoes, and offers the hospitality of his home as a space for investigation, exploration, and the cultivation of wonder. In so doing, Mister Rogers opens his neighborhood to persons young and old as a place where questions are asked, and answers are sought. He opens his door and invites in *philosophers*.

But wait, you might say, doesn't Mister Rogers primarily invite in children, and aren't philosophers that odd breed of university professor who are obsessed with bizarre and esoteric questions, like whether or not we can know if we're brains in a vat or whether to flip the switch on a run-away trolley? Doesn't the philosopher have to have gone to school and studied "Philosophy" and know about such things as metaphysics, epistemology, ethics, the Pre-Socratics, phenomenology, and more besides? Isn't *philosophy* just like other professional subjects—*economics*, *physics*, *biology*, or *history*—requiring specialized training before one can "do it" as a "job"?

In a word, No.

When Mister Rogers opens his door to his viewers—especially children—he opens his door to philosophers, because children are natural philosophers. In asking such questions as "Why are you sad?" and "Why did the light turn off?" children reflect the same inquiring mind which Aquinas and Hume displayed when they themselves wondered what makes us happy and how to understand the nature of cause and effect.

Moreover, children ask questions about what things exist, how things in the world work, and what purpose some of those things have. They ask questions about right and wrong and how we can tell. Thus, as Mister Rogers steps into his living room and begins to sing—"It is a beautiful day in this neighborhood / a beautiful day for a neighbor"—he welcomes children along and all of their questions and wonderings. In so doing, he invites them to be philosophers.

A Philosopher in Disguise: On Beauty and Curiosity

Consider with us, for a moment, the lyrics of the second stanza of the opening theme song:

> It's a neighborly day in this beautywood,
> A neighborly day for a beauty,
> Would you be mine?
> Could you be mine?

It's a wonderful stanza, but it's also a puzzling one. What is a "beautywood"? What is "*a* beauty" and how would we have one? What makes any given day a uniquely *neighborly* day?

Whatever in particular Mister Rogers himself may have meant by these lyrics (itself another wonderful question and one worthy of exploration), this much seems true, that this day—the day in which you sit down to join Mister Rogers in his living room—is one that is filled with beauty, that it is a beautiful day to live and explore and ask questions with those who are our neighbors.

Now, beauty has long held a central place—which, along with truth and goodness compose the great three "transcendentals" of being—in the history of the Western philosophical tradition. The Pre-Socratic philosopher Pythagoras (yes, *that* Pythagoras, after whom the Pythagorean Theorem is named) seemed to have found great beauty, for example, in the mathematical ratios which governed musical harmony and held that that beauty served a key role in moral education. Plato agreed and argues in the *Symposium* that seeing beauty, and learning to love beauty for its own sake, is the key to becoming wise—that is, to turn away from loving what is fleeting and to learn to love what is immaterial and eternal.

And the philosopher is, if nothing else, supposed to be a lover of wisdom (this, by the way, comes from the Greek origin of the word *philosophia*, a combination of *philos* meaning love and *sophia* meaning wisdom). St. Thomas Aquinas, following in the footsteps of Aristotle, likewise held beauty in high regard and argued that the big three (truth, goodness, and beauty) are convertible and unified in the Judeo-Christian God.

However, as Plato and Mister Rogers well understood, we don't come to see and love the beautiful *in itself* right away. Human persons are predisposed to get caught up in and distracted by what is right in front of us. We're prone to be distracted by the empirical—what we can see, hear, smell, touch, and taste—and not move any further in our quest for beauty and, thus, wisdom.

We've got to begin small; to begin by simply stopping and recognizing the beauty *in* a tree, a song, our neighborhood, a neighbor, ourselves. By inviting us into his neighborhood and asking us to share a neighborly day for a beauty, Mister Rogers draws on this rich and ancient philosophical tradition and places beauty, and a love of it, at the center of his world.

A Philosopher in Disguise: On Questions

The Greek philosopher Aristotle (a student of Plato) famously opens his *Metaphysics* by asserting, "All human beings by nature desire to know." Above, we asked some questions which arose naturally from briefly considering the opening theme of the show, and asking good questions is often considered part and parcel of what it means to be a good philosopher. But there is another side, which our reflection on the opening theme invites us now to consider: when the philosopher entertains a question, she does so without thinking that she already knows the answer.

This trait of genuine curiosity in the philosopher is underscored by Plato in another of his dialogues, the *Meno*. There, Socrates—who was Plato's teacher and plays the nebulous role of serving as the mouthpiece for Plato's own philosophy—is asked by his discussion partner, Meno, how you could search for the answer to a question if you didn't already know the answer to the question. It seems to Meno that either you *don't* know the answer you're looking for—in which case even if you find the answer you won't be able to recognize it as the answer to your question—or you *do* in fact know the answer to the question—in which case there's no need to look in the first place. Socrates's own answer to this dilemma is an interesting one involving immortal souls, the act of remembering, and more. We leave it for the curious reader to go investigate Plato's *Meno* for yourself (starting with lines 80d–86b). All that's important for us is to see that, much like Socrates, Mister Rogers both poses and investigates questions with a deep and genuine curiosity—an attitude essential to being a good philosopher.

Throughout his show, Mister Rogers frequently invites viewers to ask questions about different objects that can be found in his house or that a neighbor drops by to show him. The appearance of lightshades, batteries, balloons, dinosaurs, music, books, and more, are all occasions for wondering and questioning and learning. This questioning, however, is not limited to the privacy of his home.

No, Mister Rogers frequently invites his friends and neighbors in the Neighborhood to join him in his search for understanding, often meeting them in their own "homes" to pursue truth together. Such as when Mister Rogers visits his neighbor François Clemmons's music studio to listen to the band play several interpretations of a few of Mister Rogers's "sometimes songs" including the song "Sometimes Isn't Always"; an important exploration of the differences between universal and particular statements such as are found in Aristotelian logic (episode 1304).

When questions seem far from clear, or answers themselves not entirely forthcoming in the neighborhood, Mister Rogers turns to help from his friends in the Neighborhood of Make-Believe. For example, there is the time after King Friday and Queen Sara have gotten angry with each other that Mister Rogers asks us to join him in pretending that Lady Aberlin is trying to find out about something about the nature of feelings. What follows is an investigation into the nature of Love by means of a thought experiment (a well-used tool in the belt of the philosopher) in the Neighborhood of Make-Believe (episode 1309).

Simple Questions and Real Curiosity

Perhaps nothing better represents the ever-curious nature of Mister Rogers than his song "Did You Know." Here are the words:

> Did you know? Did you know?
> Did you know that it's all right to wonder?
> Did you know that it's all right to wonder?
> There are all kinds of wonderful things!
>
> Did you know? Did you know?
> Did you know that it's all right to marvel?
> Did you know that it's all right to marvel?
> There are all kinds of marvelous things!

You can ask a lot of questions about the world . . .
And your place in it.
You can ask about people's feelings;
You can learn the sky's the limit.

Did you know? Did you know?
Did you know when you wonder you're learning?
Did you know when you marvel you're learning?
About all kinds of wonderful,
About all kinds of marvelous,
Marvelously wonderful things?

This song was a staple of Mister Rogers's invitation to his television neighbors to come alongside him and to ask questions about our world and our place in it—appearing in no less than ten different episodes.

While Mister Rogers did not shy away from asking more difficult and sensitive questions, "Did You Know" was always sung preceding or following the investigation of ordinary household objects. In focusing on such matters, Mister Rogers, much like a good philosopher, invites us to start with simpler questions— one starts with simpler questions, because one doesn't know yet that the more complicated questions are also interesting.

Consider for instance when Mister Rogers begins to wonder about a box full of batteries. The batteries, of all different shapes and sizes, awaken a sense of curiosity in Mister Rogers and so, alongside the viewer, he began to ask questions. After laying out the batteries on his kitchen table, Mister Rogers turns to ask, "What is this battery made for?" (episode 1655).

In asking just this very small question, viewers have been invited to question what the purpose of a battery is—what its *telos* is—rather than just what they are made of or into what toys they might be inserted. Even the smallest and most mundane of objects, a battery, can serve as an occasion to engage in philosophical questions concerning teleology—the end or goal that object is made to do or accomplish. Perhaps it was not coincidental that one of his batteries powered a light, brightening the living room.

In the simple beauty of a kind and compassionate neighborhood, Mister Rogers provides space for his viewers to be curious and ask questions about ordinary objects, the building blocks of their world. The asking questions about the purpose of objects recurs throughout many of his shows, and whenever it does—particularly against the backdrop of the kindly beauty of the neighborhood—Mister Rogers not only opens his door to the philosopher, but also demonstrates himself to be a philosopher, as a person genuinely seeking answers to questions about the world and his place in it.

Mister Rogers Makes Philosophy His Way of Life

At this stage you might be wondering whether Mister Rogers shares any of those traits you might associate with those "professional" philosophers found at universities, who only occasionally leave their ivory towers. Surely, you might be thinking, such people must be among the paradigmatic examples of what it means to "do" philosophy for a living or to "be" a philosopher. However, as the late French philosopher Pierre Hadot has argued, regardless of how great the prestige is of such individuals in today's culture of learning, such a conception of the life of a "philosopher" shares little with the conception of the philosopher upon which the tradition of Western philosophy was founded.

The key to understanding the difference between the philosophical life of the "university philosopher" and Mister Rogers lies in the distinction between *discourses about* philosophy and *philosophy itself*. The longstanding aim of philosophy is the pursuit of wisdom. In his book, *Philosophy as a Way of Life*, Hadot said that for ancient philosophers, wisdom was a way of life which resulted in a unique peace of mind and inner freedom since "real wisdom does not merely cause us to know: it makes us 'be' in a different way" (p. 265).

Now the various ancient philosophical traditions each had different ideas of what it looked like to live as a philosopher. The Stoics and Epicureans, while cashing out the particularities quite differently, nonetheless each espoused a philosophy which stressed the immense value of each and every instant and thus emphasized living in the here and now (#yolo). Plato understood philosophy as a way of preparation for death. Aristotle understood philosophy as the way to inner transformation by learning to live a life of the mind. However, Hadot said that while each of these traditions differ, in its methodologies, "we find in all philosophical schools the same awareness of the power of the human self" to attain peace of mind and inner freedom (p. 266).

In understanding philosophy as a way of life which leads to peace and freedom, these traditions each view philosophy not as a series of unique puzzles and arguments about this aspect of the world and that, but as a unified act in which one simply lives out one's ethics, metaphysics, and epistemology, simply "thinks and speaks well," simply acts "in a correct and just way" (p. 267). Moreover, as Hadot has argued, within each of these ancient traditions a significant primacy of place was granted to the obligation to "always act in the service of the human community" for "human community . . . is an essential element of every philosophical life" (p. 274).

But how did Mister Rogers operate within this tradition? How did he model an attainment of peace and inner freedom? How was this done in service of the community—of the neighborhood?

A Neighborhood of Philosophers

Within Mister Rogers's neighborhood are three unique spaces that make up the neighborhood of philosophers: first, the domestic space of Mister Rogers's own home; next, the space outside the home, within the broader community; and finally, the Neighborhood of Make-Believe. Each space contributes to doing philosophy well within one's community. Each location provides a space for moving towards the freedom made possible by wisdom.

Taking a quick tour, we start in the home. There, Mister Rogers asks questions about ordinary objects like the afore-mentioned batteries or the box that he holds at the start of that episode—including whether, after a lovely moment wherein he places the box on his head, he wonders whether the box could function as a hat (episode 1655). Next, we and Mister Rogers put on our hats and step out of the living room to visit Mister Rogers's neighbors. Implicit in many of his interactions with his neighbors in the neighborhood is the question: "How should I treat others?" The answer repeatedly comes back: with kindness. For example, in one episode Mister Rogers meets Eric Kloss, a blind saxophone player. Mr. Kloss's blindness presents no barrier to neighborly interaction as the two men interact with Kloss's machine, which reads on behalf of those who can't see (episode 1654).

Finally, we can hop on the trolley and head into the Neighborhood of Make-Believe. Here in this make-believe world, as in the thought experiments of philosophers, deeper, more intricate questions can be explored through considering various hypothetical scenarios. While it may appear that in the Neighborhood of Make-Believe the questions are simple and straightforward—such as, should the kids go on a field trip or should they use James Michael Jones's learning machine?— nevertheless, even in questions such as these, deeper questions concerning the nature of learning, the limits of technology, and the importance of first-person experience are implicit (episode 1654).

In each of its three unique spaces, *Mister Rogers' Neighborhood* provides a winsome picture of what understanding philosophy as a way of life could look like when done in and for a community. The neighborhood is a place where people can ask questions about ordinary objects like lampshades and batteries and windmills, questions about happiness and sadness, questions about beauty and goodness. It is a place where we can explore our world and our place in it—which Mister Rogers himself does over and over again. It is a place where difficult questions concerning right and wrong can be asked with genuine curiosity and humility. This is a place where people can move towards wisdom and, thus, freedom.

Moreover, each of these characteristics can be seen in the way people interact in the Neighborhood. When Lady Aberlin offers encouraging words to the timid Daniel Tiger, or when Neighbor Aber tries to calm Lady Elaine's feelings about not being able to draw very well, or even in Mister Rogers's exchanges with visitors to the house, each individual speaks with respect and kindness, listening intently to what their neighbors have to say, while respecting the seriousness of each of their questions. It is no wonder then that children the world over have come to love Mister Rogers. For it is precisely these character traits, valued and aspired to in true philosophical community, which allow children to ask the most difficult questions they have. For example: Why do I get sad? Where did I come from? What are friends and how do I make them? What is death and why does it happen?

While part of the philosophical life seeks to understand the ordinary objects of this world, it is ultimately how the philosopher deals with these deeper questions, ones which even children ask, which best embody *living* philosophically. And it is in this sense that Mister Rogers philosophized with the best of them.

I'll Be Back When the Day Is New

Each episode concludes with an invitation to come back and ask questions with him.

> It's such a good feeling,
> A very good feeling.
> The feeling you know, that I'll be back
> When the day is new.

And I'll have more ideas for you.
And you'll have things you'll want to talk about.
I will too.

We all have things to talk about. New ideas to explore. Mister Rogers was no exception.

Recall our earlier discussion of the song "Did You Know?" In one of the earlier episodes in which Mister Rogers sings the song, he introduces it, with his familiar earnestness, explaining:

"You know me. I'm interested in all sorts of things, and I spend a lot of time trying to learn about things. I'm curious, and I wonder about all sorts of things. You can ask questions about the world and your place in it."

The heart of *Mister Rogers' Neighborhood* rests on the conviction that it's okay to wonder, and that not only is it more than okay to ask questions, but that doing so reflects something important about being truly human.

Mister Rogers is a master tutor, opening his door to each of us and inviting us to join him in his hunt for answers. To pursue beauty and wisdom in the community of a beautiful neighborhood. To grow in kindness and neighborly love. To be a philosopher.

4

The Gently Socratic Inquiry of Fred Rogers

BEN LUKEY AND STEVE "CHIP" BEIN

> Wonder is the feeling of a philosopher, and philosophy begins in wonder.
>
> —SOCRATES

> Our world needs more time to wonder and reflect, but there is too much fast-paced distraction.
>
> —FRED ROGERS

If you've studied any of Socrates's dialogues, you've probably been told—or maybe come to the conclusion on your own—that he was a bit of a jerk. And if you've seen even one minute of anyone's interactions with Fred Rogers, you know "jerk" is one of the last words you'd use to describe him. So the fact that we're going to compare the two may seem a bit odd.

Nevertheless, here goes.

People say Socrates was a jerk because as Plato describes him (and Plato's description is pretty much all we have), he has a pesky habit of making an ass out of powerful people. Socrates himself insists he knows nothing, and in Plato's dialogues he talks to these people to see what knowledge they have. But then he lures his interlocutors into one logical trap after another, exposing the flaws in their reasoning until they admit they're licked. (Most of them, anyway.)

This is his famous "Socratic Method," and you can imagine that if the person he's talking to is a pompous ass, this method could expose that pretty quickly. And because Socrates has these conversations on, say, the steps of a busy courthouse, he makes an ass of these people in public. People tend to think you're a jerk if you do that.

But what's often forgotten in the telling of this story is that Socrates saw the search for truth as something embedded in his community. For him philosophy was a public activity, not because it's fun to embarrass people but because philosophy happens in dialogue. It has to be conducted not in the ivory tower but in the neighborhood.

Fred Rogers knew a thing or two about philosophizing in the neighborhood. His show was a public space for his cast and his guests—and his audience with them—to think about the most pressing problems of the day. (His first antiwar statement was in the show's very first week!) He changed television by treating children as thinking beings whose inner lives are every bit as nuanced and robust as an adult's.

This was his most important contribution to children's education, and it's alive and well in certain corners of the American educational system today. This chapter will shine a spotlight on one of these corners: the University of Hawai'i's partnership with the Hawai'i public school system, where for the past thirty years kids have been practicing philosophy the way Socrates and Mister Rogers imagined it.

Philosophy with Aloha

Back in the 1960s, Columbia philosophy professor Matthew Lipman was discouraged by the poor reasoning skills of his undergraduate students. He had the groundbreaking idea to begin teaching philosophy, with a focus on logic, in K-12 schools. Moving to Montclair State University, Lipman launched the Philosophy for Children ("P4C") movement. He wrote a series of philosophical novels and a supporting curriculum that spread all over the world.

In 1984, a newly-minted philosophy PhD from the University of Hawai'i named Thomas E. Jackson attended a P4C retreat at Montclair. Inspired by Lipman's innovative approach, Dr. Jackson brought it back to Hawai'i and began to lead P4C sessions in local schools. He became known to the kids and teachers as "Dr. J," and as P4C caught on it got the attention not only of the University of Hawai'i Philosophy Department but also the Hawai'i Department of Education and even the state legislature. With their support, Dr. J established the Philosophy in the Schools Program, which later got the name it's got now: p4c Hawai'i. (And yes, we just shifted from P4C to p4c. More on this later.) That's where we, the writers of this chapter, got involved: both of us were lucky enough to be Dr. J's graduate assistants in the program, where we got p4c names of our own ("Dr. Chip" and "Dr. Ben"). Ben, the lucky bastard, still works with Dr. J on beautiful Oahu, while Chip lives in dreary Ohio.

Dr. J's focus wasn't on logic, as Lipman's was, but rather on creating a "community of inquiry" with an atmosphere of "intellectual safety." Intellectual safety predates the modern idea of "safe spaces," and in a sense they're opposites: in a safe space you're not supposed to be judgmental about *people*, while in an intellectually safe space you're not supposed to be judgmental about *questions* and *thoughts*. This opens the floor to questions that some people might not like, but if the group has created a community of inquiry—that is, a community interested in satisfying genuine curiosity about things people genuinely wonder about—then it can handle uncomfortable questions without anyone asking any hurtful ones.

The key is to be more like Mister Rogers than Socrates. In a 2001 article called "The Art and Craft of 'Gently Socratic' Inquiry," Dr. J argued that authentic thinking develops out of wonder, and that this wonder diminishes as children progress through school. As children shape their thinking to what their teachers and tests expect of them, their curiosity and wonder get squelched. p4c Hawai'i evolved as an approach to teaching and learning that nurtures students' sense of wonder, listening carefully to their voices in order to bring about meaningful and lasting change in education.

This, of course, is exactly what Fred Rogers set out to do. He made intellectually safe communities of inquiry in living rooms all over the country, talking to kids—and *listening* to kids—about any subject they wondered about. His choice of subject matter was often uncomfortable, bordering on reckless. He'd been on the air all of seven weeks when Martin Luther King, Jr. was assassinated, and it went without saying that this was not the sort of thing you talked about on a kids' show. Two months later, Bobby Kennedy was killed, and then came the fearless Mister Rogers with an episode about assassination.

This isn't the sort of thing you do if you want to keep your brand new show on the air. But it's exactly what you do if you think the inner lives of children are just as interesting, complex, and manifold as your own. That's p4c's commitment too. It says anyone can be a philosopher.

The Good Thinker's Toolkit

You can't do philosophy with children for long before one of them asks, "What's philosophy?" The textbook answer for adults goes right to the Greek: *philia* means love, *sophia* means wisdom, so a philosopher is a lover of wisdom. But ancient Greek won't get you very far with first graders, and besides, that answer isn't particularly helpful for adults. (Go ahead, define the word "wisdom." It's not easy, is it?). At p4c Hawai'i, we needed a better answer.

Dr. J identified philosophy as not a subject but as an approach to inquiry and learning. It's an approach that can be used with any subject, because just as there's room for inquiry in every subject in school, there are critical thinking skills to facilitate this inquiry. Dr. J boiled down a bunch of these into the Good Thinker's Toolkit:

W: What do you mean by that?

R: Reason (what's the reason for that?)

A: Assume, or Assumption (what are we assuming here?)

I: Inference, or If/Then (if that's true, then what?)

T: True (is that true?)

E: Evidence, or Example (what's an example of that?)

C: Counterevidence, or Counterexample (when is this not true?)

Instead of explaining them one by one, let's apply them p4c style, starting with a question we can wonder about: are children philosophers?

It makes sense to start by asking what we mean by "philosopher" (W). As an example (E) we can look to Socrates, who says in a dialogue called the *Phaedrus* that he isn't a person who understands, but rather a person who seeks understanding (lines 278c–d). Socrates says he has to do this in a community of inquiry, because "trees and open country won't teach me anything, whereas men in town do" (lines 230d–e).

There's a hidden use of reason (R) whenever you use the word "because," and an assumption (A) hiding in Socrates's statement too. Kids don't share adults' assumptions about trees, and so they might ask if it's true (T) that trees can't teach a philosopher. Maybe the kids in your neighborhood don't know about mana, but in Hawai'i they do, and certain trees are said to have lots of it. Human beings are supposed to respect it, and usually—this is an assumption (A), but usually—you learn from things you respect. If you've gained any useful understanding from trees (I), then you've got a counterexample (C) that might give Socrates reason (R) to question his initial claim. (We wonder if Mister Rogers himself might have had one, being the guy who wrote the lyric, "It's a neighborly day in the beautywood.")

You can nest these tools too. For example, if what we mean by philosopher is one who seeks understanding, then if there are any examples of children who seek understanding, then at least some children can be philosophers, and if it's commonplace to encounter children who seek understanding, then we may assume that generally speaking, yes, it's true that children are philosophers. There we've got a W, two Is, an E, an A, a T, and even a third I being used as an R.

We use these tools implicitly all the time, without ever labeling them. Daniel Striped Tiger used the W on that audacious episode of *Mister Rogers' Neighborhood* when he asked, "What does assassination mean?" Lady Aberlin's reply was a deft use of the I: inferring that he's upset, she says, "Have you heard that word a lot today?" As the episode unfolds, it's clear that Daniel isn't just looking for comfort; like so many kids that day, he's sincerely in search of deeper understanding. That's our natural state: to wonder. And the Toolkit improves our ability to wonder constructively.

What's powerful about the Toolkit is that by putting labels on these critical thinking tools, you get better at noticing your instinctive use of them. From there you get better at using them deliberately. If you've got something important on your chest—like when all the adults around you start using a new word you don't know and it's making them act all sad and somber—then the Toolkit helps you open up. It helps you ask better questions. It helps you talk about your thoughts—and even *think* about them—in a clearer way.

As kids learn to use these tools to think about their thinking, magical things start to happen. First, they become more confident in their thinking and their ability to communicate their thinking. Then they become more metacognitive—that is, more aware of their own thinking—and once they're paying attention to their thinking, they work to improve it. They also get a lot better at thinking together with other people— namely, as a community—using the Toolkit to make new connections, challenge one another, and find new paths for inquiry and learning. Together they start to play with ideas the way they play with toys, which lines up perfectly with Fred Rogers's pedagogy. (Rogers said, "Play is often talked about as if it were a relief from serious learning. But for children play is serious learning. Play is really the work of childhood.") p4c folds play and serious learning into the same practice.

Finally, as p4c develops across grades throughout an entire school, there's a wholescale shift in language. Second-graders will explain their reasoning, unprompted, and offer examples when trying to understand something. High schoolers resolve their anger with dialogue instead of fistfights. Kailua High School, one of p4c Hawai'i's model schools, has seen a drastic reduction in school violence over the past fifteen years, due in no small part to the introduction of a new school-wide Ethnic Studies and Philosophy course, taught p4c-style, where students can talk about racial and ethnic differences in an intellectually safe community of inquiry.

Mister Rogers would have approved. When he hired the opera singer Francois Clemmons to become Officer Clemmons, the Neighborhood's police officer, Clemmons became the first African American to have a recurring role on a children's TV show. That was a big deal in 1968, and Rogers wasn't done. In 1969, after national news outlets reported African American kids being attacked and forced out of public swimming pools, he invited Officer Clemmons to join him cooling his feet in his kiddie pool. He even closed the scene by helping Clemmons dry off his feet.

Kailua High School saw changes just as dramatic. In the 2003–2004 school year, when the first p4c practitioner arrived at the school, there were 368 "incidents" (disciplinary reports) and 232 students suspended. In 2016–2017 there were fifty-three incidents and forty-three suspensions. p4c can't take sole credit—discipline problems require multi-layered solutions—but its influence was profound enough that by 2010 the school adopted a new vision statement: "Kailua High School students are mindful, philosophical thinkers prepared to pursue their goals and create positive change in the world."

Through p4c, students internalize the same attitude of respect and neighborliness that Fred Rogers tried to cultivate in his viewers—and that includes adults as well as children. Rogers was a peacemaker who modeled how a community could work through challenges and differences, even when confronting uncomfortable situations and troublesome personalities. (Let's not forget, King Friday and Lady Elaine Fairchilde are hardly the sort of people you'd invite to a Kumbaya circle.) He modeled one of the key commitments of p4c: meeting people where they are, taking them seriously as individuals with important inner lives, and talking to them about what they want to talk about. It doesn't matter if it's about serious things like fighting at school, philosophical things like the nature of nothing, or fun things like who's the best Avenger. What matters is genuine engagement in the spirit of shared inquiry.

Of philosophy and Philosophy

But maybe all of this is too lowbrow for you. Maybe you're thinking of philosophy the way a university Philosophy Department thinks of it, as something requiring books written by great historical thinkers. Socrates himself distinguished between the wisdom philosophers are after and the "wisdom of the artisans," which includes things like sailing and shepherding (*Apology*, lines 22d–3). When a philosopher seeks understanding, it's understanding more than where those sheep got off to. It's supposed to involve lofty ideas, right? Ethics and metaphysics and all that.

Dr. J draws a distinction between "Big P Philosophy," which is about "official" philosophers and their thought, and "little p philosophy," which is about philosophical thought as ordinary people (including kids) do it. Big P Philosophy is primarily understood through its *content*, the -ers, -isms, and -ies that, for example, professors and their students analyze in a university setting. Little p philosophy is primarily understood through its *activity*, inquiring into our beliefs, our experiences, the ideas we encounter with others, and what they make us wonder about. If you wanted to go to college and take up a Philosophy major, ideally it would expose you to lots of big P Philosophy in order to stoke the fires of your little p philosophy. (It doesn't always work that way: sometimes the only purpose of the big P Philosophy is to see how accurately you can restate it on an exam.) But you don't have to take classes in Philosophy to do philosophy, and anyhow, not all Philosophy helps you do philosophy. If it doesn't generate genuine curiosity and wonder in you then it doesn't stoke the fire.

We believe that when it comes to what's essential for human beings, not just for their own intrinsic good but also as an instrumental social good, philosophy is more important than Philosophy. We're brazen enough to think Socrates would agree. Of course, in his day Philosophy wasn't a thing you could major in yet, but still, we think he would have been more interested in you thinking for yourself than you being able to replicate what he thought. Socrates never said philosophy begins in what the people before you had to say; he said philosophy begins in wonder.

Socrates, Fred Rogers, and Dr. J all saw great value in wonder. Socrates said philosophy begins there, Rogers said the world needs to make more time for it, and Dr. J called it "the pause button on thinking." One of the delightful little subtleties of *Mister Rogers' Neighborhood* was that the stoplight in the Neighborhood was on yellow. Rogers said this was a signal to slow down and pay attention. This is what Socrates excelled at, and it's what Dr. J intended gently Socratic inquiry to do. What he meant by "pause button" was that wonder suspends the ordinary thought process that leaps from one preconceived notion to the next.

Our minds are full of preconceived notions, and most of them are pretty handy. (Please don't get creative about what side of the street you want to drive on!) But some of them are worn out, some are downright dangerous, and many of them are set up to stifle creative critical thinking. When your brain is running as mechanically as a traffic light, making its logical leaps from green to yellow to red, wonder inserts a "hmmmm" in there. It gives you time to ask which came first, the green or the red? Why did we pick the two colors color-blind people have the hardest time with? Could we have made it easier for them by making the lights three different shapes? Why didn't we?

You Are Special, and I Mean It!

It's become fashionable to criticize Mister Rogers for telling all his guests and viewers that they're special and beautiful inside. This is the same wave of criticism that laments participation trophies, the celebration of mediocrity, and the idea that everyone's a special snowflake. (The documentary *Won't You Be My Neighbor?* features a few such critics.) We assume these critics prefer the kind of tough love that recognizes not everyone gets to be an astronaut when they grow up—or in other words, that everyone's *not* special, that there's such a thing as average, and that by definition most people fall into that category.

We won't debate the merits of that position here; we'll just point out that even the astronauts need to know they're loved. Socrates himself, who's so important in the history of Western thought that everyone before him is lumped into a category called the Pre-Socratics, still needed a booster shot of self-esteem. He said, "Oh dear Pan and all the other gods of this place, grant that I may be beautiful inside" (*Phaedrus*, line 279c). Mister Rogers's response would have been immediate and heartfelt: "You *are* beautiful inside." That's the message Rogers had for everyone, from the majestic King Friday to the meek Daniel Striped Tiger.

p4c has a similar message: if you're capable of wonder, you're a potential philosopher, and that means you have the ability to transform not only your own thoughts but also the thoughts of others. A big part of the magic of p4c is watching children discover this ability to take their internal wonder and influence those around them. They see their wisdom become manifest. If we reduce philosophy to the recorded thoughts of Very Important People, then of course only a select few will ever be significant Philosophers. But that's the very opposite of what Socrates had in mind. He insisted he *wasn't* the wisest man in Athens (despite being called that by the highest of high achievers: Apollo's own oracle at Delphi). People listened to him, but he never thought highly enough of his own opinion to charge tuition. His great crime, the one his enemies contrived to have him executed for, was getting young people to think for themselves.

Well, his enemies called it "corrupting the youth," but the inevitable question in a p4c circle will be, "What do you mean by corrupting?" However we answer that one, as Plato describes him Socrates sure looks like he's a lot more interested in doing philosophy than becoming a Philosopher. We think Fred Rogers was in the same camp. He had a philosophy—you are loveable just the way you are—but he became famous for it in spite of himself. (It was his own producer, Margy Whitmer, who put it best: "If you take all of the elements that make good television and do the exact opposite, you have *Mister Rogers' Neighborhood*.") Questionable television, maybe, but Rogers saw television the same way Socrates saw Athens: a good idea that had spoiled and was now in desperate need of shaking up.

Socrates described himself as a gadfly and Athens as a majestic horse in need of a sharp sting in the rump. It's hard to imagine Mister Rogers stinging anybody, and this is where the *gently* Socratic inquiry comes in. Because Socrates had another image of himself, and a tender one at that: a midwife, barren of wisdom but capable of delivering the wisdom of others. This was Fred Rogers's great gift, and it's p4c Hawai'i's mission too.

We see Fred Rogers and Dr. J not as Philosophers but philosophers, and we put the teachers and children who practice p4c in the same camp. History may not remember them for the intellectual *content* they contributed to Philosophy, but in their own neighborhoods they're invaluable, as persistent practitioners of the *activity* of philosophy.

II

What Do You Do with the Mad that You Feel?

5

Another Day in the Neighborhood

SYDNEY BALL AND ERIC J. MOHR

Tuesday: what a drag. I swear that Tuesday always feels like the longest day of the week; still feeling lethargic from the weekend, with mountains of work and assignments seeming to pile up, all with a due date just three days away. Yet, I always seem to think to myself "Eh, I'll get to it later." This procrastination will be the death of me. Does that song that I remember Mister Rogers singing about stopping when I want to, stopping when I wish, also imply that I can start when I want to, start when I wish? Starting things seemed so much easier back when I used to watch *Mister Rogers' Neighborhood*. Why is it easier now to stop, but harder to start?

I just feel tired all of the time, I feel old: I am old. Twenty doesn't seem that old, a mere fifth of a lifetime. But, every time I roll out of bed bent over with a back ache, every optometrist appointment where they up my prescription to match how much blinder I've gotten, every child I've babysat that looked at me with confusion when I tell them the year I was born, makes me feel ancient. Nothing snaps you back to reality faster than when a five-year-old asks "Where's your kids? Shouldn't you be married already?" as if age twenty signifies "true adulthood," as if my age is not anything but an extension of the teenage years, only now with access to more dangerous toys and ideas. Feeling old runs deeper though: I miss the energy and drive I had when I was younger.

I think it was Plato who spoke about people who are thirsty but who, for whatever reason, choose not to drink; people who are hungry, but choose not to eat. He said there's got to be something in our soul that moves and drives us toward things in the world, and something else that makes us able to stop ourselves, and overrule the thing that drives us (*Republic*, line 439c). What he called the irrational, motivating part of our us was, when I was younger, all that I seemed to have. But with age my rational side has become overwhelmingly dominant. Plato says this is a good thing, and I believe him—he says it's the key to an ordered and just soul, but I feel tired more than anything. Is feeling deflated and unmotivated a sign of justice? I miss the unbridled energy of my youth. But, who knows, maybe there's ultimately a greater freedom in this.

Sitting in front of my laptop screen, eyes glazed over behind the thick glasses that, albeit stylish, I now have to wear, I reminisce on simpler times. You never realize how amazing childhood is until you are on your own for the first time at college, or worse, forced to work nine to five. You do not appreciate the naptime of youth until three P.M. signifies the second hour of a four-hour lab discussing the nuances of yeast growth in an anaerobic environment, or perhaps the daily accounts meeting with the San Francisco branch, instead of a warm bed and an enveloping silence. The value of childhood is lost on a child; only as an adult does one truly realize the worth of youth. I wish I knew how good I had it when I was six years old, but hey, I was six. What did I know? I quickly forget about that email I was supposed to send, lost in the nostalgia. Instantly, I am transported back to a cold Tuesday afternoon fourteen years ago . . .

*   *   *   *   *

ommy plops me down in front of the television and turns on my most favorite show. I don't quite understand "TV"; it's like a magic box where little people live inside. I remember Mister Rogers saying that he doesn't actually live in the TV. To be honest, I don't think I totally believe him, but I don't care because his show is about to start. "It's a beautiful day in the neighborhood, it's a beautiful day for a neighbor, would you be mine, could you be mine . . ." I love that song, and so does my dog Hershey.

Hershey watches Mister Rogers with me every day. She's so soft and nice, but sometimes she leaves during the show and that makes me so mad, so "mad that I could bite." One time Hershey tried to leave during the show, so I grabbed her by the collar and dragged her back into the living room and she tried to bite me. That made me mad. I was so mad I grabbed her ear and bit her back and she made a high-pitched yelp and ran away from me. Mommy was so upset at me because "I should know better." Why should I know better? Hershey's older than me, I'm only six, Hershey "should know better," not me! But

Mommy said it was me that should know better, she said that "I can stop when I want to, stop when I wish, I can stop, stop, stop . . ." I didn't want to listen to her because I knew that those words were Mister Rogers's words. I didn't want to listen to Mommy, but I didn't want to make Mister Rogers upset with me, so I said that I was sorry to Hershey and now she always watches *Mister Rogers' Neighborhood* with me. Together we watch Mister Rogers on the screen, and we do just as he says. There's something calming and empowering about this gentle, slow-talking man on the screen. He helps me want to be my best self. He helps me care about how I live my life.

Then Trolley pops out from the wall and makes the beep-beeps, whisking us to the Neighborhood of Make-Believe. This is my favorite part of Mister Rogers because there, anything is possible, like when King Friday put up a wall around his castle. I was so sad when he put up that wall, but Daniel Tiger and Lady Aberlin convinced the King that his kingdom is better without walls by sending messages of peace (episode 0005). I think that I like bridges better than walls because bridges connect people, like me and my grandma. Every time I visit her I drive across a big bridge in the center of my town over the Erie Canal. Without the bridge I would not get to see her, and my grandma is my most favorite friend of all . . .

*   *   *   *   *

A text pops up on my screen, breaking me from my trance: it's from my grandmother. "Hi Sydney, it's me, Grandma. I am so proud of how good at golf you are doing. I hope school is going well, I love and miss you—Grandma Judy." I miss her so much. I love the way she texts me. She always signs it like it's a love letter even though I tell her over and over again that she doesn't have to, that I would know that it's her, but she still signs them anyway. I sometimes wish I went to school closer to home, but that thought only lasts a moment. I truly love going to school out of my home state. I've been afforded so many wonderful opportunities here and I've met people whom I love more than I ever thought I was capable of, and for that I'm grateful. But, I still miss my grandmother, I miss my dog Hershey, I miss New York, and I miss all my friends and family there. I am not necessarily homesick; I love going to school in Pennsylvania. Sometimes I just miss what I once had in just a few minutes' distance and a bridge away.

School is going well, but the new responsibilities take some getting used to. There're so many interesting events and activities that I want to attend. But I can't do everything. I don't know how some of these kids do it. I guess they think that with more freedom comes more fun, but I'm beginning to realize that I must do what I have to do on my own, even if it's not what I most want to do. There's no one breathing down my neck here, making sure that I do what I'm supposed to. Immanuel Kant had a word for this: he called it "autonomy." He was a bit like Plato in stressing how our behavior should be guided by reason. The key to goodness, he thought, is self-directed behavior; not doing what you're told, but doing what you should, without needing to be told. Did I learn some of this from Mister Rogers so long ago? Who knew Kant and Mister Rogers were on the same wavelength? I suppose he taught me how to be a bit more "autonomous."

Nevertheless, I think organic chemistry might actually be killing me. The equations and bond structures and nomenclature distinctions seem not only endless, but pointless. I'm a Pre-Med-Biology major, so why am I forced to take yet another chemistry class? I ask myself this question after every class, after every lab, after every time someone dares mutter the word "carbon" to me, yet I continue to study, even if it gives me no pleasure. I have always wanted to be a doctor and there is no way that I am going to let something as trivial as organic chemistry stand in my way. I am determined, I want to be the best I can possibly be, I want to do it all.

Perking up, I realize forty minutes have passed and my homework is all but completed, but I'm burning daylight, and I need to run to the store quickly before it gets cold and dark out. I walk out to my car and buckle myself in. As I drive, the monotony of the road starts to melt into my subconscious and I find myself reminiscing about my younger years once again . . .

*   *   *   *   *

Mommy clicks the belt on my car seat and away we go. Our car bumps and bumbles all across the road. With every stop the snow crunches underneath us. Snow is so weird; I don't understand it. We never talked about snow in school, but I feel like it's a surprise every time. Where does snow even come from? The streets are so white and clean. I really like the white. It is like a clean sheet of paper ready for crayons and paint. Crayons are my favorite thing to draw with; Mommy says I am a good artist like daddy. Daddy thinks so too, but he says I can't be an artist when I grow up. He says I need to get a good job so I can make lots of money to pay for my art supplies.

Daddy works with computers, but I do not like them. I don't like their stupid buttons. I never am able to hit the right ones, and it makes me so frustrated, but Daddy loves them. Daddy wants me to be a doctor like my aunt when I grow up, and I do too. My Aunt Jennifer is a special tooth doctor called a dentist. All my friends are scared of the dentist, but I'm not because my aunt loves me and she does a good job of taking care of my teeth, and after every visit she lets me pick a prize out of the special treasure chest for being such a good patient. Mister Rogers says that we shouldn't be afraid of doctors because they are just trying to help us, and I believe him. Mommy says I don't have to be a doctor. She says that I can be anything I want as long as it makes me happy. I like this: I like how open and expansive she allows the world to be for me. The freedom she gives me makes me happy. I like being happy; it makes my insides feel warm and my smile grow big. But I think that being a doctor will make me happy too, so I've decided: when I grow up I am going to be a doctor.

Stop, go, stop, go. We stop and go so many times on the way to the store, but then we stop one last time. Mommy gets out of the car and unbuckles my belt. I climb out of the car with my stuffed doggy Wishbone in hand and Mommy snatches my other hand, but I let her. Mister Rogers says it is important to look both ways when crossing the street and to let adults help, so that's exactly what I do. And with that Mommy and me enter the store through the magic doors that open all by themselves. When we are inside, Mommy grabs the bag of salad we need for dinner, and she rushes me to the checkout so we can beat Daddy home from work.

I like how bright it is in here, I can see myself in the floor. I drag my stuffed dog on the ground, right through my reflection. Back and forth, back and forth, but then, I see a little boy in front of me and Mommy in the line, staring. He's staring at my doggy, he's staring at Wishbone, but I stare too. The boy has a teddy bear, the most beautiful bear I've ever seen with a yellow ribbon around its neck. I have my doggy and I love him, but I want the bear. I want the bear so much; I feel my face get hot and my eyes start to well up as I start to cry. I cry and I cry, and Mommy picks me up, but I still want the bear. I can't stop crying. I want the bear so much! I don't know why, but I think that the bear should be mine. Mine, not his, mine. It should be mine. Mommy quickly gives the lady behind the counter some money and shuffles me to the car. She straps me in and we drive back home, my tears dry up and I start to feel better, but I am afraid that mommy is upset with me for making a scene. I ask

Mommy if she is upset because I am like this, she smiles and says "of course not," and like she always does, she borrows Mister Rogers's words and said "I like you just the way you are." And I believe her.

*   *   *   *   *

I park without issue for once, not a single sideways glance nor lewd gesture necessary to ensure a close parking spot. I beeline it for the produce department and grab a bag of spinach salad mix, the same brand my mother used to buy, and I head for the register. I quickly get into line before the after-work rush of mothers and fathers arrive, picking up boxes of macaroni and cheese and chicken nuggets: the two staple foods of childhood. The lights overhead are hauntingly bright and the floors shine a brilliant white. I look at the woman in front of me and think, "who goes grocery shopping in such high heels?" Standing there, as the line inches forward, I'm drawn back to that vapid thought about the woman's shoes. I really love them, yet I feel so strange, so uneasy, I think that I might be jealous.

My mind wanders back to the Neighborhood of Make-Believe, back to Henrietta Pussycat, probably because I feel a little like she felt when Grandpère's fancy-pants Parisian granddaughter, Collette, visited the neighborhood (episodes 1176, 1177). I remember how Henrietta had started to dress in the fashion as Collette did and how angry she was at all of the special attention given to Collette, Henrietta feels like she's being replaced, and that "meow was here first, meow!"

I have no reason to be jealous: I could easily have shoes like that if I really wanted to. I wonder why I feel this way then. This isn't like me. Am I being "inauthentic"? I feel like Martin Heidegger would call it that. It's an inevitable part of our being, sure. I mean, Heidegger had his own share of inexcusable inauthenticity. But he's got a point especially when he describes the way we have a tendency to "fall prey" to what he calls "the They." It's a phenomenon of being absorbed, or dissolving, into others, into a group of indefinite, anonymous others. "In this inconspicuousness and unascertainability, the real dictatorship of the 'they' is unfolded," Heidegger says. "We take pleasure and enjoy ourselves as *they* take pleasure; we read, see, and judge as *they* see and judge; likewise we shrink back from the 'great mass' as *they* shrink back; we find 'shocking' what *they* find shocking" (*Being and Time*, p. 164).

Jealousy is such an ugly feeling, I just want it to stop. "I can stop when I want to, I can stop when I wish." I think I can do this, I can make it stop; I can conquer this. I tap the woman in front of me in line on the shoulder and I stop all of my uneasiness in five little words: "I absolutely love your shoes;" and with that I feel better. I felt like the real "me" again—my "authentic self," perhaps. I feel now a bit like Henrietta Pussycat who eventually overcame her jealousy of Collette and her fanciness, and rose to the task of introducing Collette to the rest of the neighborhood: an expression of goodwill (episode 1180). The fancy woman in the checkout line—maybe her name is Collette, who knows—smiles with gratitude towards me and turns her attention back to the cashier. Once again, I'm alone with my thoughts in this crowded supermarket. There is just one thought in my head, but it is one that sparks something deep within me, something that I haven't felt since I was six years old, and with that, I think to myself, "Sydney, I like you just the way you are."

"I like you just the way you are. I like you just for being you."

6
Peace through Emotional Development

NATHANIEL J. MCDONALD AND
FRANK SCALAMBRINO

There isn't anything quite like *Mister Rogers' Neighborhood* on television. An episode is as distinctive today as it was forty years ago. Obviously, Fred Rogers himself is the reason the program is unique, but not because of his personal eccentricities as a television host. His show is unique because Mister Rogers carefully crafted every moment of every episode to speak directly to children.

Calling for adults to "Please, think of the children first," he intentionally avoided the cheap thrills that other television programs deliver to children through sensory "bombardment." As entertaining for parents as *Mister Rogers' Neighborhood* may be, the mission of his philosophy was to serve the needs of children—especially their emotional development—through the medium of television, even at the expense of all other priorities such as production value, entertainment, or commercial success.

In this way, Rogers's philosophy produced a fundamental innovation in television programming in that he took the developmental needs of children as his starting point. His philosophy of absolutely prioritizing the needs of children involves two important principles.

- First, his philosophy acknowledges that the needs of children are different from the needs of adults. This involves the existential principle that life consists of a series of developmental stages, the navigation of which allows us to construct a mature self.

- Second, his philosophy is generally based on the humanistic principle, closely aligned with the idea of "unconditional positive regard" from the thought of psychologist Carl Rogers, which emphasizes the dignity of all humans. Fred Rogers understood that the feelings children experience are as real and as valuable as the feelings experienced in adulthood, and every aspect of his work is grounded in this understanding.

Rogers felt that most television programs for children essentially ignore these principles. So, he took it upon himself to study child development intensely, learn about the particular needs of children, and ground the theme, message, and content of every episode in a scientific theory of child development.

Around the turn of the twentieth century an Italian physician named Maria Montessori had observed that traditional methods of education were not based on a scientific understanding of child development. Like Rogers's sentiments regarding television for children, Montessori felt that education was fundamentally misguided because it did not prioritize children or an understanding of their needs. And, like Rogers, she turned to developmental psychology for a deeper understanding of the particular needs of children.

Montessori's Planes of Development

Drawing on the work of early developmental psychologists such as Jean Piaget, Montessori designed a developmental approach to education. She identified four stages, or "planes" of human development, roughly divided by age 0–6, 6–12, 12–18, and 18–24.

At each plane of development, the child is particularly sensitive to acquiring certain skills, or integrating certain components of personality or identity. For example, children in the first plane literally need to learn how to be in the physical and social world, so they have an insatiable drive to use their senses, to move, and to understand how to communicate.

According to Montessori, first plane children are in a "sensitive period" for use of the senses, movement, and language. Thus, they learn to walk and talk, and they do so without anyone teaching them. The sensitive period for language is one of the best examples of her theory of planes of development: a child between one and four years old can learn multiple languages perfectly simply by interacting with people speaking those languages. Although adults can study and learn other languages, fluency is almost always compromised or requires an extraordinary and intentional effort. It is as if toddlers have a superpower for learning a language.

The other planes of development have particular needs, tendencies, and characteristics as well. The second plane of development (6–12 years old) is focused on learning the knowledge necessary to enter society. The third plane (12–18) involves "adolescence," so the primary drive is social, especially with respect to the formation of identity and development of independence. The fourth plane (18–24), then, calls for the consolidation of identity and independence. Fortified with an understanding of these planes of development from developmental psychology, Montessori set out to painstakingly prepare learning environments optimized for the particular needs, tendencies, and characteristics of children in each plane.

In this way, each Montessori classroom is a "prepared environment," specifically designed to meet the particular needs of the children in the environment. Embracing the same "Humanistic" philosophy that Fred Rogers would later adopt, she theorized that a child who has the opportunity to exist in a succession of prepared environments has the best chance of optimizing their own potential as a human being. In fact, Montessori resisted her ideas being classified as "education," preferring instead the notion that her prepared learning environments were an "aid to life;" that is, a method to facilitate the process of self-construction involved in each individual's natural development toward maturity.

This process of self-construction is the child's *"work"*—their mission as an individual. A primary philosophical ideal in this vein is for the adult to trust that the child is driven toward self-construction. Therefore, an essential aspect of implementing this ideal is to *trust the child to be able to act independently in the prepared environment*. The prepared environment of a Montessori classroom provides children with freedoms appropriate for their plane of development. This freedom to make their own choices, direct their own activities, and manage their own time, provides children the opportunity to work toward self-construction regarding the truth of "freedom and responsibility," that is, the idea that with increasing freedom and independence comes increasing responsibility.

Rogers's Prepared Environment

Maria Montessori and Fred Rogers shared a philosophy characterized by the same branch on the tree of developmental psychology and the same archetypes of Western spirituality. Rogers consulted directly with the child psychologist, Margaret McFarland, about nearly every episode, and McFarland was directly influenced by the contributions to developmental psychology from such luminaries as the pediatricians Benjamin Spock and T. Berry Brazelton, and the psychologists Erik Erickson and Jean Piaget. Along with sharing such influences, Montessori and Rogers even both invoke Jesus, the Christ, to frame the work of self-actualization as an existential vocation.

It was against this philosophical backdrop that Mister Rogers characteristically explained, "When I look at the television, I see one person" and "I give an expression of care every day to each child." He sought to make his thirty-minute television program a prepared environment to meet the social and emotional developmental needs of the child watching the program. Like a Montessori classroom, the *Neighborhood* set was painstakingly designed to ensure that every detail was developmentally appropriate and contributed to the goal of helping children develop key emotional skills and competencies such as self-regulation, communication, rationality, and emotional and social awareness.

Why did Mister Rogers deliberately enter and exit his home in the same consistent way, singing the same transition-oriented song? Assuming his audience was pre-school to early elementary-aged children, he directed the show with regard to their sensitivities and the work of their developmental planes, which includes making clear distinctions between reality and fantasy. Thus, everything in his TV studio "home" was always in the same place—the bench Mister Rogers sat on to change his shoes, the closet where he hung his coat and sweater, Trolley's route to the Neighborhood of Make-Believe, the fish tank, and so on. This allows for a consistent and coherent anticipation.

Similarly, the show was consistently organized with careful attention to making a clear transition between each short segment so that the child would not be startled or confused. The child can depend on the show beginning and ending in the same way. Likewise, he always orally introduced the puppetry segment in the Neighborhood of Make-Believe with Trolley moving down the track, as the screen fades from Mister Rogers to the puppets. Such stability provided a visual and aural context in which he could directly, and carefully, address common issues related to feelings. Rogers said that "feelings are mentionable and manageable," and through the puppets he attempted to demonstrate both how to communicate about and manage feelings appropriately. The puppets, and the human performers interacting with them, express, discuss, and work through feelings like fear, jealousy, sadness, and anger deliberately, modeling the process for the child-viewer.

Rogers determined the themes and substantive content with the attention to emotional development characteristic of preparing a Montessori classroom. For example, based on his study of child development, he believed that learning self-discipline requires self-esteem, a healthy self-concept, and arises over time through practice. Many of the songs and the themes of episodes revolve around communicating an appreciation for each child as an individual "just the way you are." And Mister Rogers delivers the message in clear, simple language with a genuine earnestness that cannot be misinterpreted as anything but an authentic statement of a true belief. Consider the lyrics to the song "It's You I Like":

> It's you I like.
> It's not the things you wear.
> It's not the way you do your hair,
> But it's you I like,
> The way you are right now,
> The way down deep inside you,
> Not the things that hide you.
> Not your toys.
> They're just beside you.
> But it's you I like,
> Every part of you,
> Your skin, your eyes, your feelings,
> Whether old or new.
> I hope that you'll remember,
> Even when you're feeling blue,
> That it's you I like.
> It's you yourself.
> It's you.
> It's you I like.

Invoking Carl Rogers's philosophical principle of unconditional positive regard as fundamental for education, Fred Rogers explained, "I don't think anyone can learn unless he is understood exactly as he is." And every episode ends with the song, "It's Such a Good Feeling," which sometimes includes a spoken bridge where Mister Rogers looks straight at the camera (the child viewer) and says: "You always make each day such a special day. You know how: by just your being you. There's only one person in the whole world exactly like you, and that's you yourself, and people can like you exactly as you are."

It should be clear how the foundation and goal of education—which naturally and logically follows from the efficacy of the philosophical principle of unconditional positive regard—is peace.

Individual Self-fulfillment

In his now-famous testimony before the United States Senate committee considering funding for public television, Fred Rogers spoke about the possibility that a child can learn to manage his emotions—namely, anger—successfully, and feel a deep sense of accomplishment as a result of being able to "stop when you've planned a thing that's wrong." He expresses serious concerns about the content of children's programming on television, but strikes an optimistic tone about the possibilities associated with his program, describing it as "constructive."

Rogers undoubtedly used that word deliberately. Children who advance effectively through the stages of social and emotional development will be more balanced, mature, and productive adults. In other words, invoking the philosophical principles noted above that humans naturally develop their potential for having a self, given appropriate conditions humans can do the work of developing their potential to a point which may simultaneously be characterized as self-actualization and self-construction.

In her affirmation of these philosophical principles, Montessori was explicit that the goal of education is peace. "Preventing conflicts is the work of politics; establishing peace is the work of education. We must convince the world of the need for a universal, collective effort to build the foundation for peace." Montessori's foundation for peace was a simple syllogism, as follows:

- **First, as the poet William Wordsworth put it, "The Child is father of the Man"—children are nothing more nor less than the next generation of adults in development.**

- **Second, when society dedicates sufficient time, attention, resources, and expertise to the unique developmental needs of children, the result is adults who have had the opportunity to develop optimally and reach their full potential as individuals who understand the interconnectedness of all things.**

- **Therefore, these adults will be peaceful and create the conditions for a just and lasting peace.**

Montessori explored the concept of peace in depth in a series of lectures given around the world in the 1930s, that is, after World War I and as the thunderclouds of World War II were gathering in Europe. Through these lectures she specifically discussed a negative and a positive concept of peace. She defined the negative concept of peace as the absence of war. She acknowledged that the negative conception of peace can be achieved through armed conflict after which the victor imposes its will on the defeated. However, she also noted that peace through subjugation is a vicious cycle that can only be sustained through further conflict or unremitting oppression of some by others. In contrast to the negative concept of peace, she passionately advocated for a positive concept of peace which could be obtained through education.

Affirming both the existential and the humanistic principles noted above, Montessori explained, "our hope for peace in the future lies . . . in the normal development of the new man . . . What we can and must do is undertake the construction of an environment that will provide the proper conditions for his normal development."

In this way, Rogers and Montessori share a positive view of children and the potential of self-actualized individuals. Their prioritization of the interests of children, while for the benefit of the children themselves, is also for the benefit of society. Just as Rogers assumed that children have the same intrinsic value as adults and, therefore, deserve the same respect and attention to their particular needs, so too Montessori felt that each child is "an independent person who must be considered in terms of his own individual self."

So, conflict resolution clearly involves "feelings," and a productive, independent adult who understands and self-regulates his or her own emotions can develop healthy social relationships. Further, for Mister Rogers, self-worth is the foundation of other skills and competencies, and children who develop skills to self-regulate, manage their own emotions, and communicate about emotions, are stronger, more resilient, and more productive adults. This is what we can do by working through the mad that we feel.

Mister Rogers—Father of the Millennials?

A common criticism of Mister Rogers is that he enabled children to feel good about themselves without accomplishing anything. This, in turn, is said to have fostered a destructive sense of entitlement, narcissism, and weakness in a generation of adults who watched his program as children.

On the one hand, this criticism agrees with one premise of the Montessori syllogism; namely, that the education of children influences the character of a society by determining the character of its adult members. This is the existential principle noted above viewed at the societal level. But, on the other hand, it cuts straight to the heart of Rogers's approach, contradicting the "intrinsic value" or "unconditional positive regard" premise of the Montessori syllogism and challenging the validity of his commitment to providing unconditional positive regard—"I like you just the way you are"—to children.

A similar critique of Montessori schools claims that children have too much freedom in the classroom, and use that freedom to engage in unproductive activities. In general, the criticism may be articulated as suggesting that children should receive *conditional* (rather than unconditional) positive regard, and be given less freedom, if they are to achieve their full potential as independent, productive, self-regulated adults. But why should positive expressions toward children only be understood in terms of "behavior reinforcement"? Isn't there value in expressing positive regard toward a child so as to help the child develop its natural capacities for self-regulation?

A philosophical defense of *Mister Rogers' Neighborhood* might at least involve the following two insights. First, the entitlement critique of Mister Rogers's prepared environment may be an example of the logical fallacy that "correlation implies causation." While it may be true that a sense of entitlement and lack of resilience and persistence are significant problems for many children today, *Mister Rogers' Neighborhood* might not be the *cause*. Second, the misinterpretation of any theory can lead to deviant practices and aberrant—even antithetical—results. Parents could misinterpret Mister Rogers's message of unconditional positive regard as a rationale for consistently low expectations and no accountability. Likewise, teachers misinterpreting Montessori's theory regarding independence and self-direction might allow students too much freedom, including the freedom not to work at all.

7
Feelings, Mentionable and Manageable

JONATHAN R. HEAPS

There's a video of Fred Rogers that I must watch once a month and probably more often than that. Maybe you've seen it? An almost unrecognizably youthful Fred Rogers sits at a wooden table, a microphone in front of him. He's got on a dark suit and narrow tie that suggest a serious purpose. The camera looks down at him from above and a little to his right. Across from him, a mustachioed Senator John Pastore (D-RI) stares with swaggering authority down the lens of the camera. The video is immediately strange, because we know our television neighbor already. We know his voice, deliberate and sincere. By contrast, Senator Pastore blusters, though he clearly means for it to lighten things up. He's playing to the room. It's his room. Still, the way he addresses Mister Rogers—interrupts him—is startling, like someone accosting a kitten.

Mister Rogers is before Congress to ask the United States government for funds to continue his new experiment in public television. He tells the story of his television program and explains a bit about the philosophy behind it. "We deal with such things as the inner drama of childhood," he says. He tells them that each program offers children a "neighborly expression of care." By now, Senator Pastore has softened. His hand finds his cheek. His head is tilted. He's listening. He gently asks questions. It has now become Mister Rogers's room. His testimony, still in that familiar, gentle voice, reaches a zenith. "I feel that if we in public television can only make it clear that feelings are mentionable and manageable we will have done a great service for mental health." Pastore acknowledges, despite his reputation as a "tough guy," that Rogers has given him goose bumps. Mister Rogers smiles demurely and asks for permission to recite the lyrics to what is now a classic in the Neighborhood canon: "What Do You Do with the Mad That You Feel?"

Feelings

"What Do You Do with the Mad that You Feel?" is a song about a feeling: feeling mad. But there are lots of songs about feeling mad. Some of those songs have lyrics, though many don't. You may remember when Wynton Marsalis visited the neighborhood. Mister Rogers asked him to share with us what kind of music he would play on his trumpet depending on what feelings he had (episode 1563). In the wordless way that music can, his trumpet evoked and expressed the joy or sadness or anger we feel. This song, however, also names a feeling. It "mentions" it. These are the lyrics:

> What do you do with the mad that you feel,
> When you feel so mad you could bite?
> When the whole wide world seems oh, so wrong,
> And nothing you do seems very right?
>
> What do you do? Do you punch a bag?
> Do you pound some clay or some dough?
> Do you round up friends for a game of tag?
> Or see how fast you go?
>
> It's great to be able to stop
> When you've planned a thing that's wrong,
> And be able to do something else instead
> And think this song:
>
> I can stop when I want to
> Can stop when I wish
> I can stop, stop, stop any time.
> And what a good feeling to feel like this
> And know that the feeling is really mine.
> Know that there's something deep inside
> That helps us become what we can.
> For a girl can be someday a woman
> And a boy can be someday a man.

You may notice that not only is it a song that mentions our feeling mad, but it is also about "managing" our feeling mad. What do we do with the mad that we feel? That simple question—a question so simple little children can understand it—has a profound assumption buried in it: that our feelings are not just felt, nor even simply named, but that having felt them, we can do something about them. Mister Rogers told us, through time and television, that mentioning our feelings is part of managing them.

Perhaps you already know that Mister Rogers was right about this link between feeling, mentioning, and managing. Perhaps you still are skeptical. Either way, we might ask, "How?" How is it that mentioning our feelings helps us manage our feelings? That's a reasonable question, whether driven by our curiosity or by our skepticism. But I want to couple that reasonable question with a question that perhaps hasn't occurred to you. It's a question that might seem so obvious that it doesn't merit a question at all: how is it that we can mention our feelings in the first place?

Of course, we know *that* we mention our feelings. But it's a philosopher's job and privilege to ask "Why?" and "How?" and "What is it?" about all kinds of seemingly obvious and familiar things. That's what we're going to do together here: ask how it is our feelings are mentionable and how mentioning them helps us to manage them. It will turn out that being mentionable and being manageable are tightly woven together in our relationship to our feelings.

In the following, I rely on Eugene Gendlin's theory of "experiencing" and the various functions of symbols as he spells them out in one of his philosophical texts, *Experiencing and the Creation of Meaning*. However, Gendlin was also a clinical psychologist and if you are interested in how Gendlin used this philosophy in his practice, you might look at his popular work, *Focusing*.

Experiencing

If you're awake and reading this, then you are experiencing right now. You are experiencing the words on the page, either by looking at them or hearing them or perhaps feeling them by braille. So long as you are reading, you are paying attention to what you are experiencing.

But you are also experiencing things that you pay little or no attention to, like the sound of the HVAC system humming away or maybe the way your shoes are hugging your feet. Whether it's the part you are focusing on or the part that's "in the background," all of these are part of your experiencing. You can move your attention from one part to another because they're all part of your experiencing right now.

But there's another part of your experiencing and it's the greater part. This biggest part is the experiencing itself. This part isn't the experiencing "of" something, like the words on the page or the HVAC system. It is the presence you have to yourself in order for the words or the hum or the hug to be present to you. It's your experience of you, experiencing. But this can be the hardest part to pay attention to.

You probably picked up this book because Mister Rogers means something to you. Mister Rogers means quite a lot to me and that's why I was so excited to write something for *Mister Rogers and Philosophy*. When I think of Mister Rogers, I can picture all kinds of things about him: his sweaters, the red trolley, the jazz piano. I can also pay attention to how Mister Rogers makes me feel. Now, that could mean, "Mister Rogers makes me feel happy," or "Mister Rogers makes me feel safe." But we can also pay attention not to this or that feeling about Mister Rogers, but to how I feel when I'm experiencing my memory or my imaginings or my feelings about Mister Rogers.

We might call this feeling of experiencing something or someone the "quality" of my experiencing. Try this: think of Daniel Tiger and try to focus your attention on how it feels to experience that thinking and what that thinking feels like. Don't just think (like the words of "It's You I Like," say), about his hair, or about the things he wears. Don't just imagine his voice, but try to think "all about" Daniel himself. You may find that the way you are "experiencing" feels different from the way you are "experiencing" if you think "all about" King Friday or Lady Aberlin. We experience our images and thoughts and memories of these characters differently because they each mean something different to us.

It's important not to mix up our particular feelings (anger, sadness, or anxiety) with this over-all quality of experiencing them. It might help to distinguish these two ideas this way: when I feel anger ("the mad that you feel"), there is the anger and there is also feeling-the-anger. Feeling-the-anger is experiencing. The quality of our feeling-the-anger is a clue to what our anger means to us.

When X the Owl is getting too bossy while he and Henrietta are making fruit salad, Henrietta feels mad, but also knows why she feels mad. She knows what her anger means to her. It means, she tells us, that she feels unfairly controlled by X (episode 1508). However, if we aren't paying any attention to our own experiencing, but only to what we experience, we will remain oblivious to what our feelings mean to us. We won't understand why we react to our feelings the way we do. If we don't pay attention to our overall experiencing, we won't know what our feelings mean to us, and so we won't know what to do with the mad that we feel.

Mentioning

Feelings are mentionable because they are meaningful to us. We don't just experience them, the way we experience colors or sounds, but we care about experiencing them. Still, this only answers part of the question. It tells us why they *can* be mentioned, and so why mentioning them is possible.

How, though, do we go about mentioning our feelings? We use symbols. The symbols can be very simple: we turn our attention to our experiencing and we pick out "this feeling." "This feeling" names the experiencing we are focused on. So a word ("this" or "mad") can pick out a feeling, point our attention to it.

It doesn't even have to be a word. It could be a picture or some music, even a smell directing us to our feeling and to the quality of experiencing carrying what it means to us. Symbols can also help us say (even if just to ourselves) what it is they mean. We might say that our anger is "like a big scary animal on a chain," or that our sadness feels "like a deep hole that doesn't have a bottom." These images say what our feelings mean to us, what experiencing those feelings is like. By symbolizing the experiencing of our feeling, we get clearer to ourselves and with others about what our feelings mean.

When Mister Rogers sings to us, "What do you do with that mad that you feel?" his question offers us a symbol: the word, "mad." It turns us to our experiencing. What am I experiencing? Do I feel something that I would call "mad"? Now, the answer to these questions is just a fact. Yes or no; I feel mad or I don't. They are answered by paying attention, by putting a symbol to what I find in my experiencing, and by seeing if it tells the truth about how I feel. We discover that our feelings are *mentionable* by symbolizing them. We discover that our feelings are *meaningful* to us the same way: by paying attention to experiencing and symbolizing them. I feel mad and that feels like a burning fire or a dark cloud. We can mention our feelings to the people around us, but we can also mention them just to ourselves. That can be helpful when we aren't sure what we're feeling or why, and especially when being unsure is upsetting in itself. Which leads us to our final question: how does mentioning our feelings make them manageable?

Managing

When we mention our feelings, the quality of experiencing those feelings changes. Mentioning our feelings changes our experiencing, because now we feel the feeling along with the symbol we gave it. Once it's connected with that symbol, the meaning of experiencing that feeling becomes not *just* experienced, but also attended to, and even understood. But this changes what the feeling means to us now. Experiencing that feeling as meaningful, and naming that meaning and understanding that name, all of these are now part of experiencing that feeling. Mentioning our feelings transforms them.

This implies something remarkable: by paying attention to experiencing our feelings and by expressing what it means to us, we are capable of changing our experiencing of feelings itself. If experiencing a feeling is bothering you, you might be tempted to try to ignore it, to not give it your attention. But as I said before, just because you aren't paying attention to something doesn't mean you aren't experiencing it. Instead, you might pay attention to how you're feeling, and especially to the quality of experiencing that feeling. You might try to say what it means to you, to express it as clearly and as truly as you can. But you might also try to express your feeling in other ways, by making music or even sewing a quilt like Mister Rogers does in an early episode (episode 0041). Almost anything can be a symbol to help mention and manage your feelings. Whatever you choose, you may find that, all of a sudden or gradually, experiencing that feeling means something different to you. That means that you are experiencing it differently. Maybe now it doesn't bother you so much, though there's no guarantee. In any case, you can have that good feeling of knowing that you have made this feeling, as the song says, "really mine."

The good news is that, because experiencing that feeling has changed, you can turn to it yet again and symbolize it yet again. You can change its meaning and quality yet again. You're free to symbolize and re-symbolize, mention and re-mention your feelings as many times as you need to. You're never completely trapped in experiencing your feeling one way forever. Because we can always mention our feelings (even if it is hard), we always have the chance to make our feelings manageable. As you mention your feelings, as you render them more manageable, you may find that the process of paying attention to and symbolizing experiencing your feelings gets easier and easier. You may find that you get better at it over time. Many of us will have to develop this skill as an adult.

What Mister Rogers offered to us, through time and television, was a chance to grow in mentioning and managing our feelings when we were still young, so that we "can be someday a woman" or "someday a man" who feels and mentions and manages her or his feelings deftly.

What We Have Learned

As a university teacher, I sometimes show my students clips from *Mister Rogers' Neighborhood*. They always remark how calmly and how directly he turns to face difficult topics and feelings, whether divorce or disability or death. Mister Rogers could do this because he knew that making feelings mentionable helped to make them manageable.

As good philosophers, we ourselves have turned to ask, "How?" and "Why?" making feelings mentionable makes them manageable. It may well be true, but we wanted to know the reason it's true. We also asked how it is that feelings are mentionable at all. We started by distinguishing experiencing in general from what we happen to be paying attention to. We noted that along with our attention to something or someone, there is an experiencing of the attention and that it has a quality of its own. We can pay attention to that quality for its own sake and we can symbolize it, whether minimally ("this feeling") or more descriptively and even creatively.

With a theory about how feelings are mentionable in hand, we turned back to our central question about how mentioning feelings helps to manage them. We discovered that mentioning our feelings helped to change the quality of experiencing them. This change resulted from the way in which the feeling is now not just experienced, but experienced as meaningful and as, to some extent, understood. This change in the quality of experiencing the feeling changes the experience of the feeling.

Because I'm the one who can decide what to pay attention to and how to symbolize my experiencing, I am able to do something to help manage my feelings. I can do this as many times as I want, because each change of feeling carries a new meaning to me and a chance to come up with new symbols to express it. Finally, the more I practice this management of my feelings through mentioning them, the easier it becomes.

With time, I might learn to turn to face my feelings about difficult things with the confidence and gentleness of Mister Rogers.

III

By Pretending
You Can Be Most
Anything You Can
Think About

8
The Virtues of Art

DAVID BOERSEMA

In the 1984 movie, *The Karate Kid*, seventeen-year-old Daniel LaRusso moves into a new home in Los Angeles where he meets the apartment's handyman, Mister Miyagi. Daniel befriends a high school cheerleader, which draws the attention of her ex-boyfriend, skilled in a vicious form of karate through the Cobra Kai dojo. When the boyfriend and some of his buddies attack Daniel, Mister Miyagi intervenes and, through his knowledge of karate, single-handedly defeats the five attackers with ease.

Amazed, Daniel asks Mister Miyagi to be his teacher. Daniel's training starts with menial chores, such as waxing a car and painting a fence, tasks that he believes are pointless to his interests. When he becomes frustrated, Mister Miyagi demonstrates that these actions have helped him to learn defensive blocks. Mister Miyagi was teaching Daniel more than he, Daniel, realized by assigning those seemingly pointless chores, and Daniel was learning more than he realized.

Just like Mister Miyagi's interactions with Daniel, one of the profound virtues of Mister Rogers and his approach to others, especially children, is exactly the same: his gentle use of arts, particularly music, was to help and teach about not only the virtues and values of arts, but also about becoming a virtuous and happy person. Through his songs and other arts, maybe he was teaching us more than we realized, and maybe we were learning more than we realized. And like the vicious form of karate, as presented in the movie, other art-forms can be and have been created and used in non-virtuous ways and for non-virtuous goals.

We can all identify many examples of arts in the service of violence and abuse (for example, pornography, stereotyping of groups, war propaganda). Arts are powerful, but Mister Rogers felt them and used them in ennobling ways and for ennobling ends. Let's explore some ways that Mister Rogers uses art to connect with his television neighbors, as well as some philosophy of art, or what is typically called Aesthetics.

Affective Meaning

Think of the different connotations between, say, "wilderness" and "wasteland" or between "environmentalist" and "tree-hugger." The first words in those pairs seem more complementary and positive than the second words. Or, think of the difference between these examples:

- **Lady Elaine is firm; X the Owl is obstinate; King Friday is pig-headed.**

- **Mr. McFeely is devout; Lady Aberlin is committed; Henrietta Pussycat is fanatical.**

- **Daniel Striped Tiger is flexible; Prince Tuesday is indecisive; Hula Mouse is wishy-washy.**

The three words used in each case speak to the same trait, but they have different connotations. Being firm, obstinate, or pig-headed all speak to being resolute, but you'd probably rather be considered firm than pig-headed, right?

The point is that the literal meanings are all the same (or nearly enough), but how the different words affect you can be quite different. This is often referred to as affective meaning (as opposed to literal meaning).

Similar to affective meaning, there is also affective behavior. We all can tell the difference in someone's tone of voice or body language, often as an unspoken feeling. If someone says to you, "Nice haircut," you can usually tell if those words are spoken genuinely or sarcastically. Or King Friday and Queen Sara could perform the same action, such as visiting a sick friend, but if Friday does it grudgingly out of duty and Sara does it happily out of kindness, we can usually feel the difference, and that difference matters to us.

While Mister Rogers sought to communicate ideas, he did so first and foremost at an emotional level, through making "felt" connections. In particular, he used the arts, especially music, because "music is the one art we all have inside."

We may not be able to play an instrument, but we can sing along or clap or tap our feet. Have you ever seen a baby bouncing up and down in the crib in time to some music? When you think of it, some of that baby's first messages from his or her parents may have been lullabies, or at least the music of their speaking voices. All of us have had the experience of hearing a tune from childhood and having that melody evoke a memory or a feeling. The music we hear early on tends to stay with us all our lives (*The World According to Mister Rogers*, p. 18).

This quote speaks not only to the immediate emotional impact of music (and more broadly, the arts), but also to the meaning and virtues of the arts themselves for who we are and who we can become. Mister Rogers consciously and intentionally used what he saw as the virtues of the arts in his goal of helping children become fulfilled and virtuous persons.

Being Affected by Art

Have you ever been moved by a musical performance? Consider what it is about that experience that makes it *aesthetically* moving. We can be brought to tears by experiencing physical pain and we also can be brought to tears by experiencing a deeply moving artwork; what's the difference between those experiences and what makes the one aesthetic but not the other? It's obvious that with art, at least some art, we feel an immediate connection that can be difficult to enunciate or explain. We just feel it! This more aesthetic, emotional connection can also happen when we encounter a beautiful view of nature; there, too, we have a felt connection that moves us.

Mister Rogers was keenly aware of this aesthetic experience and made it a central element of the show. Consider for moment the way Rogers's opening song makes you feel: "It's a beautiful day in this neighborhood, a beautiful day for a neighbor. Would you be mine? Could you be mine?" By beginning this way, he means to establish that immediate felt connection with his audience. But while there is an emotional immediacy, the aesthetic experience it evokes also has a cognitive component that is presented for us to understand. The song is meant to express a particular, literal message, that it's a beautiful day and he wants us to be his neighbor (and friend).

In using the affective nature of aesthetic experience, one of the components of Mister Rogers's teaching was to emphasize that art is both product and process. When we think of works of art, we often (perhaps usually) think of the product like paintings, sculptures, and novels. Besides being objects, such as paintings, artworks can be events or performances, such as dance, theatre, or music. Still, a dance performance or music recital is a product. However, arts can also be thought of in terms of the creative production of those products, or their process.

The *Mona Lisa* didn't just pop into existence! If you have ever attempted to create a painting or song or poem, you know very well that the process is a matter of a lot of blood, sweat, and tears. The distinction between art as product and art as process is not a sharp line. There are impromptu and spontaneous acts of artistic creation. So, you might think of product and process as points on a spectrum rather than separate categories or components.

Mister Rogers saw, and encouraged his audience to see, art in both senses: product and process. In one of the episodes where he talks about art specifically, he invites his viewers along with him to visit the studio of an author, Eric Hill (episode 1645). At the studio Mr. Hill talks about the process of creating one of his books and shows how he draws and paints his characters. In another one, he talks with an artist who demonstrates the process of making a pot from clay and is given a hands-on lesson in pottery (episode 1644). The subtle message in these, and numerous other episodes, is to see art both as a finished product and also as a series of steps and decisions in the creative process.

Expression and Representation

Something we hear a lot about art is that it is a subjective mode of expression. We feel or think certain things and certain ways, and we put those feelings or thoughts out into the world through paintings or writings or by dancing. Mister Rogers spoke repeatedly of this, both in the show, and in his own writings:

> In order to express our sense of reality, we must use some kind of symbol: words or notes or shades of paint or television pictures or sculpted forms. (*The World According to Mister Rogers*, p. 28)

> The more I wrote [songs], the better the songs became, and the more those songs expressed what was real within me. (p. 123)

And in the show, he sometimes states the importance and value of art as self-expression. At one point Lady Aberlin tells King Friday about a portrait she likes, and the king remarks that she should show it to all the neighbors and have them copy it for themselves. But she convinces him that art comes from within each person, and so each of the neighbors should make their own artworks (episode 1641). More commonly, though, he simply creates a piece of art and implies its importance and value, like when he works on an art project using sand (episode 1762), or when he and a neighbor mix clay and create pottery (episode 1763).

A fundamental value of art, then, is as an avenue of self-expression, especially for children, because of its affective nature. It allows us to engage with the world in a way that exhibits and enables our agency, or our ability to meaningfully act and create change.

Communication and Community

While self-expression is important, many artists and non-artists alike have noted that communication is more important in the creation of art than "mere" self-expression. They say that self-expression is merely a one-way street; it's an artist expressing herself, but that's all. A more important feature—and virtue—of art is its power as a tool of communication and of building community with others. Art should be a two-way street; it should be an artist using art as a means of connecting with others, not merely stating or announcing their feelings or beliefs. Throwing a temper tantrum is an example of self-expression, but it ain't art! Even further, a goal and virtue of art is to have an impact on others as well as on oneself.

One reason that art is seen as communicating and creating community is because much of it is a matter of working collaboratively with others. Despite the stereotype of the lone artist painting pictures in a garret, much art is collective and collaborative. The performing arts especially—theater, music, dance, film—all involve the creative collaboration and cooperation of many artists. Theater involves actors, script writers, stage managers, costume designers, lighting designers, sound technicians, and others. A dance performance involves dancers, choreographers, stage directors, musicians, costume designers, lighting designers, and so on. The point is that for the creative process to work, this involves collective collaboration, working well with others.

For Mister Rogers, these notions of communication and community are front-and-center in his engagements with others. In one episode he arrives with various drawings of Trolley that were made by some of his young "neighbors" (episode1765). He talks about sharing creations with other people you care about and sharing your creative art as a demonstration of love, with the clear message again of using art not simply to express yourself, but to connect with others. In another episode this point is demonstrated when Dr. Bill Platypus, Handyman Negri, and King Friday all play various musical instruments to create a harmonious rendition of *The Bluebells of Scotland* (episode 1764).

From the perspective of the audience, communicating and creating community can result from encountering works of art. A simple example comes from my own experience teaching a course on the Middle East. As might be expected, my students had a number of stereotypical conceptions of people in the Middle East, most of them quite negative. However, when I played samples of Arab hip hop and rock music for them they loved it! They came to see that their peers in the Middle East were in many ways (but certainly not all) like themselves, and were much more open to listening seriously to the views and concerns of those others and to seeing them more positively. Music was an avenue for opening minds and hearts.

This connection of arts for the audience occurs in numerous episodes of Mister Rogers's show. As just one example, Lady Aberlin and others are working on royal portraits. Lady Elaine refuses to help and says that she is tired of seeing portraits of King Friday. But after Queen Sara asks Robert Troll to create a portrait of Lady Elaine, she comes to realize that people care about her, too, and comes to be more accepting (episode 1645). For Mister Rogers, this points not only to how art can help us connect with others, but also how it can lead to personal transformation.

Change and Transformation

Another important virtue of art is its power to evoke a response in others and, ultimately, to create change, transforming both the artist and the audience. As Mister Rogers himself reflected on the transformational power of music:

> Music has given me a way of expressing my feelings and my thoughts, and it has also given me a way of understanding more about life. For example, as you play together in a symphony orchestra, you can appreciate that each musician has something fine to offer. Each one is different, though, and you each have a different "song to sing." When you sing together, you make one voice. That's true of all endeavors, not just musical ones. Finding ways to harmonize our uniqueness with the uniqueness of others can be the most fun—and the most rewarding—of all. (*The World According to Mister Rogers*, p. 154)

Besides affecting the artist, another sense of art as affecting change is with respect to the audience, that is, the rest of us who encounter that art. Sometimes the change can be unintentional; we experience some poem or painting or song, and it resonates with us so profoundly as to change us. Sometimes the change can be intentional, in the sense that the poem or painting or song is meant to help us (make us?) see the world differently, and may even be a means of social and political activism. This certainly is not new. It is as old as Aristophanes, writing in the fifth century B.C.E., with his comedic play *Lysistrata*, and as current as the public artist Banksy. The novels of Charles Dickens have long been recognized not simply as illustrations of the difficult and harsh conditions of life for many in nineteenth-century England, but also as a form of protest intending to instigate change. Other well-known examples include Harriet Beecher Stowe's *Uncle Tom's Cabin*, Upton Sinclair's *The Jungle*, and Ralph Ellison's *Invisible Man*.

Mister Rogers's approach to using art for social change was, of course, subtle, given that his focus was on children. Mister Rogers arrives, in one episode, with a small tree that he is looking after for Mr. McFeely. He draws a picture of it and sings a song, "You're Growing." Meanwhile, in the land of Make-Believe, Mayor Maggie visits with Henrietta Pussycat and X the Owl, who are waiting for the arrival of Cousin Mary Owl. When she does arrive, she talks about making videos, in particular of the sycamore tree where she lives. Back at the house, Mister Rogers talks about love of trees (and nature) before singing another song, "Tree Tree Tree" (episode 1761).

The subtle point here, especially for children, is to appreciate nature and to help it thrive by feeling its importance and value in our lives. And in another episode he feeds some fish and sings a song, "I Like to Take Care of You," and later remarks that he always makes sure that the fish are fed and taken care of (episode 1642).

But Mister Rogers's social activism is reflected even more explicitly in his remarks addressed to adults:

> I often think of what Will Durant wrote in *The Story of Civilization*: "Civilization is a stream with banks. The stream is sometimes filled with blood from people killing, stealing, shouting, and doing things historians usually record—while, on the banks, unnoticed, people build homes, make love, raise children, sing songs, write poetry, whittle statues. The story of civilization is the story of what happens on the banks." (*The World According to Mister Rogers*, p. 161)

Additionally, he noted, "Peace is far more than the opposite of war!" (p. 177). Genuine peace (both for individuals and society) involves a sense of self-worth and also meaningful and respectful interactions with others. As he noted, "We all have only one life to live on earth. And through [the art of] television, we have the choice of encouraging others to demean this life or to cherish it in creative, imaginative ways" (p. 158). What's true of television, for Mister Rogers, is true of the arts generally; they can be used to demean or to cherish.

The American philosopher John Dewey once remarked that art is not a thing, but an experience. We live in the context of many environments: physical, cultural, historical, and others. Art, he claimed, is a natural response to the conditions in our various environments and also a basic way of creating meaning and shaping those very environments in which we live.

For Dewey, art is a verb. It is a way of being. The same was true for Mister Rogers, and like Mister Miyagi, he tried to teach that to us in his own heartfelt, gentle, and thoughtful ways.

9
Fred's Felt Friends

DANIEL LEONARD

You are a young child. You feel ready to play. You go to a place in your home where you keep your toys and take some out. You pause. This last plaything is not one you know well; it is new. It feels soft in your hand. Some of it is made of plastic, like other toys, but most of it is made of fabric, like the clothes you wear. It has eyes, a nose, and a mouth, like a doll, but it has no legs; instead, it has an opening big enough for a hand, like a mitten. You put it on.

* * * * *

Why do young children love the puppets of Make-Believe? There are exceptions, of course. Lady Elaine Fairchilde, the scofflaw part-witch part-clown, saw her share of hate mail. But by and large, Fred Rogers's host of hoisted helpers kept his toddling target audience riveted to the screen. His characters work wonders to this day.

The televised puppets speak so directly to growing minds that Rogers fielded fan letters and inquiries on the slip-on celebrities' behalf. In one case, a toddler named Joe wrote, enveloped, stamped, and mailed a note—likely with help—simply to ask, "Why aren't there hands on Daniel's clock?"

Many of us once wondered why Make-Believe's Big Ben wears a blank face, but few had the gumption to sleuth it out like Joe. In Rogers's reply, he says something profound: "We decided we would pretend there was no time in Make-Believe, like the timelessness of love." When Rogers's hands take a break from view, so do time's. He hits pause on the onrush of reality that makes daily life so challenging by shifting our circumstances and removing us from positions of comfort. This

75

insight about "puppeternity" can help us to adjust, and then answer, our opening question: *How* is it possible for children to respond to puppets they see on TV? What makes toddlers adopt the values and attitudes of fuzzy objects onscreen as their own?

The timelessness of Rogers's puppet world lets it do something special. What it does is similar to what children's first possessions do for them—their blankies, teddy bears, and other objects, usually soft ones. The similarity between the Neighborhood's puppets and children's own toys and stuffed animals is no coincidence; in fact, some of the puppets began, in earlier incarnations, as Rogers's own toys when he was a child.

Such objects do a few important things: They can help a child learn to cope with being alone. They can enable a child to spread emotional investment from a relationship with a mother or primary caretaker out into the rest of the world. And they can give a child a way to establish and maintain a distinction between inner and outer reality while remaining connected to both. These are the tasks that belong to a "transitional object."

*   *   *   *   *

A face moves! It looks like it could be alive. You have seen faces move that aren't alive: on machines, in cartoons. But this face is different. It looks alive because your hand is alive. You turn your hand, and the face turns toward you. Its eyes are looking into yours.

*   *   *   *   *

Transitional Objects: How One Thing Leads to Another

In 1953, while Fred Rogers was undertaking his first televised puppet work on Josie Carie's show *Children's Corner*, psychoanalyst Donald Winnicott published a groundbreaking essay that names and describes transitional objects and how they work. His article, "Transitional Objects and Transitional Phenomena—A Study of the First 'Not-Me' Possession," describes how children use these objects creatively to build a bridge from their inner lives to the world around them.

In the womb, no bridge is needed; the umbilical cord lets fetus's needs be met instantly, no willpower involved. After a baby is born, a good mother works hard to feed her, change her diapers, and quell her cries. (We'll call this the role of "mother" even though it needn't be filled by a woman, nor even a parent—just someone who cares.) From the perspective of an infant, all this rapid need-filling can feel like it's the direct result of wishing: I wanted the bottle, then I got it, so I guess I made it happen. The infant has the illusion of being all-powerful to meet her own needs, with the mother remaining simply an extension of the infant's body and will. And this is a natural result of *good* parenting!

Fortunately, the story of reaching maturity doesn't end here. The illusion arises only to be shattered. As the baby grows, the mother spends more and more time parted from her and allows her to experience unsatisfied needs for increasing periods of time. It's at this stage that a baby starts to develop self-soothing behaviors like putting her fist in her mouth or sucking her thumb. The baby discovers by experimentation that she can use what's most ready to hand—literally, her own hand!—to stand in for the mother's bosom. In these ways, the baby learns to replicate some of the satisfaction of breastfeeding on her own terms, enough to tolerate the first brief periods of being left on her own.

But the experimentation continues. Soon the baby gets objects involved: while holding a blanket or a piece of cloth, she brings its edge into her mouth along with her fingers, or she uses it to caress her face. The baby's nerve endings don't inhabit the soft item, so the item's touch feels like it's coming from outside her body in a way that her hand can't. The object feels more like the bosom in this way, replicating a further aspect of the breastfeeding experience. In some ways the object is under the infant's control, to be picked up and used at will. It brings feelings to the baby's inner life as desired. In other ways, though, the object is its own entity. It submits to gravity; no matter how intently the infant summons it in her mind's eye, it sits where it's left until she physically reaches for it. It changes by accumulating stains and smells and showing wear, it occasionally gets lost, and, if the baby puts her hands behind it while playing with it, it sometimes appears to move on its own.

*   *   *   *   *

What kind of look is it giving? A friendly one? Angry? Curious? Bored? Whichever it is, you notice. Then the looker moves its paws. Toward you, in greeting? Away in fright? Upward in exhilaration?

*   *   *   *   *

Did Fred Rogers see and affirm the importance of transitional objects? Of course! Even the younger puppets in Make-Believe have special dolls, blankets, and animals that accompany them at bedtime. This shows Rogers's perceptive awareness of a few key traits of transitional objects.

First, a child develops an initial attachment to *one* object in particular. Whatever that object is, it comes with the child everywhere. To her, it's unique and irreplaceable.

Second, it's important for others to recognize that the child makes a unique claim on that object. The child shouldn't be asked to share it, and it's best for caretakers only to clean it or alter it only with the child's approval.

Third, the object is especially important at times of high stress and anxiety, bedtime particularly.

Children eventually outgrow their sole devotion to their object and spread their investment across a broader range of less purely consolatory toys. Eventually, as children struggle to let the outside world fulfill their needs, they're willing to include the most curious and complex type of "object": other people! Even then, the original object may remain important for falling asleep and at other stressful times.

Fred Rogers uses his puppets as ideal models and reassurers about bedtime, both in slumber-centric episodes of his show and in other published materials for parents and children. The critter crewmembers lend themselves to this task because of their object-ness. They approximate the material items children naturally use to bear being left alone and to surrender conscious control and awareness for the night.

A time comes when a child puts down her transitional object for good. Winnicott writes, movingly, "It is not forgotten and it is not mourned. It loses meaning." It simply finishes serving its purpose. But the "transition" isn't over; it never is. The "transition" of a transitional object isn't a one-way movement from infancy to maturity, but a both-sides holding-together of imagination and reality, of the subjective and objective worlds.

Older children and adults keep these realms connected through what Winnicott calls "transitional phenomena." For children, these include games, hobbies, and other forms of play. For adults, childhood activities broaden to include endeavors like the arts, sports, advocacy, even religion—areas that mediate between inner and outer reality. Fred Rogers recognizes how these activities serve as bridges. In his book *You Are Special*, he refers to them as filling a "gap":

At the root of all art and all science there exists a gap—a gap between what the world is like and what the human creator wishes and hopes for it to be like. Our unique way of bridging that gap in each of our lives seems to me to be the essence of the reason for human creativity.

Each person has his or her own realms of experience that satisfy the need to find links between the mind's wishes and the world's facts. Many of adulthood's meaning-making communities—social groups, fandoms, churches—consist of people who bond by the way they inhabit one particular realm or another. That includes, of course, fans of *Mister Rogers' Neighborhood*— viewers like us! The conversations that make up this very book are part of a transitional space. We come together as authors and readers to share our experience with the show, try to understand how our experience affects us, and find links with others through it.

*   *   *   *   *

She—you've realized she's a she—wants to say something. Her voice is going to be different from yours. You know this because you've seen adults holding friends like this one: the adult's mouth moves while the friend speaks. Usually it has a voice like the adult's, but high and gentle, or jumpy, or raspy. Your friend is ready. What will she say?

"Hi there," she says to you in a gentle voice. She tries again, her voice a little clearer: "Hi."

"Hi," you say. You wonder about her name.

"My name is Lucia," she says. "It's nice to meet you."

At the edge of the room, your parent is watching and smiling.

*   *   *   *   *

Transitionvision: How Puppet Programs Come in Handy

Puppets usually don't serve as transitional objects in the way Winnicott defines them. By the time children are ready to speak and act through a toy, they're past the stage of drowning an object in slobber around the clock. Still, the sense of company, even friendship, a puppet can offer is a more refined form of a transitional object's satisfaction and soothing. It too depends on a child's separation from her mother. Think of the games mothers play with their infants: making silly faces and voices, feigning surprise and other emotions, bouncily touching the child's nose, asking questions in jest. Puppets perpetuate these pastimes in a form that places the mother in the background, pulling strings without presenting herself as the agent. When children who experience puppetry in this way are ready, they can pick up puppets for themselves and do as they've seen.

Why do children imitate what they see their parents and other authority figures do? We all know intuitively that mimicries like "shaving" with Dad or "playing house" with friends express a child's desire to grow up, and they also help to make it happen. These behaviors lie within what's technically called "observational learning"—or, less technically, "monkey see, monkey do."

Psychologist Albert Bandura describes observational learning as a process that happens in four stages. When a model performs a behavior, the observer must first engage in attention (notice the act that's happening), then retention (remember it for later), then initiation (have the abilities needed to do the act), then motivation (want to do the act). Puppet play lends itself well to being taught to children through this process. It's highly attention-getting and memorable, it needs only simple skills to perform, and it offers ample motivation in the form of fun.

Observational learning helps to explain not only why children *play* with puppets, but also why they *imitate* puppets like those in Make-Believe. When the puppets in a show receive rewards from other characters for demonstrating prosocial behaviors and attitudes, even simple rewards like words of approval, this qualifies them as models for observation in children's eyes. Since young children are accustomed to treating doll-like objects as bridges between fantasy and reality, the fact that the puppets aren't actual people is no barrier.

On *Mister Rogers' Neighborhood*, the puppets gain further in status as models, since the affirmation they receive often comes not only from other puppets, but also from living adults who reside in Make-Believe. Many of them inhabit the "real" Neighborhood as well, where they earn young viewers' trust and provide motivation by making their approval feel valuable. The show's structure helps with the first three steps of observational learning, too. Its measured pace and tight focus promote attention, its repetitive themes, songs, and segments bolster retention, and its direct suggestions to the viewer— "Maybe you could try this with your family" and "Won't you sing with me?"—encourage initiation. Children's fascination with Daniel Striped Tiger comes in part from his compelling honesty about childhood fears and feelings, but it also comes from his close relationship with Lady Aberlin, whose motherly "ugga-mugga" nuzzles and words of support offer children an incentive to, so to speak, earn his stripes.

*   *   *   *   *

Now you are watching TV. On this show, a man welcomes you to a house and calls you his neighbor. He shows you things he brought home today, tells you things he's thinking, and even sings to you. Over time you have come to trust this man, maybe even love him. He also takes you—by trolley!—to the Neighborhood of Make-Believe, a different place where small friends like Lucia live alongside adults like ones you know. Today Lady Aberlin, your favorite adult, is talking with Daniel Striped Tiger, a small gray friend made of cloth. They're talking about mistakes.

Daniel has a small gray voice; it's familiar somehow. He says he isn't like other tigers, and he wonders if he's a mistake. Lady Aberlin looks at him lovingly, not interrupting as he goes on to speak about his question, then sing about it: "Most of the time I'm weak and I'm mild. Do you suppose that's a shame?" When he's done, Lady Aberlin sings back, "You're not a fake. You're no mistake. You are my friend." Finally, she and Daniel sing together—he still asks his question, but his question and her answer sound lovely together. Lady Aberlin is holding his paw. In his house, he's high up, so they can look at each other. You're looking at them. When it's over, the man will have something to say to you about it. You don't see him right now, but you know he's watching along. Lucia is too.

*   *   *   *   *

Display Play: The Power of Parasocial Interaction

We've let one last theoretical problem go unstated. Yes, the transitional objects of very early childhood pave the way for receptivity to puppetry later. And yes, children involve themselves in puppet shows and alter their behaviors and attitudes in response thanks to observational learning. But how is it possible to care about models, human or otherwise, presented on a TV screen? Doesn't the lack of living, realtime presence and of back-and-forth interaction, or at least the potential for it, detract from children's investment in what's said and done? Who cares what a flat face on a glowing box thinks? If it presents a challenging idea, can't you just turn it off?

If you've ever cheered till your face was red for a sports hero, been shocked and bummed by a celeb couple breakup, or felt warm fuzzies about man-myth-legend Fred Rogers, you know that our social brains never turn off completely, even when the relationship only goes one way. We engage routinely in what Donald Horton and Richard Wohl call "parasocial interactions"—relationships where we serve as audience to a mediated persona. Thanks to the power of illusion, we feel and even interact in such relationships in ways we do when relationships are reciprocal.

TV shows invite us to imagine that what's happening is genuine and present, and the camera places us in the same room as the action. We understand characters' emotions by appeal to our own, so it makes sense to envision ourselves as part of the scene as a way to develop feelings about it more thoroughly. Some shows, especially children's programs, foster parasocial interaction by speaking directly to the viewer. From the faux-collaborative mystery-solving of *Blue's Clues* to celebrity endorsements of hygiene products, media culture takes advantage, for better and for worse, of our inclination to respond to familiar faces, even when they're boxed in.

There's a special kind of safety in these interactions: they let us imaginatively try out behaviors and attitudes without the risk of failing, suffering rejection, or harming others or ourselves. If the trial seems promising, it gives us confidence to test the new pattern in real life. Parasocial interactions like those we develop with Fred's Neighbors, then, hit pause—paws?—on the stresses of reality. This lets them offer resources for maturation and personal growth that can make a permanent difference, in the right hands.

*   *   *   *   *

oudon't quite remember, but you have heard of children being called mistakes, or happy accidents. Part of you has noticed that most people are bigger and stronger than you are; you want to do things they can, but you try and someone laughs. Sometimes you cry or pout and someone tells you to stop being a baby. Other times you want to ask someone to give you a hug or say they love you, even though they recently did. These things live somewhere inside you. After the show, the place they live feels smaller. There are other places you can stay than that place, and it's easier to stay in them as you grow. You're learning this; you're watching the show.

* * * * *

In Safe Hands

The puppet stage is the centerpiece by which *Mister Rogers' Neighborhood* works as a transitional space. We come to care about X the Owl, King Friday XIII, Henrietta Pussycat, and all the rest, both as companions and as inspirations. By disappearing during the Make-Believe segments, Mister Rogers offers his puppet play as a transitional phenomenon—it "weans" children from *him* so that they can learn to cope with a caregiver's absence.

Meanwhile, the puppets resemble the soft items toddlers remember using as their first tools of self-comfort, and the puppets participate in creative play that echoes infants' own innovative coping techniques in a more advanced form. The show as a whole directs children's attention away from their real-world caregivers for half an hour at a time, giving them a cardigan-sweatered surrogate parent to tide them over.

Mister Rogers' Neighborhood is responsive to the pivotal role televised media can play in a child's life. Sometimes TV even serves as a proxy babysitter for kids whose caregivers aren't present. Accordingly, the show takes seriously its responsibility to tend children's needs while also leaving gaps in which independence can grow. When Mister Rogers sings his promise to be back when the day is new, it's more than a formality. He's helping the young to reconcile their inner world's wishes with the outer world's limits.

We adults who long for Fred to return from where he has gone—"promoted to Glory," he liked to call it—can rest in the timeless space of his love-land whenever we wish. And when, in our visits, we see his squeaky-voiced play-beings work through their feelings together caringly, we're handed gifts that help us to be whole.

10
Play in the Real World

Elizabeth F. Cooke

In so many ways Mister Rogers uncovers reality for children. In each episode of *Mister Rogers' Neighborhood*, he reveals what lies beneath the masks and mysteries of everyday things and activities that children encounter. When we learn how crayons and macaroni are made, we learn that these things don't arise out of nowhere.

We're also introduced to musicians and artists and learn how they do their work. Often Rogers asks the artist whether she had to practice hard while learning, or whether she made mistakes along the way. The child learns that making beautiful art is not magic. In the set of episodes on work, Rogers even shows us his own job of making television shows for children. The camera pans out to reveal the whole studio. The audience sees that Rogers's house is really a film set, they see the neighborhood as a miniature model, and the stage set for the Neighborhood of Make-Believe (episode 1530).

Rogers even shows us the puppets we normally see only in the Neighborhood of Make-Believe, and Mr. McFeely delivers pictures of Rogers working the puppets. Rogers also shows us his musical score with his own handwriting to teach us that the song we hear him sing regularly, "It's You I Like," comes from his thinking about the words and notes and then writing them down. The show is not magic, the characters in make-believe are not animated magically and the music we hear is not magic either. It's all part of the work of putting on this show.

Rogers understands that children want to know about reality. In the week's episodes on families, Rogers takes us to a "well visit" at a doctor's office (episode 1553). Before the visit, Rogers sings a song about how he likes to be told when he's going somewhere, how long it will be, if it's going to hurt, and so on. The song teaches parents more than children. Children want to know and grown-ups need reminding. Rogers tells the child to ask a parent or grown-up if she's wondering about something. Rogers first shows us an otoscope that doctors use to look in our ears. When he visits the doctor, Rogers asks the doctor whether she can see what a child is thinking and feeling when she looks into his or her ear. Rogers knows a child might wonder whether an otoscope can see into her mind, so he dispels that illusion. Knowing more about reality is empowering for the child, and puts her at ease. Rogers is a master at teaching children about reality because he recognizes that they want to be told the truth and because he understands that they sometimes come up with their own versions of reality based on appearances that are not real. Sometimes reality is hard to figure out. So much of our real world is confusing and covered. And we forget to tell children what's *really* going on.

Rogers's Philosophy of Pretend

Despite devoting so much of his show to uncovering reality, Rogers spends almost as much time in the Neighborhood of Make-Believe. In those episodes on work, after showing us his puppets in the real world as unanimated dolls, and pictures of him working the puppets, Rogers invites us into the pretend world where the puppets go back to being animated and the puppeteers are invisible again. Now it's time to pretend.

Rogers makes pretend time explicit for the child, saying something like "Let's have some make-believe." He presses a button for the neighborhood Trolley to arrive, and talks about what's going on in the pretend world, that he calls "the Neighborhood of Make-Believe." This world is not to be confused with our own. Psychologists and contemporary philosophers recognize that children are able to keep these two worlds apart at a fairly young age, and yet clearly children get reality wrong sometimes. Rogers helps them recognize that the pretend world is distinct from our shared real world, and that some things in make-believe do not apply to reality.

In the week's episodes titled "Be Yourself: That's the Best," X the Owl wants to give flying lessons, not just to birds, but to anyone who wants to learn. Upon returning to his television home, Rogers asks us whether we think that X the Owl can teach people and things like trolleys how to fly. He answers "anything is possible in make-believe" because make-believe is like a daydream. Rogers talks about how it's fun to pretend all sorts of things, like being braver or stronger than we are. But "the best thing is to know that we're really just fine the way we're growing," says Rogers, and "that people can like us exactly for what we really are way down deep inside ourselves" (episode 1716).

Despite keeping the two worlds distinct for children, Rogers spends so much time in the pretend world because we can uncover reality when we pretend, too. Here we see an important common theme between Rogers's philosophy and some American philosophers who suscribe to a philosophy called Pragmatism: Charles S. Peirce, William James, John Dewey, George Herbert Mead, and George Santayana. These philosophers were interested in doing philosophy in a way that makes sense of our everyday lives and everyday practices, rather than constructing theories and ideals with little application to life.

The pragmatists rejected Plato's view that ultimate reality exists only in the realm of immaterial ideas, and that the material world of tables, rocks, and buildings is mere illusion. You simply can't *live* Plato's philosophy, these pragmatist philosophers thought. They also rejected Descartes's skepticism which left us questioning whether this world was nothing but a dream, again because that philosophy can have no real effect in our lives. But even though they believed that skepticism is not a live option, knowing reality is neither simple nor straightforward for the pragmatists. Knowing the world is difficult work and requires asking questions and investigating everyday practical activities. Rogers, like the pragmatists, realizes that we learn from experience but not always directly from experience. Experience is mediated through our concepts, our preconceived notions and beliefs, as well as through our bodies interacting with our world. So learning is best done by engaging the world, manipulating it, experimenting with it, and asking questions about it.

Learning is not passive; it's active. We learn when our active engagement with the world is rational, thoughtful, and creative. So, for Rogers, make-believe is not escape. Viewers of Rogers's show know this. We don't visit the Neighborhood of Make-Believe to hide from problems. Instead problems often arise for our make-believe friends, and these problems often resemble the ones we face in our own world. Rogers knows that pretending offers an important opportunity to learn because sometimes parts of reality can be seen and understood more clearly from the perspective of the pretend world.

Pretend and the Self

In the essay, "The Soul at Play," contained in his book *The Birth of Reason and Other Essays*, George Santayana makes the case for the importance of pretend play, and like Rogers, Santayana also refers to pretend play as a dream. He says that pretend play is a "holiday," or a "midsummer truancy" from reality, but "these silly runaway impulses are parcels of our very selves; truer, in one sense, than the rational self they shatter" (pp. 35–36). We are freer when we pretend and so better able to get in touch with our truer selves. Rogers holds the same.

The Neighborhood of Make-Believe is filled with characters and events that are not real, but some truths uncovered in the pretend world echo truths in our real world. These talking cats and tigers are a lot like us after all. And sometimes in this make-believe world, we understand our shared reality and our truer selves. In the week's episodes on making mistakes when Daniel Striped Tiger wonders if he's a mistake, we learn that while we all make mistakes, no person is ever a mistake (episode 1578). And, at another time, when Daniel Tiger copes with the disappointment that a community swimming pool cannot be built, viewers realize things don't always work out the way they hope (episode 1530). Rogers often explains how the lesson learned in make-believe applies to our real world, after Trolley arrives back at his television home. We learn lessons about reality when we pretend because a shared reality exists between the two worlds, and because in pretend we can abstract from the contingencies of our real world and get at what is most essential.

Mister Rogers understands the child's instinct to leave reality and to "flout nature," in Santayana's terms, but also the child's equal pull to understand reality. But these instincts to know reality and to leave reality only seem to be opposites. Both in the real world and in pretend we aim to get at what's most important, the underlying reality. According to Santayana, "children are not empiricists; they want to understand, to know what things are *really*, not what they are obviously: they want to know what supplement their dream should add to the data of sense, so to round off the tale, and know the whole story" (p. 37). Empiricism is the theory that our knowledge of the world is derived from the evidence of our senses—from seeing, hearing, and touching things. Both Rogers and Santayana see the limits of simple empiricism. Rather than simply opening our eyes, we have to work to get at reality.

We have to pretend and create. "Nothing in nature behaves as its sensible essence," writes Santayana, and "everything behaves in a fashion which can only be explained (if explained at all) by a network of subterranean processes" (p. 38). For Santayana, pretend teaches us about this "network of subterranean processes," what lies beneath the surface of sensuous reality, but also what lies deepest within ourselves. We enter the world of pretend play, and feel comfortable knowing we never lose our true selves exploring a make-believe world.

As Santayana writes of pretend play in "The Soul at Play," "in this carnival of disguises and recognitions the soul feels quite at home, for her own life runs beneath the surface" (p. 38). Fred Rogers emphasizes this lesson time and time again. It's not what can be seen by others that makes us special and important, but what's underneath. As the song goes:

It's you I like,
It's not the things you wear,
It's not the way you do your hair,
But it's you I like.
The way you are right now,
The way down deep inside you,
Not the things that hide you.

Children become individuals through pretend play, through exploring different ways of being, and by learning what's most important about people and themselves.

Rogers explores a further dimension of pretend which helps the child to develop into an individual. By inviting the child to explore a pretend world, Rogers shows the child how to take different perspectives in pretend. Rogers shares this philosophical view of perspective taking in pretend with the philosopher George Herbert Mead, who says that in pretend we become socialized, and through socialization, we become an individual self. The child pretends to be a teacher, a mail carrier, cashier, or a mommy, and when she does she begins to develop a sense of what it's like to be another person because, in order to pretend, she must take that other person's perspective. But in so doing the child also begins to see herself in a different light. For Mead, pretend is essential to learning about others and oneself. As the child matures, she becomes capable of taking the perspective of any number of people in her community, and she utilizes this understanding in interacting with others in the real world.

We see Rogers address many relationship issues which require taking another person's perspective in the Neighborhood of Make-Believe. In the set of episodes about competition, Lady Aberlin discovers that Henrietta Pussycat is worried that X the Owl doesn't like her anymore because X has another friend (episode 1482). We understand both Henrietta's worry and Lady Aberlin's view that Owl can like two friends at the same time. And again, Handyman Negri realizes that Lady Elaine Fairchilde thinks people won't like her unless she wins contests. By watching their conversation, we see both points of view. We learn to take the perspective of others in order to understand them, and consequently learn something about ourselves too.

Play in the Real World

Not only does Mister Rogers bring lessons from the pretend world to bear on our real world, but he also explores pretend and play within our real world, the kind done by grown-ups and children alike. Rogers teaches us about this kind of play in his regular visits with artists and musicians and craftspeople. We're introduced to some of the best in the world, such as cellist Yo-Yo Ma, children's illustrator Eric Carle, and the group of percussion performers, Stomp. Rogers consistently tries out the new medium demonstrated by the expert, and shows courage in trying something new and taking lessons from the very best.

But Rogers never aims at perfection. We need not mimic the expert exactly. He lets the viewers see him fall far short of the expert's skill level. And that's okay, because the point isn't about producing a beautiful or perfect work. It's about empowering the child to try a new medium and to set off on his or her own path. The point is to have fun trying it out ourselves. Rogers makes this point explicit in the competition episodes when he draws with crayons and tells his viewers that he's not very good at drawing, but it's all about the fun of doing it. He goes on to draw a simple house and a tree and a stick person (episode 1481).

Charles Peirce develops a theory of imaginative play which resembles Rogers's practice of open-endedness. Peirce calls play "musement," and describes it as "esthetic contemplation" and "distant castle-building" (*Essential Peirce*, Volume 2, p. 436). We play for the fun of it, for its own sake. We meander in thought in an open-ended way, without a particular purpose in mind. We may develop a great idea or a beautiful work of art in play, but that is not why we do it initially. We do it initially because it is our nature, because all children (and all adults) love to play.

Earlier we saw how pretend helps the child develop as an individual, but playing and creating are also ways children develop as individuals. Your own work is valuable because it comes from you. It's special just as it is because each of us is special just as she is. Rogers explores the art world with a respect for these acts of creativity themselves, not only for the beauty they create. Acts of creativity express our individual autonomy. Autonomy, the philosophical concept of freedom, is more than just a concept; it is a practice for Rogers, just as it is for pragmatists. Being a free individual doesn't just mean making your own decisions every once in a while. It means doing things in your own way on an everyday basis. Rogers teaches us to be comfortable with that and even to embrace it. We can and should admire greatness, but we should embrace the everyday greatness that comes from being a unique individual.

For the pragmatists, more than just trying to understand reality, we must also recognize that we're part of reality too. We are agents, actors, and creators in this real world. Creativity has instrumental value because it helps us create in art and discover in science. But creativity is also "our condition." William James writes in his book, *Pragmatism*, that "in our cognitive as well as in our active life we are creative." Our creativity adds to reality: "The world stands really malleable, waiting to receive its final touches at our hands" (*Writings 1902–1910*, p. 599). What is most important in understanding Rogers's view is what James says after this last point: "No one can deny that such a role would add both to our dignity and to our responsibility as thinkers" (p. 599).

For Rogers, like James, understanding reality as well as creating reality adds to our dignity. Rogers respects children as knowers and actors in the world. The unifying project of his living philosophy is to uncover what matters most, what is most real. Part of this reality is the world we make through our own practical actions.[1]

[1] This paper could not have been written without helpful conversations and comments from R. Abrams, A. Abrams, and Jerold J. Abrams.

11
Mister Rogers's Pseudonyms

HOON J. LEE

No depiction of *Mister Rogers' Neighborhood* is complete without a trolley ride to the Neighborhood of Make-Believe. On my desk I even have a Mister Rogers Funko Pop! figurine holding the famous trolley. The land King Friday XIII rules is the setting for stories and lessons, which in turn forms the backbone of the show.

Trolley rides to this other-world lead the audience not towards an escape into fantasy, but towards an opportunity to see reality with a new perspective. The make-believe world is not a momentary respite from life issues, but a way by which Mister Rogers can help us through important life issues, *indirectly*. And, of course, it's also where we fall in love with X the Owl, Henrietta Pussycat, Daniel Striped Tiger, and others.

As inseparable as this make-believe world is to the show, Mister Rogers never makes an appearance in this world. Certainly, Rogers is behind the puppeteering and voicing of characters, but he never appears as himself. This is not simply due to a matter of logistics, as there are others who are involved in the puppetry. The nature of this magical land lets us understand how the concept of indirect communication plays an integral part in Rogers's philosophy of communication and language.

As all are aware, *Mister Rogers' Neighborhood* is about more than just entertainment. Rogers communicates a message of contemplation, love, with helpful emotional support. Indirect communication serves as a key methodological component to this endeavor. Specifically, by separating reality from a make-believe world and by hiding himself behind his characters, Rogers exemplifies Johann Georg Hamann's and Søren Kierkegaard's methodology of indirect communication.

First, there is a distinct break between the real and make-believe worlds. This intentional divide is reminiscent of Kierkegaard's strategy of addressing the self. Reflection about oneself, and especially criticism of oneself, is always difficult. Self-defense mechanisms preserve the self from harm by minimizing faults, deflecting on others, and turning a blind eye.

Kierkegaard realizes that the best strategy for addressing the self is through indirect address. His works are often narrations of events that happen to imaginary figures. These works allow the reader to examine matters with neutrality and without any need for self-preservation. It is not until after this indirect examination that the readers apply the lessons of the study to themselves.

That's exactly what Rogers does in the Neighborhood of Make-Believe. It's easier to talk about issues such as anger, sadness, and self-confidence in a land of puppets than in the real world. The various puppets allow for the working out of issues in a detached and indirect way. After addressing these issues from a distance, the trolley returns to the real world and the sequence of indirect communication is complete.

Mister Rogers and his persona belong to the real world. He reaffirms the lessons of the Neighborhood of Make-Believe with plain speech and direct communication. He does not confuse his role in the two worlds. For the Neighborhood of Make-Believe to be able to do what it does with indirect communication, and for Mister Rogers to work with direct communication in the real world, the two cannot be blended.

Second, for Hamann and Kierkegaard, the use of pseudonyms is a literary device to indirectly communicate authorial intent. Though they never write in their own names, their use of pseudonyms is never to hide their identities, as everyone knows they are the authors of their works. Instead, their intricate system of pseudonyms intends to indirectly communicate a different learning experience that fosters greater reader participation.

For Rogers, pseudonyms are not a literary device, but nonetheless, carry the same force of indirect communication and authorial intent. By masking himself behind puppets, Rogers can indirectly communicate his message. The puppets serve as his voice piece.

Kierkegaard uses pseudonyms to provide a variety of perspectives. Some of them are: Johannes De Silentio (*Fear and Trembling*), Vigilius Haufniensis (*The Concept of Anxiety*), Hilarius Bookbinder (*Stages on Life's Way*), and Anti-Climacus (*Sickness unto Death*). He never asserts a straightforward expression of his thought, and the pseudonymous authors do not align with Kierkegaard's own understanding. Rather, the numerous pseudonyms represent the different voices within the real world.

Rogers too uses "pseudonyms." Whereas Kierkegaard's pseudonyms are his puppets, Rogers's puppets are his pseudonyms. The anonymity is to the point where figuring out which puppet is the real Rogers becomes a guessing game. Throughout the years, the most common guesses, ironically, have been puppets with polar opposite personalities: King Friday the XIII and Daniel Tiger. The same guessing game is applied to Kierkegaard's various pseudonyms. But figuring out which character or which author represents the real Rogers or Kierkegaard is not the point.

The purpose behind pseudonyms is to engage the audience and foster participation. When direct communication is absent, the audience is encouraged to become an actor within the dialogue. Rather than being told what to think, the audience digests the material for themselves. This produces a deeper learning experience for the audience. As Hamann describes the process, the author provides a balled fist, and the reader does the hard work of unclenching the fist, finger by finger. Rogers provides a conversation about emotions and the child participates as the issue is worked through by the various puppets.

The Neighborhood of Make-Believe is a manifestation of Rogers's philosophy of communication, centered around his use of indirect communication. We can see this poignantly in the episode following the assassination of Robert Kennedy. In the aftermath of the horrific event that gripped the nation, Rogers recognizes the vulnerability of children. Their emotions are taken seriously as Trolley goes to the Neighborhood of Make-Believe. Through indirect communication, children are given an opportunity to work through their confusion and fears as Daniel Tiger asks Lady Aberlin what assassination means.

Contemplation in Silence

After his graduation from Rollins College, Rogers set out to enter church ministry. In a fateful turn of events, Rogers becomes mesmerized by the possibilities of television. This innovation sets Rogers on a new life trajectory that would impact millions of lives.

It's not so much what Rogers sees, but rather what he did not see that interests him. Television shows, especially shows for children, are filled with hysteria, loudness, and constant action. What is sorely missing is contemplation.

Contemplation requires time and silence, things not normally associated with television shows. Rogers realizes that
contemplation is not something that necessarily needs to be
directly taught, but rather something that should be indirectly
nurtured. Indirect communication becomes a tool to foster
reflection by making room for slowness and quiet. The visibility
of Rogers's indirect communication in the Neighborhood of
Make-Believe is mirrored in the things not seen or heard.

For instance, Rogers addresses the counter-intuitive measure he would take to get children to talk to him. You do not get
children to talk to you with direct dialogue. This can produce
shyness and hesitancy. Rather, the best way to get children to
respond is with silence. Contemplation and response are
encouraged by the gentle method of indirect communication.
By remaining silent, enough room is made for a child to contemplate and respond. By waiting, rather than directly talking,
the opportunity for the child to think and speak is indirectly
nurtured, which leads to a more open dialogue and authentic
conversation.

The same reasoning is applied to the aesthetic values of the
show. From the start in local Pittsburgh television to the
numerous seasons that captivated national audiences for
decades, *Mister Rogers' Neighborhood* possesses an intentional
aesthetic that indirectly fosters contemplation. Despite the
show's rising fame and the accompanying larger budget,
Rogers maintains his indirect communication of the value of
reflection through the simple aesthetics of the show. These aesthetics become the visual language of contemplation and indirectly immerse the value of reflection in the structure of the
show.

Reflection is not fostered by flashy lights or constant action.
Nor can we get children to contemplate simply by telling them
to contemplate. Rather than being told to spend a moment contemplating, audiences simply watch as Rogers merrily feeds
the fish. Sometimes this exercise is accompanied by a song, or
a lesson, or just with silence. Whichever way it is done, it is
never rushed. The process is always given time and energy, setting the tone and pace of the episode. By adding these aesthetic
values and taking out some of the traditional fanfare of children shows, Rogers indirectly communicates the importance of
contemplation and reflection.

The simplicity of the set, which some will call spare, inserts
within the show enough room for contemplation. The absence
of things and sounds allows for the indirect communication of
reflection. For instance, in one episode, the audience sits and

watches Rogers pipe a cake. The process is slow and deliberate. But within these few minutes children are encouraged to think about a parent's love, what it means to persevere, the short-comings of jealousy, and how simply wishing something to be true does not actually make it true.

Love in Numbers and Swimming Pools

Over the years, Rogers received many awards and delivered many eloquent and heartfelt acceptance speeches. Notably, his speeches are often injected with ten seconds of silence. These seconds are not an awkward pause or a lapse of memory. Rather, they were requested by Rogers as a moment for the audience to recall all those who loved them and helped them to become who they are now. No award or occasion was too big. Whether it was when he accepts a lifetime achievement award or was inducted into the TV Hall of Fame, Rogers requested ten seconds to remember how you are loved.

Love is the central tenet of *Mister Rogers' Neighborhood*. Before, and outliving, the monotonous *Teletubbies* and their song of love, Rogers cultivates an environment and message of love. It is the most common subject matter the show deals with.

Certainly, he directly communicates this through his songs and outright statements of love. However, this crucial message is also coupled by indirect methods. The significance of love is expressed both directly and indirectly.

For instance, love can be seen indirectly communicated through his beloved number 143. The numbers 1, 4, 3 represent the numbers of letters in "I love you." The numbers are repeated and appear in countless episodes. 143 becomes a way to indirectly include love in all aspects of life. The "code" of 143, or the open secret of 143, provides a way to talk about love in matters such as the 143rd day of the year, to Rogers's email address of zzz143@aol.com, and to his own body weight.

Love is also indirectly communicated in the simple pleasure of soaking your feet in a plastic kiddie pool. After the assassi-nation of Martin Luther King, Jr., Rogers thought it best to tackle social unrest and the issue of racial inequality. He had recently hired François Scarborough Clemmons as the first African-American with a recurring role on a children's televi-sion program. Not only is Clemmons's hiring unusual for its time, Rogers goes a step further and establishes Clemmons as a police officer.

While African-Americans were barred from swimming in public pools, Rogers fights segregation with a kiddie pool. In the episode, we find Rogers soaking his feet on a warm sunny day. Officer Clemmons enters the scene, and Rogers invites Clemmons to join him. Both men are seen with their feet in the pool, enjoying the moment. The scene ends with a biblical allusion to foot washing and Rogers drying the feet of Officer Clemmons.

This scene of love and its indirect communication is repeated over twenty years later. In Clemmons's last appearance on *Mister Rogers' Neighborhood,* the pair re-enacts the pool scene. What has now become Officer Clemmons's most famous scene and cherished song "Many Ways to Say I Love You," began as an indirect way to address the evils of segregation, racial equality, and an expression of love of neighbor.

Emotions in Communication

In 1969, *Mister Rogers' Neighborhood* and other public television shows were on the brink of cancellation. The Senate Subcommittee on Communications were deliberating on the fate of public media. The proposal was to cut funding to public media, which would bring an end to many public television shows. Rogers appeared before the Senate subcommittee to make an appeal on behalf of public television. The original plan was to read a "philosophical statement" that Rogers had prepared in advance. Instead, Rogers decides to put aside his papers and just "talk about" the philosophical statement.

In his testimony, Rogers addresses matters of pedagogy, early child development, and the significance of emotions. He states that *Mister Rogers' Neighborhood's* budget of $6,000 could pay for two minutes of cartoons, which Rogers calls "bombardment," or it could pay for a specific "kind of communication."

The drama addressed in Rogers's show is not what is depicted in a gunfight, but of the "inner drama of childhood." The drama does not have to appear on the screen, since the drama is already within the viewer. That is the specific drama Rogers wants to wrestle with.

The educational television that he provides is centered around emotions and feelings. His show communicates that emotions are "mentionable" and "manageable." By dealing with emotions with a "neighborhood expression of care," the show is a "service for mental health."

What allows for such direct speech is the truth of Rogers's words. Rogers and his team built a show that did exactly what he is claiming. The show addresses emotions and feelings on a daily basis. Pivotal to the success of the show and its ability to deal with emotions is Rogers's philosophy of indirect communication. Whether it is through the Neighborhood of Make-Believe, the visual language of the show's aesthetics, or the central tenet of love, indirect communication forms the foundation to which Rogers could directly speak about emotions.

The two types of communication are intertwined in a show that favors watching someone get a haircut more than watching someone getting "bopped" over the head. The two types of communication make possible a show that communicates the importance of emotions. Rogers ends his testimony with the lyrics of a song about the management of anger and how you can get so angry that you want to bite someone. Instead, the song suggests, you can possess an inner feeling that helps you become a different kind of person. With the conclusion of the song Senator Pastore gave a quick response and awarded public media funding of $20 million.

Becoming a Neighbor

It is uncertain whether Rogers ever read Kierkegaard, and it is doubtful that he was familiar with Hamann. But, his use of indirect communication is clear. Behind the affable and gentle person of Mister Rogers lies a sophisticated philosophy of communication centered on indirect communication.

And, as strange as it may sound, this sophisticated philosophy ends up teaching us how to be a neighbor. Thanks, Fred.

12
Puppets Are People Too

Sara Lindey and Jason King

> Life is good. Being a person is good. Breathing air is good.

> —Puppet King Friday XIII, puppeteer Fred Rogers

Mister Rogers and Big Bird once got into a fight.

Rogers had invited Caroll Spinney, the actor who portrays Big Bird, to appear on *Mister Rogers' Neighborhood* in 1981. Rogers's idea was to have Big Bird appear in the Neighborhood of Make-Believe and Spinney appear in Rogers's neighborhood to show how he worked the costume. But Spinney didn't want to appear outside of the costume, fearing he would undermine the magic of Big Bird.

They reached a compromise. Spinney agreed to appear as Big Bird only in the Neighborhood of Make-Believe. In the regular neighborhood, Rogers would don a large giraffe costume, show children how it worked, and tell his audience that there was a person inside these large costumes (episode 1483).

True to his view of puppets, Rogers repeatedly explained to children that he and other adults worked the puppets in the Neighborhood of Make-Believe, in about a dozen episodes over thirty years.

The Big Bird fiasco gets to the heart of Rogers's approach to puppets. Rogers insists on the connection between people and puppets because he believes that the imaginative world helps people see and understand the real world. This revelation can give people confidence to know how to act, helping themselves and others.

Nowhere is this more important than in our environment.

People in the Anthropocene

Environmentalists name our current epoch the Anthropocene. Generally, it means that human beings have become the dominant influence on the environment. The effects of human dominance began with the Industrial Revolution and have grown exponentially since then. It has caused rising CO_2 levels, global warming, melting of the polar ice caps, deforestation, water and air pollution, and extensive species annihilation in what is now called the sixth mass extinction. While many register the Anthropocene in terms of scientific measures of the environment, philosophers examine the problematic notion of the human person at the root of Anthropocene.

The Anthropocene understands human beings as separate. They are considered creatures that are distinct from the rest of creation. Some philosophers chart human exceptionalism through the existence of a soul or the capability to reason. Human beings can ask questions about the meaning of their lives and contemplate their own deaths. Some find their uniqueness in a human ability to transcend their biology or their environment or their culture. Regardless, human exceptionalism leads to human privilege.

With humans at the top of the hierarchy, all other inferior things have little to no intrinsic value. This kind of thinking about people and their relationship with the world leads toward exploitation. When human beings are valued above all other animals and things, the world is filled with resources, or things to be used and manipulated, instead of things to be treasured and respected. This easily leads to the idea that everything can and should be merely used by human beings, regardless of the effects it might have for the things themselves. In short, it turns the world into puppets or puppet-like things, yet covers up the connection between people and the environment, the way Spinney resists the connection between puppets and people.

Through puppets, Mister Rogers turns the idea of the singular and separate self on its head. He takes the thing that is usually manipulated to show its value and, in doing so, shows the value of all things.

Puppets Are People

Henrietta Pussycat has a personality of her own, her "meow, meow" way of talking, and her shy demeanor. She is loyal and tender, insecure and lovely. Live actor neighbors continually support her, often singing her the song "You Are Pretty," which happens in eleven different episodes over thirty years.

Its first verse in particular—"You are pretty / You are black / You are beautifully dressed in lovely fur / Finely curled / Perfectly / You are pretty / Elegant / You are black"—seems to anthropomorphize her. This means that viewers see her as more human, and so might see in her a reflection of their own skin color, and benefit from the acceptance and praise the song offers.

Daniel Striped Tiger is his own person, too, a lovable, timid, curious, sensitive tiger-child. In 1968, reeling from Martin Luther King, Jr.'s assassination and in response to Robert Kennedy's assassination, Rogers produced a special where Daniel asks Lady Aberlin what "assassination" means. Continually voicing children's worries, Daniel Tiger, in a touching duet with Lady Aberlin in 1987, wonders if he's a mistake, being the one and only tame tiger in existence (episode 1578).

During Thanksgiving week, in the 1986 set of episodes on "Playthings," puppet King Friday XIII pronounces, "Life is good. Being a person is good. Breathing air is good" (episodes 1566–1570). Despite the fact that King Friday is not conventionally alive, let alone breathing, Rogers here grants him his own human breath, and a personhood that expresses real gratitude.

King Friday continues to expand a puppet's capabilities, implying that they can feel and act by singing the chorus of "You've Got to Do It": "You've got to do it. / Every little bit, you've got to do it, do it, do it, do it / And when you're through, you can know who did it / For you did it, you did it, you did it" (episode 1567).

Following the weird logic in Timothy Morton's book *Humankind: Solidarity with Nonhuman People*, it is as if Rogers suggests that we re-think species. If the puppet can be a person, animals can be people, too. Rogers allows us to think of a nonhuman person, be it animal, puppet, or thing. Morton, in a move that just may ring true for Rogers, asserts that "humankind" exposes the two meanings of "kind" by revealing both the reality of inter-species affinity and the human drive toward compassion. Both Rogers and Morton propose that humankind is in "solidarity" with nonhuman people.

Rogers's puppets represent humans, animals, and the puppets themselves as full of life, unique, valuable, and capable of giving and receiving love and care. These anthropomorphic animal puppets have their own inner lives that are so much like our own. By thinking about puppets in this way, Rogers resists

anthropocentrism (the idea that humans are the only important things in the world) precisely by means of his anthropo-
morphism (viewing things in the world as human-like.)

In making puppets people, Rogers works against the separate and superior human being of the Anthropocene. He does so
not by devaluing people but, in his typical fashion, by lifting up
every creature to make them valued like people.

Puppeteers Are Cyborgs

During the 1986 Thanksgiving week, where King Friday pro-
claims his own personhood, Mister Rogers includes a drama in
the Neighborhood of Make-Believe about the nature of puppets. Neighbor Aber showcases different sorts of playthings
and explains how puppets are special toys. In Make-Believe, he
shows the puppet schoolchildren how he moves and voices the
puppet H.J. Elephant III, speaking as the puppet and then as
himself to illustrate.

This demonstration raises a metaphysical puppet quandary.
Daniel Striped Tiger and Ana Platypus ask if they are toys, too.
Neighbor Aber replies, "You could be." In protest, puppet Prince
Tuesday insists that he's a prince and not a toy, and Aber
explains, "You see, in Make-Believe, toys can be real if you want.
Anything is possible in make-believe." Daniel Tiger encounters
this existential crisis with good grace, accepting that he might be
connected to another, remarking, without his customary anxiety,
"I never thought of that" (episode 1567).

Rogers does not allow the puppets to magically come alive
on their own. Instead, he goes so far as to hint that his puppet
Daniel Tiger might realize his connection to Rogers, who is his
puppeteer. Rogers's surreal scene figures the puppet as both its
own individual self and as a vehicle for Rogers's voice and
imagination.

Even though Rogers's puppets are people, they are not separate from those who play with them. Puppets are more than
dolls. They require human beings to pull their strings, or, in
Rogers's case with hand-puppets, animate their bodies. The
puppet becomes an extension of the self and so helps us better
understand ourselves.

But because puppets appear to be separate from their puppeteer, they provide a "double vision" to help children access
the parts of themselves that seem contrary or just different
from the other part of themselves, especially to manage uncomfortable feelings. When speaking through puppets, one can
communicate with a version of the self that is both estranged,

into the puppet body, and is still connected to the self, articulated by one's own voice. They do, as Donna Haraway says in "A Cyborg Manifesto," what cyborgs do: trouble the boundaries between human, animal, machine, and nonhuman entities.

Playing with the King Friday puppet lets the puppeteer exert unbridled control; yet Rogers ensures that the puppet's personality and the caring neighborhood context inform playing about authority. Rogers insists on a critique of absolute power while celebrating the loving and imperfect parent as he plays ruler of the Neighborhood of Make-Believe.

King Friday is a stubborn, conceited, imperious, softhearted, and generous patriarch. King Friday often misuses his authority in short-sighted decrees. Yet his family and his subjects respectfully tolerate and question him, and King Friday eventually listens and often changes his mind and his actions. He is loved and accepted, with all his faults, as is everyone in the Neighborhood of Make-Believe. Susan Linn, a puppeteer and psychologist who worked with Rogers and performed Audrey Duck on the show, maintains that this radical acceptance of the imperfect person and their contradictory emotions and actions is crucial for emotional intelligence and growth. She argues that Rogers models this acceptance through his puppets.

In helping us do emotional work, Rogers's puppets make us cyborgs. Cyborgs are people who have technology connected to their bodies which enhance human powers. The enhancement, however, is typically thought of in terms of fire power—with more strength, or speed, or weapons. Instead, Rogers's puppets make humans a cyborg because they enhance the emotional power of people.

Although low-fi and low-tech, puppets enable us to see, understand, and accept our own emotions that are reflected through the puppets. Moreover, in seeing the emotional life of the puppet that is both separate from, and connected to us, we can see animals and other parts of creation similarly. They have their own lives, their lives are connected to our own, and we enhance each other. Rogers's puppets suggest an ecological vision that—in contrast to that of the Anthropocene—sees humans not as separate, but closely connected to everything in the world.

We Are Family

King Friday, the puppet patriarch, is uncle to Lady Aberlin, a live actor. She and puppet Prince Tuesday are cousins. Puppet X the Owl's cousin is Mary the Owl, an actor dressed up in a costume. Rogers insists that puppet animals and human animals are family. Beyond play about interspecies kin, Rogers uses adoption to more clearly cross species and connect people with loving affiliation.

The week-long series "Mister Rogers Talks about Families" first aired in November 1985, during Thanksgiving (episodes 1551–1555). In this week, Mary the Owl, an actor in an owl costume, comes to visit X the Owl, a puppet, who is her cousin. Mary the Owl plans a cousin reunion, but the party causes problems for Bob Dog, an actor in a dog costume, who has no cousin. This drama is resolved when platypus-child puppet Ana offers to adopt Bob Dog. Everyone, then, is welcome at the cousin reunion. Rogers's make-believe makes a literal point: we are all cousins—humans, animals, and puppets.

Adoption is further discussed as humanoid puppets Betty Okonak Templeton and James Michael Jones adopt a baby, Carrie Dell. Rogers discussed the adoption of his own sister and shows a video of the real families of actors on *Mister Rogers' Neighborhood*. He maintains that all families are real, and all are based in love. Rogers visits penguin families at Sea World. He plants an orange seed and talks about how oranges grow into trees, and later shows a picture and a video of birds who have made a tree their home. He visits with Mrs. Shiono who makes origami birds and a puppet for Mister Rogers. Birds, like puppet X the Owl, are lovable, and so are their homes, the trees that grow like children do. Rogers associates animals, trees, paper, and puppets to access multiple avenues to celebrate interconnection in a universal family love.

By making these familial connections, Rogers pushes his viewers to expand their own connections among entities. As he asks us to listen to the voice of the puppet, he asks us to listen to the voice of other people and ourselves. Puppets allow Rogers to help children think and care about their relationships with the environment, animals, and other people. Unlike the Anthropocene that sees the world in terms of utility, Rogers's puppets suggest people should care about the world and those around them as if they were family.

Puppets Save the Environment

The relevance of puppets for addressing the Anthropocene can be seen in Rogers's 1990 week-long series, "Caring for the Environment," which aired the week before Earth Day's twentieth anniversary that inaugurated its international enterprise (episodes 1616–1620).

During this week, a trash cataclysm threatens the Neighbor-hood of Make-Believe. The dump, located in Someplace Else, is full, so full in fact that it is threatening to overrun Harriet Cow's school for the Neighborhood children and Donkey Hodie's farm. They are building a fence around it to stave off the impending mountain of trash.

Through the story of the trash problem, Rogers shows his idea of family at work. The viewer has to listen to all the differ-ent voices and each voice generates concern for others as if they were family. The threat to Harriet Cow's school and Donkey Hodie's farm become our own concern. We see how the stink troubles X the Owl and Lady Aberlin. We feel the exhaustion of Hilda Dingleboarder, who is furiously manufacturing nose-muffs, and Handyman Negri, who is constantly waving fans, both helping deal with the garbage's overwhelming stench. We even extend our concern to the relatively unknown Westwood and Southwood, discovering they, too, have the same problem. Puppets and people, known and unknown, all of these are brought into our circle of concern and become like family.

Because they are like an extended, caring family, the people in the Neighborhood of Make-Believe seek out a solution. Some of the first attempts at this come from Lady Elaine Fairchilde, but so many of her ideas are bad. She suggests throwing the trash in the ocean or sending it on a plane to Just Anywhere. When Lady Aberlin reminds her that the fish in the ocean and the people of Just Anywhere might not like the trash being dumped on them, Lady Elaine says, "I never thought of that" (episode 1618). Just like when Daniel Tiger had never thought that he could be connected with another, Rogers asserts that new ideas are not threatening when they come from caring neighbors.

Solutions are difficult to come by, especially when the prob-lem is so complex as environmental ones. When Lady Elaine realizes that her ideas don't work, she doesn't sulk but rather starts reaching out to others. She calls her friend Betty Okonak Templeton in Southwood to see if they can use their dump, and so finds out that Southwood is having a similar problem. Finally, she has a splendid idea to fly King Friday's rocket to the television studio of the talk-show "The Universe Today" to ask the galaxy to come together to solve their garbage cata-clysm. She assumes that they, like her, will want to help.

Not afraid to get it wrong and not afraid to ask for help, Lady Elaine shows us the value of continuing even if we fear making mistakes and, more than that, how, when we reach out to others, we will often find them similar to us, or at least in a similar situation. She is the low-fi and low-tech enhancement that we need to become cyborgs with emotional power that can connect us with ourselves and others. Resonating biographically, she is the namesake for Fred Rogers's adopted sister, and she does the most work during this environmental crisis to bring people near and far together to care for each other, each neighborhood, and our common and universal home.

Finally, it is the others, the puppets that are people, who save the Neighborhood of Make-Believe from the environmental apocalypse. Old Goat and New Goat arrive from Northwood. They are not there to eat everything, a false belief about goats that Rogers dispels earlier in the weeklong series. Instead, the Goats bring their animal wisdom. They come up with a plan to "divide and conquer": divide up trash into different piles so that much of it can be reused or recycled (episode 1620). Their wisdom is complemented by the engineering genius of humanoid Hilda Dingleboarder who makes a device that creates new things out of old, thrown-away things. Instead of being stereotypes, the puppets have their own gifts. They use them to help address the problem, and so they show their value, not in acting superior to others, but through caring for them. They are true people, these puppets.

Big Bird Is a Person Too

Big Bird's visit to *Mister Rogers' Neighborhood* was preceded by Mister Rogers's visit to *Sesame Street* a few months earlier. When Rogers shows up, Big Bird can't believe his eyes and wonders if he's pretending Mister Rogers is there. Rogers insists on the difference between reality and pretend, saying that reality is full of tangible things that interact with each other, just as he interacts with Big Bird.

Big Bird eventually acknowledges, "There is a big difference between imaginary and real" (*Sesame Street*, episode 1575). The encounter ends with Big Bird and Mister Rogers hugging, bringing together the real and the imaginary. This culminating hug enacts an embrace that spans human and puppet creatures, holds together diverse television shows for children, and extends love and care to all entities in our environment.

Rogers is unlike the other adults in *Sesame Street*. Big Bird's own neighbors do not believe Big Bird. They explain that he must have imagined seeing Rogers and, for years, almost fifteen, in fact, *Sesame Street* adults never take his "imaginary friend" Mr. Snuffelupagus seriously. In fact, four years later, in the premier of the 1985 season, Big Bird arranges a stratagem so his grown-up neighbors finally meet Snuffy in person.

It turns out that Big Bird has always seen things clearly, which the muppets and children watching *Sesame Street* realized. The adults apologize for disbelieving Big Bird for so long (*Sesame Street*, episode 2096). The confusion in *Sesame Street* between pretend and reality allows Big Bird to be mistreated. Puppets seem to represent children, and *Sesame Street* finally lets the joke about Big Bird's "imaginary friend" go, in order to respect children.

In contrast, Rogers, from the start, listens, helps, and respects Big Bird. For Rogers, Big Bird is a person, too.

Rogers celebrates the ability for the imaginary to illuminate the real. Instead of human beings as separate and superior, puppets help us to see we are connected to others—people, animals, and the environment—and such connections enhance us.

Instead of viewing everything as something to be used and manipulated, we are to see them as people and even family who work together for the greater good. This view makes puppets more important than playthings confined to imaginary worlds. It is a view that connects puppets to us in a loving embrace and, through this, can compassionately connect us to all other things. We are people, and Rogers makes all things have the value of people by making puppets people, too.

13

Won't You Be My Posthuman Neighbor?

FERNANDO PAGNONI BERNS

There are so many things that continue to make *Mister Rogers' Neighborhood* compelling today, all these years after its heyday: the well-known songs, the charming guests, the moral and practical lessons, and the make-believe kingdom: the place where everything is possible!

The Neighborhood of Make-Believe is especially interesting, not only for the adventures that take place there, but also for its inhabitants, many of them hand puppets. King Friday XIII, Prince Tuesday, X the Owl, Henrietta Pussycat, Lady Elaine Fairchilde, and Grandpère Tiger, to name a few.

They chat and interact with each other, but also with human beings, such as Lady Aberlin or Handyman Negri. There seems to be no difference whatsoever in the way the hand puppets communicate with other non-living beings, such as other puppets, and the way they engage with humans. Any clear distinction between humans and objects (puppets) becomes ambiguous.

The hierarchy separating humans from non-living objects is a concern for posthumanist philosophical investigations. Posthuman philosophers explore the implications of making room for non-human objects. In her book, *The Cinema of Things: Globalization and the Posthuman Object*, Elizabeth Ezra considers "what happens when they take on a life of their own." The status of human existence is complicated when objects, which have consistently been declared as inferior in our anthropocentric worldview, become alive. Through philosophy, we can question what it means to be alive in a world where technologically created body parts (including vital organs), cells and minerals are becoming valued components of our conception of life. In this way, we can see the Make-Believe Neighborhood as a land of posthumanism.

Many of the hand puppets represent animals, such as Old Goat or Harriet Elizabeth Cow. There seems to be no difference between the interplay of humans with human-like hand puppets or animal-like hand puppets. What could this mean?

Moving Beyond Humanism

But perhaps we're getting ahead of ourselves. What the heck is posthumanism?

Posthumanism is the broad name encompassing various efforts to supplant the conventional *humanist* paradigm. Traditional Western thought has been and still largely is dominated by humanist philosophy, where things are described and understood largely in human terms. The humanist way of describing humans is to build on difference, to define a human against everything non-human: the environment, animals, plants, minerals and machines, all of them seen as "essentially" inferior to human beings.

Posthumanism wishes to break down such differences. As medicine advances in its developments, replacing flesh and body parts with plastic and artificial organs, the frontiers dividing the human from the non-human becomes increasingly thin. So it's necessary to give the proper value to objects while pointing out that the values of "humanity" are mere cultural constructions. There is still a greater objective, though. Besides objects, posthumanism tries to attack the norms that ground discrimination against non-human animals as well.

As inferior beings, they are "thingified," becoming objects and instruments to be used and mastered by humans. Humanists would argue that humans are superior because of some "essential" traits possessed by humans, such as intelligence, or having a soul. The center of any system of thought, for humanism, is the human.

But beware!

"Human" does not actually mean "any human," but those who actually construct the systems of thought that they want to naturalize. Let's be honest: "human" usually ends up meaning the white, heterosexual, Christian, Western bourgeois man. Women, African Americans, homosexuals, and so many others end up with the short end of the stick here, as though they (we?) lack humanity in some way.

But there's good news, folks! This system of thought can be destabilized by posthumanism, a discipline that helps us imagine a world without a strictly "human" center. To posthumanism, humans are just another species sharing the world with animals, plants, minerals and objects. Posthumanism is not about "killing" the man but about the end of a universe where (the white) man is the measure of all things. Not too bad, hmm? Now let's see how Mister Rogers destabilizes humanist think-ing in his show.

If It Behaves Like a Human and Looks like a Human, It Must be a Hand Puppet!

Posthumanism works with the provocation of localizing man at the same level with other less-human beings; with this shift, posthumanism abolishes any form of social and cultural hier-archy. In this sense, the opening of any episode of *Mister Rogers' Neighborhood* is strongly posthumanist.

If you pay close attention, you'll notice that each episode opens with a wide shot of a neighborhood completely con-structed by toys. Each house, each tree, each street was made using toys. Even the bus passing through is a toy. The scene blurs and we're in Mister Rogers's house, where he invites us to get in and share a moment of learning and playing with him.

Some questions arise from this simple opening scene. Is Mister Rogers living in the neighborhood fabricated with toys? It seems so, right? But if he lives there, is Mister Rogers also a toy? Or is he living in a normal neighborhood? If so, why is it represented by toys? In other episodes, the camera pans towards a particular toy building, for example, the Brockett bakery, a penguins' sanctuary, or tuba player Sam Pilafian's apartment (nice place, by the way!). It then cuts to the interior of the place, the latter populated with real people, thus confus-ing the limits between object and human. Are all those people living in toy houses? Are these people human-like toys?

What each opening of the TV show does is blur boundaries, putting the human (Mister Rogers) within a crisis of cate-gories. Humanism loves with passion the borders separating the human from the non-human because these limits help it to differentiate between more and less important beings, between humans and everything else. Mister Rogers, who is certainly not a toy, may however be making a certain statement in being "reduced" to one.

Has Mister Rogers been "downgraded" to the level of human-like toys? Or are the toys "upgraded" to paralleling the human scale? Never mind: posthumanism is completely disin-terested in foolish things such as "downgrading" or "upgrad-ing." All these terms only serve to favor exploitation: being considered as object-like, animal-like, and even female-like are "bad" words because they constitute a lacking, the impossibility of reaching complete humanism, complete "perfection" (the Western white man ideal). And being "less" implies a destiny of bondage to those considered (according their own terms!) as "better." The best thing to do is to discard all these "humanist" categories.

Philosopher Bruno Latour writes in his *Pandora's Hope: Essays on the Reality of Science Studies* (1999) that there is no obvious differentiation between objects and subjects, as neither humans nor technologies exist one without the other. Latour speaks of some objects as "non-humans." This can be baffling for many: it is not obvious, you say? Of course a vacuum cleaner is not human!

But follow me in this: inanimate things have traits that can be characterized as human-like. What Latour finds human-like in objects is the fact that they help us to channel our desires, our (completely human) needs. Thus, they are "quasi-human." Think about a human playing a game against a computer. The machine is not human but it behaves like one to make the game compelling. On the other hand, the human playing the game finds a channel to express his or her (completely human) desire to play a game. This channel is an object rather than a human partner. Thus, the object acquires some human traits (and be honest: how many times have you accused your computer of cheating when you know that's completely impossible?).

Let's find some examples in our beloved show. In one of the episodes, Mister Rogers shows a music box with a figurine, a ballerina, at the top. He winds up the little machine and the little ballerina starts to dance. While the ballerina might be "fantasy," it (she?) works just like a human being, at least, in appearance; she dances to the music like real ballerinas do.

Mister Rogers wants to talk about ideas and technology. He wonders about how amazing it is that someone thought of a music box with a ballerina and later created it. In other words, someone has created voice and expression in a little contraption which looks human-like. Immediately after he shows us the music box, the telephone rings, another apparatus that gives voice to humans.

One day, Mister Rogers arrives at his house with a set of leg braces and a pair of crutches. He explains that some people need them to help them walk, a way to "express" themselves (episode 1322). And in another episode, Susan Linn, a puppeteer ventriloquist who works at the hospital for children, acknowledges the fact that sometimes it's easier to say some things with a puppet (episode 1576). The puppet, Audrey the

Duck, is a clear example of a "quasi-human" object that says, "sometimes *I* say things," the "I" turning the duck into a being with a voice all of her own.

Okay, non-living objects such as telephones or video games interact with humans in a way that they seem to be "human-like" or "quasi human." Still, there is no better example than the puppets themselves. The Neighborhood of Make-Believe is populated by hand puppets that pass for humans. To make things even more posthuman, real humans not only interact with the hand puppets, acting as if they do not notice any difference, but some human characters are relatives of puppet characters. The most common example is that Lady Aberlin (portrayed by Betty Aberlin) is King Friday's niece.

I know what you're thinking: people watching the show know that these little persons are, in fact, inanimate things and that the voice that audiences hear is coming from hidden human beings. To adults, yes this is obvious, but to very small children it's not. Children's fantasy is allowed a certain degree of *freedom*. They can believe in the life of puppets (it's a land of make-believe, after all!). This belief of children is the dream of posthumanists: the abolition of the frontiers that divide the all-supreme human from other beings and things. A child is the posthumanist's best friend.

Still, the Neighborhood of Make-Believe wants to play even deeper with the borders. Rather than resting in a univocal reality such as "hand puppets are human beings in this magical place," this special neighborhood wittily shifts from one position to another, discarding any sense of security. In one of the episodes, Lady Aberlin is sharing orange juice with everyone. She offers some to Trolley, who (which?) denies the juice. Of course it (he?) does! We all know that little trolleys do not drink orange juice. Thus, we reach a conclusion: the Trolley is an object, not a human-like creature. At last, some humanist certainty!

The clear divide, however, evaporates when audiences realize that Trolley is capable of using language, precisely to reject the juice, thus assuming human-like capabilities. At the end, we can ask: is Trolley an object or a subject with will? This complication is what posthumanism tries to highlight to demonstrate that the borders separating one and the other have been established by humans to secure their supreme position. The human might say: only humans have language and so, they speak on behalf of everything else. But Trolley can speak for itself (himself? Herself? So confusing!), mocking these "natural" boundaries.

But the Neighborhood complicates things even further. It's really a posthuman, witty place. In one of the episodes during the weekly theme on music, Lady Aberlin is preparing a big party for King Friday. One of the guests is dressed as a bass, thus transforming the human into an inanimate object. Later in the episode, Lady Aberlin uses her real bass as a dancing partner, given human features to the inanimate object (episode 1547). So, a human becomes an object and, later, an object becomes "quasi human." It is confusing, I know, but posthumanism wants to keep things confusing, fluid. That is better than "fixed"; a 'fixed' world creates hierarchies and sustains dichotomies (male/female; human/animal; superior/inferior) and that can't help but come with exploitation and domination.

Animals and Plants Are Your Neighbors Too

Following the humanist logic, man is the origin of all meaning. Animals and entire landscapes can be exploited due to their inferiority to humanity: all that is considered non-human must serve the social progress of humanity. Animals and plants can be killed and entire species annihilated. Why not? They are all inferior beings that exist only to serve human needs.

Since the 1970s, but even more since the advent of posthumanism, the term "non-human animals" is increasingly used to downplay humanity to the level of other animals or upgrade animals to human level. The term "non-human animals" is really hurtful for the humanist heart because it explicitly declares humans to be just another species of animal sharing the globe. (And not even the most interesting one!)

The humanist hierarchical system localizes the human at the measurement of all things. All things "inferior" exist to be exploited (as food, as entertainment, as pets). This criterion discriminating between "superior" beings and those "poor, inferior" creatures creates ideological forms of oppression which spread outside the sphere of the animals to infect everything. So, people considered animal-like and "primitive" must be conquered "for their own good", so they can make "progress." Plants, meanwhile, are considered especially inferior due to their passivity.

But this way of thinking commits two sins. First, it ignores the fact that vegetable life can indeed move, though at a very slow pace. Second, it endows passivity with negative connotations in contrast with speed and strength. Why is "passive" coded in a negative way? In a capitalist humanist world that links human with "man" and man with action, everything else is "primitive" or having a form of "lacking."

Mister Rogers' Neighborhood destabilizes the humanist view thanks to a lack of separation between the human and the human-like puppet. Not all the hand puppets, however, resemble humans. In fact, "people" like King Friday XIII or Prince Tuesday are in the minority here. The majority of the inhabitants of the Neighborhood are animals. These animals, however, are not there to be passively observed (this is not a zoo!), but they interact with human-like puppets and with Lady Aberlin without making any distinctions.

X the Owl, Henrietta Pussycat, or Grandpère Tiger are animals. But Lady Aberlin never talks to them differently than she does with the "human" puppets like King Friday. Further, animal-like hand puppets behave the way humans do. For example, Daniel Tiger gives good advice to Lady Aberlin, pushing her to be honest with King Friday. Prince Tuesday shares the classroom with animal-like hand puppets as if humans and animals can cohabit common spaces as species alike.

I have mentioned that the show constantly shifts between object and human. Of course, there is also a displacement taking place between the animal and the human as well, presenting a recurrent sense of fluidity. Henrietta Pussycat is a good embodiment of posthumanism: she speaks blending together feline "meow, meow" sounds, intermittently, along with human words. Is she human-like or animal-like? Who can pin her down? Basically, she is a blurring of categories.

This shift between the human and the animal or plant goes further, to the point that nature and inanimate objects bleed into each other. Fruits can be objects such as an "orange-o-gram," while Mister Rogers pretends that his shoe is a bird and talks about different kind of birds and their behavior.

In one of the episodes, X the Owl is unable to recognize Audrey the Duck even though they are friends. For X, Audrey "does not look like a real duck," thus acknowledging that this particular animal is just a hand puppet ("But I'm a real duck!" exclaims Audrey, justifiably offended). Or is X the Owl implying that this particular duck looks too human-like? After all, Audrey is an inanimate object (a hand puppet) who behaves like a human (she talks and dresses like one) but who is still an animal (a duck). Audrey is offended and X feels sorry for that. Later in the episode, Audrey is at the school. She is learning the letters, and when she comes to D (for duck), she cries.

AUDREY: Am I a duck?

CATALION: Of course you are

AUDREY: Am I a real duck?

CATALION: Oh? You're as real as you want to be.

Audrey seems to worry. Is she an animal? A human? A hand puppet? All the above? When her friend the lion tells her to be as real "as she wants to be," he's making a posthumanist affirmation. He's not talking about the reality of things, but about putting under the spotlight the boundaries between humans and other animals, as well as between the living and the non-living. And in so doing, he offers the sweet surprise of seeing that there could be *other ways of being*. The human, the object and the animal collapse together in the figure of Audrey the Duck (episode 1576).

The radical difference that divides "us" (the white heterosexual man) from "them" (non-human animals, women, black people, homosexuals) is blurred when posthumanism states that "man" is just a fantasy, just a way of being in the world.

Posthumanism undoes humanism by removing the hierarchical positions that enthrone the human/male in the world as a God-like creature. In *Mister Rogers' Neighborhood* nobody seems to care if you're human, an object or an animal (or a stone or a plant): you can be a good neighbor if you're ready to let your human privileges drop and, like the king himself, share your world with humans and animals alike.

IV

You Are My Friend, You Are Special to Me

14

A Party to Celebrate the Personal

Eric J. Mohr

Mister Rogers begins the weekly theme "Everybody's Special" by reflecting upon his reflection in a mirror: "There's only one person in the whole world exactly like me," he says, "and there's only one person exactly like you: nobody else but you. Each one of us is unique. Unique means one of a kind. Only one like you! Only one like me!" But, in the Neighborhood of Make-Believe, Prince Tuesday is struggling with who he is, and whether it's merely his royalty, and specifically his royal cape, that makes him special (episode 1686).

Meanwhile, the neighborhood is preparing a surprise birthday party for Cornflake S. Pecially. Chef Brockett plans to bake him a very special (and quite unique) birthday cake with raisins and nuts in it. What better way is there to celebrate Corney's specialness (Corney's "corny-ness") than by throwing a party designed just for him, by people who see how special he is?

In contrast to all of this talk about difference and specialness, there's also a segment that week about how ceramic plates are made. It's a highly mechanized process where the goal is to make sure all the plates are *exactly the same*. In fact, there's a worker whose job it is to eye the plates that come off the conveyor belt and to remove and recycle any plate that is noticeably different from the rest. What an ironic and strange juxtaposition! What's valued in the factory is sameness. What's valued in the neighborhood is difference.

A Rebellious Mister Rogers

The ways that things are the same, and the ways in which they're different has played a central role in philosophy even before Plato and Aristotle made philosophy cool. The earliest philosophers were metaphysicians, which means they thought more in terms of categories or kinds of beings, and tended to emphasize our sameness. Since all human beings are commonly human, it stands to reason that we must in some basic way all be the same.

On the *inside*—on the level of the "soul"—we're all the same kind of being. Aristotle famously called us "rational animals." But on the *outside*—on the level of bodily appearance—we're different. It's our "matter" that individuates us, they thought. This means that you and I are distinct individuals because your body is separate and different from mine, but our "insides" (to use Rogers's phrase) are basically the same. The soul is a higher kind of being than the body, and the highest kinds of beings, in this classical metaphysical worldview, are also the most formal and universal. Aristotle even calls the soul the "*form*" of the body. And while we each may live out our human lives in different ways, the way of life that is most fulfilling of our common human, rational nature has to be the one *correct* way to live, for everyone.

These early metaphysical considerations about a common nature and the extent that we are, and are not, different from each other (and from other kinds of living things) have their place. It's important to define such things and say what a human being is according to our very nature. But chances are this idea—that your inside, essential self is also the same for everyone else, and that your differences are merely incidental, outside stuff—doesn't square with your experience of yourself. While it's true we're beings of the same kind, we're somehow also *one of a kind*. The word "special," after all, is derived from the word "species," and from where we get our term, "specific." It's as though, while we belong to a common species, we may also be a species unto ourselves. Okay, probably this isn't what Rogers has in mind when he calls you special, but if you really are the only person exactly like you, then when you're gone there's something (whatever it is) that will never, and can never, exist in the same way ever again, for all time. This is to me one of Rogers's most profound messages, but it's also philosophically perplexing, and it complicates traditional metaphysical categories.

Prince Tuesday goes into significant depression at the thought that who he is might be no deeper than his social status and princely garb. He ends up taking off his royal cape and leaving it on the ground (as if what makes him special is so incidental that he can just take it off). Mayor Maggie and

Neighbor Aber are confused as to why he doesn't want to wear such a special garment. "I don't want to be special!" Tuesday cries. Aber assures him that he'll always be special, whether he wears the cape or not. "It's what's inside you that makes you special," Aber explains. "It doesn't have to do with capes or names or any outside stuff."

"It's true." Mister Rogers affirms back at the house. "Each one of us is special, and that's because of who we are *inside*." Whether he knows it or not, Rogers is challenging a long-standing rationalistic view of the human being by ancient and medieval philosophers, and what was later on called the "person" by Immanuel Kant (1724–1804). The deeper we look into the interior life of a human being, we'll come to encounter *more* of his or her individuality, not less. Perhaps the bodily differences that exist between people pale, by way of comparison, to the differences with respect to their inner *personal* being.

Mister Rogers's Personalism

Mister Rogers would have had a good amount of philosophical backing of his view that everyone is special by the time the show began in 1968. In fact, one such backer of this view died in 1928 in Frankfurt, Germany just three months after Fred Rogers's birth in Latrobe, Pennsylvania. During his life, Max Scheler was at the forefront of a growing movement of phenomenology, and was a key contributor to a certain kind of philosophy called Personalism.

Scheler's main work on ethics and the person is horrendously titled *Formalism in Ethics and Non-Formal Ethics of Values*. He says that defining the person on account of our reason leads to a "depersonalization." It turns the person into something impersonal. If the person were only a subject of rational acts, then it refers to everyone in the exact same way, and as "something *identical*" in all of us. We could therefore not be distinguishable from each other by virtue of our personal being alone, and the very idea of an "individual person" becomes a contradiction in terms. So the traditional view had it backwards. The inner, essential part of you is not a form, but rather something "non-formal." The more external, physical parts of us are more in common; our interior space is more personal. The deeper we go the more difference we'll get.

As Mister Rogers does implicitly, Scheler explicitly challenges the traditional metaphysical perspective that denies individuality to our inside self. But it's a difficult business trying to figure out what it means to be a person, generally. Could there be a universal definition that's also not impersonal? And it's tricky to figure out what exactly inside us makes us personal and one of a kind. But let's give it a shot.

In the course of the set of episodes about specialness that I mentioned earlier, we are shown the process of certain things being made. In addition to the manufacturing of ceramic plates (episode 1686), we are shown the similarly mechanized process of how kazoos are made (episode 1690), where sameness is also privileged, but maybe a little less so.

Then we see how wooden shoes are made (episode 1687). It's still a mechanical and heavily routine process, but it requires a greater degree of human skill and involvement. While the shoe-carver basically aims for sameness in each of his products, there are inevitable, but acceptable differences in them. They are specially designed for specific foot sizes and maybe even for specific people. We see also how guitars are made (episode 1688), which again, are made by means of a template-based sameness, but are also made in all different types, to account for personal preferences.

The more removed we get from mechanized manufacturing, and the more a person is involved in, and close to, the process, the more those products bear particular differences that can be traced back to the hands of the artisan. Each of the products bear a certain personal stamp. When I say that something I've made is "mine," I mean more than just who owns it. I mean that something of myself is in it. We can learn a lot about a person from what he or she makes. Handyman Negri comes into the house to play his guitar after we see how guitars are made. The kind of music and the way he plays disclose something of himself, rooted in Mr. Negri's love of music and guitar playing.

And at other points in the week, Mister Rogers sits down at the kitchen table to make a spoon puppet and a birthday hat, each bearing the unique touch of Mister Rogers himself. I happened to think that the hat he made was terrible, and not at all how I would have made it. That's okay, though, because he made it as well as he could and in the way he wanted. With such crafts, we don't aim for sameness like they do in factories, but we want the stuff we make to be our own, and be genuine expressions of ourselves.

The Seat of the Personal

Have you ever asked someone what they're thinking? If you asked a stranger or someone you just met, they probably wouldn't tell you anything too deep. If you asked a more intimate friend or romantic partner, they might express something more intimate, or even their deeply *personal* thoughts and feelings. Thinking itself is not personal, but your own particular thoughts are, some maybe more than others. Some thoughts you have are maybe so private that you won't share them with anyone for your entire life. The seat of the personal is deeper than the mere act of thinking. You are what you think about, or that to which your thinking (and the other things you do) gives expression. But let's go even deeper.

What *do* you think about? (Or, should I ask, what do *you* think about?) Scheler thinks that we're beings who love even before we're beings who think, and so we most think about what we love. In fact, you probably don't even notice certain things in your environment unless they relate to what interests you. Might I suggest then, that, in a certain respect, you are what you would want, or want to do, for your birthday? I know that sounds corny. Naturally, I'm referring here to Corney's birthday party which culminates the week's theme of specialness. But maybe there's something to this. The birthday cake (specially made with nuts and raisins) and the party refer to such a height of personal expression that it would be too impersonal even to call them "products."

Corney asks Mayor Maggie what most people do on their birthday, thinking that all birthday parties would have to be the same. "Different people do different things," she says, and asks Corney what *he* likes to do on his birthday. (His party should be especially for S. Pecially!) Interestingly, he says he wants to do the things that most people do: sing the birthday song, and have cake, balloons and play hide-and-seek. But that's what interests Corney. His wish for that kind of party expresses something about himself.

Scheler speaks of the person as that deepest part of your being that lives in and through all of your conscious acts: in your thinking, willing, wishing, hoping, believing, feeling, preferring, loving, hating, and so on. There's hoping itself, and then there's *your* hoping. There's loving itself, and then there's *your* loving. And of course, there's thinking, and then there's *your* thinking. Your person is a kind of spirit that permeates all you do, contained in every one of your acts of consciousness without being exhausted in any of them. There's a unique quality or moral tenor to all that you do, which discloses to others that personal part of yourself. It's what Scheler calls your "individual value-essence." This is the seat of your personal difference, which makes you special on the inside.

You cannot encounter the personal being of another by just looking at them, but—even so—you could spend your whole life with someone without ever recognizing their personal value. Scheler insists that only in love is the personal value of others disclosed; hatred, on the other hand, closes off our ability to see others as individual persons. There's an individual value-quality to Corney, too, which his friends, who love him, and can therefore see that value, celebrate in the birthday party they give him.

An Edict of Conformity

By referring to our differences so much, don't we run the risk of abolishing that which makes us all politically, and even morally, equal? The idea of equality seems to rely on a certain sameness. I think of Dash, the kid "super" from the movie *The Incredibles* who can run really fast. When he wasn't allowed to try out for sports because of his speed, he expressed a popular sentiment: saying everyone's special is "another way of saying no one is." But personal uniqueness doesn't have to indicate superiority or inferiority, nor should it. In fact, such designations indicate a blindness to the personal value of others—a consequence of a *lack* of love. Maybe a sign of a thriving community is that everyone helps each other be most themselves through discovering and living out (and celebrating) their personal differences.

Fred Rogers once wrote a short book for children called *Everyone Is Special*. It begins with King Friday XIII summoning everyone in the neighborhood to the castle for an announcement:

> Friends and citizens of the Neighborhood of Make-Believe. I have decided that life would be much simpler if all of us looked alike. And since I am your king, I feel you should look like me. You will begin at once to make masks for yourselves—masks that look just like my face. . . . And no objections!

There was much consternation throughout the neighborhood, but everyone begrudgingly complied. Soon they were all wearing robes and King Friday masks. Now, instead of there being lots of different people around, there were just lots of kings. But things were not made simpler (surprise, surprise!). It took a much longer time to find certain people. King Friday couldn't find the Queen and missed seeing her face. And nobody could tell anymore who the real king was.

> "Don't you know that people look different and act differently for a reason?" Lady Elaine Fairchilde asked the (real) king.
> "What reason?" the king inquired.

"Why, the best reason in the world! If everybody's different, then everybody's special!"

"Do you mean," King Friday asked, "being the only person who really looks and acts like me makes me special?"

King Friday realizes that if he were to be like everyone else, or if everyone were to be like him, then that would make him less special and unique, not more so. But don't we tend to assume the opposite: that we're more special and likable the more we "fit in" with certain people or certain kinds of people? This can be misleading, though. I hear it said often that people have such different views and opinions, yet it seems to me that people think too much alike, and that there should be a greater diversity of views than there is.

But some are unsettled by the fact that people are different, and resist difference. Following upon certain interpretations of early philosophers, they think that if everyone thinks rightly, then everyone will think in the same way. If everyone lives rightly, then everyone will live in the same way. Sameness indicates a rightness; difference indicates a wrongness.

Scheler doesn't think this way, and I don't think Mister Rogers does either. It's far more likely that certain individuals are "called," or feel a moral imperative, to live in a wide range of different ways, based upon the particular ways that individuals recognize values in the world. There is nothing that prevents you from experiencing the call of a genuine good (or a "good-in-itself") that is also just for you. It is an imperative that emerges from the values you see in the world, and "whispers: 'for you'."

Maybe this is a little bit of what Lady Elaine means in her response to King Friday's realization that being the only one like him makes him special. "But there's a catch," Lady Elaine continues. "Being yourself makes you a special person, but you have to work at making yourself the best person you can be!" While it doesn't take any work to be special, it does take work—and perhaps a little bit of courage—to live out your difference and uniqueness in the world.

A Personalist Community

King Friday thought about what Lady Elaine had said to him, about how being special gives us a responsibility to live out his specialness in the best way we can—to become his best self. This makes him realize how mistaken he was to make a rule that everyone should be like him. This is not the best way to be king. This is not the best way to live his own personal uniqueness.

> "You mean that I should help people be themselves instead of making rules that they should be somebody else?" King Friday said at last, nodding and looking very wise.
> "You said it, [Toots!]," Lady Elaine called back happily as she left.

One thing I like so much about this exchange is that Rogers has King Friday coming to the realization for himself that he should help people be themselves rather than Lady Elaine needing to tell him. But notice that in challenging his rule of conformity, Lady Elaine helps King Friday come to a realization that helps King Friday be himself in a better way. She does for him a little of what he should be fostering in others throughout the neighborhood.

When Scheler had given some thought to how society should be in the context of his personalism, he gave several guiding ideas about the value of the person and its social implications. The first one we've just about mentioned already:

A person isn't considered valuable because she's rational, rather a person is valuable because she's a unique and unrepeatable individual.

The value of the person for Scheler begins in the fact that, as Mister Rogers says, each one of us is the only one of us, and the only one there will ever be. But for Scheler, it also refers to our particular capability to intuit, or recognize the values of the world in our own way, according to our individual essence, and also to realize new values in the world, in our own way. To "realize" means here to bring about into reality, or to make real. The idea is that if even just one person is destroyed, there will be forever lost not only an unrepeatable being in her own right, but also a subtly particular recognition and realization of values that only that one person is able to see and has the potential of bringing forth. Think of it like this: if all the values (and all possible values) of the universe were a whole infinite pie (let's call this God), each one of us would have, within ourselves, our own finite piece of that pie.

If this is true, then Scheler's second idea gains importance:

A person shouldn't be regarded as valuable only to the extent that she's helpful for the growth and development of community, rather community is valuable to the extent that it is helpful for her growth and development as an individual person (who can then in turn freely offer service to the community).

The greatest social concern within this personalist context is something like King Friday's rule of sameness, and the variety of other ways that undervaluing personal differences undercuts the ability for the unique value of each person to "come to the fore." Any social order that treats people as the same, or pressures conformity, to the extent that it does, is depersonalizing. This includes treating people merely in terms of fixed social roles, reducing them to their class, race, gender, or to other social or political categories, their status as "consumer," or even as "citizen," and using someone merely as a means for gain, economic or otherwise.

Rogers echoes a nearly identical sentiment:

> as human beings, our job in life is to help people realize how rare and valuable each one of us really is, that each of us has something that no one else has—or ever will have—something inside that is unique for all time. It's our job to encourage each other to discover that uniqueness and to provide ways of developing its expression.

Scheler would support this view socially. He says that if the satisfaction of the needs of human development is a condition that allows for us to grow and develop as persons—to be fully individual and of unique value—then the social goods and tasks required to satisfy those needs must be equally available to everyone. They must be available for everyone equally so that personal differences do not remain hidden and concealed, as if by a (King Friday) mask! Any social policy that halts and disrupts human development effectively places a mask on those people, concealing their true faces, and their personal selves.

Eventually King Friday comes around and realizes it was a mistake to try to conceal everyone's differences. To correct his mistake, he makes another announcement:

> Friends and citizens of Make-Believe, my rule was unfair. You no longer need to wear a kingly mask and robe, and I invite you to come in the castle for a Party to Celebrate Our Differences.

"Everyone had a great time at the party. Some danced, and some sang. Some laughed and played. Some happily sat and watched everything that was going on."

But one thing was the same for everyone in the Neighborhood of Make-Believe: everyone was glad they were different. They were glad they were special.

15

I, Thou, and the Neighborhood

JAMES MCLACHLAN

. . . and you'll have things you'll want to talk about. I will too.

Fred Rogers often related a story about an experience he had
one summer while vacationing in New England. At the time he
was studying at Pittsburgh Theological Seminary and was
learning how to preach a sermon. On Sunday he decided he
would visit the local church in the small town he was visiting.
The regular minister was out of town and he sat through a sermon by an older pastor who was filling in that week. He
remembered thinking he was listening to the worst sermon he
could have ever imagined. Rogers sat in the pew thinking, "He's
going against every rule they're teaching us about preaching.
What a waste of time!" But then he overheard the person sitting beside him whisper through her tears, "he said exactly
what I needed to hear." At that moment he realized that something important had happened. The woman beside him had
come in need, and the words of this incompetent preacher, who
had given what was, by the rules, a poorly crafted sermon, had
spoken to her heart. Rogers, on the other hand, had come in
judgment and heard nothing but faults. He called this one of
the great lessons of his life. "The space between the person trying to deliver the message and the listener is 'holy ground'." He
said the experience that day had taught him to be a better
neighbor and listener.

The German-Jewish philosopher Martin Buber (1878–1965)
described a similar experience he had as a young Professor at
the University of Vienna. At the time, Buber who had been
raised a secular Jew, had discovered religion and, in particular,
mystical religion. He was interested in religious and mystical

experience, not merely studying them, but having them. At the time, religious experience meant for Buber that the transcendent broke through into ordinary life. This "otherness" didn't fit into the everyday, but lifted one out of the world in ecstasy and rapture. He had been upstairs in his rooms meditating and praying one morning, fully engaged in deeply religious intensity, when there was a knock at his front door downstairs. He was taken out of his spiritual moment and went down to see who was at the door. It was a young man who had been a student and a friend, and who had come specifically to speak with Buber. But Buber says it was an "everyday" event and lifted him out of this enthusiasm.

On that afternoon in the late summer of 1914, after a morning of "religious enthusiasm" during the visit with the young man, Buber said he was not present to the visitor "in spirit." He was polite, even friendly, with the man but was also hoping to soon get back to his meditations. They spoke for a time and the young man left. Buber never saw him again. The man died at the front in World War I. Later, Buber learned from a mutual friend that the young man had come to him that day in need. He had a question that he never asked, and Buber had not even attempted to discern that this might have been the visitor's purpose. Had he been "present," Buber might have noticed. The man had come with a need to understand his life and was trying to figure out what life meant. He wanted help.

Just as Rogers didn't hear the sermon, but only its mistakes in form, Buber had not recognized the young man's need at the time because he had been concerned to get back upstairs to his prayers and meditation. He had been polite and friendly, but he was not listening. He had not been present in the way that one person can be present with another, in such a way that you sense the questions and concerns of the other.

After that Buber said he gave up on the religious in the sense of the exalted, exceptional, and enthusiastic. He says he gave it up for the "everyday." Every moment demands we be present to others. It is our responsibility. Fullness was not to be found "out there" but rather, in the present moment with the present person, in the present world.

Everyday Relations in the Neighborhood

Take a moment to think about your own interactions with other people during your day. Martin Buber said that we can approach the world, and others in it, in two distinctly different ways. In the way that he called "I-You" (or "I-Thou"), we encounter the other as unique, a person with whom we are open to dialogue. In the other way that he called "I-It," we see the other as an object in the world to be used, manipulated, enjoyed, or overcome.

Fred Rogers attended Pittsburgh Theological Seminary at the height of the influence of 'dialogical philosophy' in American theological thought. Whether explicitly or not, he seems to have incorporated something like Buber's notion of dialogue into what he was trying to do on television. He wanted to create a neighborhood on TV, a place where children entered a relation. Even though there was no verbal dialogue happening between Mister Rogers and the viewer, Rogers was always present to his "television neighbor."

According to Buber, the world is the theater of creation. It is in the everyday world, not the mystic beyond, where persons can create meaning through relation to each other. Buber claimed that no one should deceive himself into thinking that there are places too commonplace as to be excluded from creation. You ought not think that if you work in such a place, you can only return to creation, to a meaningful life, when your shift is over, and you go home.

> No factory and no office is so abandoned by creation that a creative glance could not fly up from one working place to another, from desk to desk, a sober and brotherly glance which guarantees the reality of creation which is happening. And nothing is so valuable a service of dialogue between God and man as such an unsentimental and unreserved exchange of glances between two men in an alien place. (*Between Man and Man*, p. 37)

Don't you find this to be a common experience? Think of being bored stiff while waiting in a line at the DMV. Suddenly someone smiles or tells a joke about the monotony of it all, and the place is softened, humanized. Buber thought that reality existed "between" persons in the relation created there through simple activities of recognizing the uniqueness of the other person, the "You." No place was so dehumanized that it couldn't be restored by the action of recognition between two people. This was not an interior mystical experience but rather the space of "the between," where relationships occur and unfold. From this perspective, the psychological, the subjective experience, that which happens within the souls of each, is only the secret accompaniment to the dialogue. The meaning of any dialogue is found in neither of the two dialogical partners, nor each of them combined together, but rather in and within their interchange.

Fred Rogers saw the children's programming of his time as a kind of wasteland, what Buber described as the It-World. The programming was devoid of meaningful relationships. Most of it sought only to entertain children, to sell them products, and make money for the advertisers. Rogers launched his project at the beginning of the age of television. This commercial juggernaut was just emerging that would fill most every home in America. He moved against the tide. Rogers did not want to aim at the mass market of children, but was concerned with the development of individual persons. He used the simplest props, language, and storytelling. Like Buber, Rogers referred to the space between him, in the television set, and the viewer as "holy ground."

> I'm not that interested in 'mass communications,' . . . I am much more interested in what happens between this person and the one watching. The space between the television set and that person who's watching is very holy ground. ("About Us")

The Everyday Holy

It's hard to watch an episode of *Mister Rogers' Neighborhood* without encountering the everyday, the usual. Even in the Neighborhood of Make-Believe there are no overwhelming special effects just simply made puppets and people talking to them. Fred Rogers often spoke of his disappointment with children's television. He would comment on its loudness, the explosions, violence, and the pies being thrown in people's faces. In a way, Rogers's disappointment with children's television resembled Martin Buber's critique of "the religious." In both cases the aim was at the emotional impact of the exceptional, the enthusiastic.

Think about how this has worked in "religious" movies. In the 1923 version of *The Ten Commandments*, Cecille B. DeMille recreated the parting of the Red Sea using large amounts of Jell-O and trick photography. People were impressed but the impression didn't last. In 1956, DeMille did it again with much more impressive special effects. But seen in 2019, it might still be cool to watch but doesn't move us to religious ecstasy. In 2014 Ridley Scott used CGI and a budget of 200 million for *Exodus: Gods and Kings*. The illusion was, again, impressive. All three movies aimed to help us escape the everyday in which we live. Yet fabulous "effects" age quickly.

Rogers and Buber devoted their lives to meeting the other person. It was right here in the everyday—not in escaping it—

that that meaning happened. Rogers described the eternal as shining, but everyday moments. He called them "twinklings" and said that eternity was made of them. They are moments when human beings recognize and relate to one another.

> In the external scheme of things, shining moments are as brief as the twinkling of an eye, yet such twinklings are what eternity is made of—moments when we human beings can say "I love you," "I'm proud of you," "I forgive you," "I'm grateful for you." That's what eternity is made of: invisible, imperishable good stuff. (*The World according to Mister Rogers*, p. 88)

No, Hell Isn't Other People; They're Neighbors

Rogers once said, "You bring all you ever were and are to any relationship you have today." For Buber this would mean that we must be fully present to the other person. In *I and Thou*, Buber makes his famous distinction between the I-You relation and the I-It relation. Basically, I-It is when I confront the world and others as objects for my use, as customers for advertising, digits in the television ratings wars, obstacles or useful tools, or merely as things sitting around before me. This isn't necessarily evil. We need to be able to use things. The food I eat, I consume as a thing. The wood I use to build a house is a thing. When I visit the supermarket, I see the persons working there in their functions as employees who facilitate my purchases. In one way they are just filling a role in the machine that is society. The problem is in seeing them as only things, or ultimately things for my use.

Buber's contemporary, the existentialist philosopher Jean-Paul Sartre, thought that our problem as human beings was that we all desired to be God. This sounds rather grandiose, but it's really just an everyday desire for power, according to Sartre. We want to be the center of things, one way or another. We want to be in control. In Buber's terms, we see everything and everyone essentially as a thing, an *it*. But this is also the source of conflict. Other people also want to be the center of the universe and they oppose my fantasy that I'm in charge, that I'm the hero of the story. So, in Sartre's famous words, "Hell is other people." Sartre wanted us to get past this. He shared that with Buber and Rogers.

For Buber and Fred Rogers, the other is my neighbor. Rogers once said: "One of the greatest paradoxes about omnipotence is that we need to feel it early in life, and lose it early in life, in

order to achieve a healthy, realistic, yet exciting, sense of
potency later on" (*The World according to Mister Rogers*,
p. 111). For Rogers, to grow up is to lose the desire for omnipotence, the desire to be God. Buber thought we shouldn't even
think of God this way, as omnipotent. To do so was to worship
power. St. Augustine interpreted the famous story of Moses
meeting God in the burning bush as a manifestation of the eternal omnipotent God. When Moses asks God his name, the deity
replies *ehyeh asher ehyeh*. This usually gets translated "I am
that I am" kind of like Popeye saying "I am what I am and that's
all that I am." Augustine liked this translation, because God is
portrayed as pure being, an unchangeable power.

Buber, and his friend Franz Rosenzweig translated the
Bible into German in the 1920s. They rendered this phrase differently as "he who will be present." I am a faithful presence on
whom you can count. Mister Rogers spoke at times about
superheroes and about little boys who wrapped towels around
their necks so they could be Superman. But then he redefined
superheroes as people, neighbors, who help each other, and as
little boys in wheelchairs who don't give up, but give of themselves to the people around them. The people are heroes who
embody Buber's translation of the name of God more than
Sartre's or Augustine's.

Presence to the other person is central to Buber's I-You relation. The other is unique. This is what it is to be a superhero for
Rogers. It's to be love, and love is to be a good listener.
"Listening is a very active awareness of the coming together of
at least two lives. Listening, as far as I'm concerned, is certainly a prerequisite of love. One of the most essential ways of
saying "I love you" is being a receptive listener" (p. 92).

I-You and the Neighbor

Fred Rogers's two most famous songs are probably "Won't You
Be My Neighbor?" and "It's You I Like." In the first, he invites
the viewer to be his neighbor. The other person is asked to participate in the space between each member of a relationship.
In, "It's You I Like," he describes the uniqueness of the other
person with whom we enter a relation.

> It's You I Like It's you I like,
> It's not the things you wear,
> It's not the way you do your hair,
> But it's you I like. The way you are right now,
> The way down deep inside you,

Not the things that hide you,
Not your toys, they're just beside you. But it's you I like, every part of
    you,
Your skin, your eyes, your feelings
Whether old or new. I hope that you'll remember
Even when you're feeling blue
That it's you I like,
It's you yourself, it's you,
It's you . . . I . . . like!

The words of the song fit nicely with Buber's distinction between the I-You and the I-It. Buber tells us that how we approach others determines not only our attitude toward them but who we are ourselves. The I-You can only be spoken with our whole being. We must be completely present to the other person, or even animal, or God. When we're not present to the other, or see the other as an object for our use, we speak the basic word I-It. When we say It, the "I" of "I-It" is said too. When we approach the other as an "It," we see her as a thing and not as a person. We don't really approach her and we don't speak the "it" with our whole I, our whole self as we do when we approach her as a "You." The other person is a collection of characteristics, a list of things ("the things that hide you"). In Buber's words, "The basic word I-You can only be spoken with one's whole being. The basic word I-It can never be spoken with one's whole being" (*I and Thou*, pp. 53–54).

To approach the other person as a You is, according to Buber, to encounter them in their uniqueness. But for Buber, to appreciate the uniqueness is not just interpersonal. It is to see the uniqueness in each person, but also in animals, plants, even rocks. In *I and Thou* he gives the example of a Tree. When I stop seeing the tree as a mere object, the sum of my observations, the power of the exclusiveness of the tree draws me into relationship with it. Reciprocity is the meaning of relationship. I stop seeing things as mere objects in my world for me to manipulate. Speaking to the uniqueness of persons, Mister Rogers gives us a Buberian reflection:

> The older I get, the more I seem to be able to appreciate my "neighbor" (whomever I happen to be with at the moment). Oh, sure, I've always tried to love my neighbor as myself; however, the more experiences I've had, the more chances I've had to see the uniqueness of each person . . . as well as each tree, and plant, and shell, and cloud . . . the more I find myself delighting every day in the lavish gifts of God, whom I've come to believe is the greatest appreciator of all.

16
Loved into Being

SCOTT F. PARKER

> Love is at the root of everything. All learning, all parenting, all
> relationships. Love or the lack of it.
>
> —FRED ROGERS

When I think of the teachers who have made the longest and
deepest positive impacts on me, I notice certain common characteristics. Each of them has been enthusiastic about his or her
subject and able to make that enthusiasm contagious. But a
charismatic lecturer can do this much. The teachers I have in
mind did more.

Each of them took me seriously as a student, as a thinker,
and *as a person*. They treated me with respect; they listened to
my questions and ideas affirmingly; they encouraged me to
push myself to think more deeply and take on new perspectives. They were open about themselves, and they were willing
to think *along with* me. This last, above all, confirmed for me
my status as an active learner. Because they took me seriously,
I learned how to take myself seriously.

Everything I'm mentioning about these teachers has to do
with how they carried themselves, and not with any particular
information they imparted to me. Although in each case I
learned a lot of "content" over the course of the relationship,
that content, while not entirely beside the point, is not the
main point.

Two examples: Norm Baird taught me how to solve certain
kinds of physics problems, but more significantly, he taught me
how to be curious, to pursue my interests, and to be open-
minded. And he did this mostly by being himself, thereby modeling these traits for me. Debra Gwartney taught me, among

other craft elements, to be aware of the difference between the narrator-I and the character-I in my nonfiction, but what mattered more to me than such nuts and bolts were her warmth, commitment, care. With both teachers, I felt myself growing from the relationship, not just with respect to the subject at hand, but, more profoundly, as myself. This, of course, is why I recall them here.

Can it be an accident that at each period of my life the teacher who made the most profound positive impact on me taught in the field I was primarily interested in? Professors who have had students visit them in their offices to tell them that an inspiring class has led to a change in major will appreciate the power of a positive learning relationship. And when the new major is a good fit for the student, there is particular satisfaction.

These examples stand out for me because they're rare. I hope my reminiscence triggers your own and that you are lucky enough to have had some good teachers. If you have, I ask you to consider whether your good teachers share some of the characteristics I've described in mine.

One person who may occur to you in this context is Fred Rogers. We know Rogers primarily as the television character Mister Rogers, but it's important to note who that character was and how the man himself understood his role. Rogers considered himself an educator rather than an entertainer. His music and puppetry and acting were instrumental for him, means—like the medium of television itself—of conveying his teachings. When I think back to watching *Mister Rogers' Neighborhood* as a boy, what I remember primarily are not the particular things Rogers taught me, like how to make a banana boat (episode 1473) or why divorce happens (episodes 1476–1480), but the character of the man himself, with his directness, sincerity, and compassion. I appreciated the respect with which he spoke to me.

In a clip from the documentary, *Won't You Be My Neighbor?*, Rogers recounts an exchange he had while visiting a nursery school. There, he was greeted by silence and stares from the children until one boy said, "My doggie's ear came off in the automatic washer." Rogers interpreted the statement and the silence that resumed after it to mean, "This is your test, Mister Rogers. Are you still in touch with childhood?" His response, which seems so simple but actually demonstrates a keen awareness of the boy's concerns and needs, was to say, "Sometimes that happens to toys, doesn't it? Their ears come off or their legs come off. But that never happens to us.

Our ears don't come off. Our noses don't come off. Our arms
don't come off." Hearing this, the boy got excited and said, "Our
legs don't come off." Rogers responded, "No, they don't."
Immediately the other children started to ask questions. He
had passed the test.

This is how I remember Fred Rogers and how I encounter
him now as I revisit his neighborhood with my son. I want to
think here about how he excelled at forming healthy relationships with kids (even from the remove of television), how he
helped so many of us (and continues to help so many of our children) understand our feelings and ourselves, and how important these things are to growth and well-being. And to do this, I
want to start by introducing another Rogers: Carl Rogers.

Rogers, the Psychologist

Carl Rogers (1902–1987) was an American psychologist who
played a foundational role in the emergence of humanistic psychology in the early to mid-twentieth century. This "third force"
in psychology developed in response to the earlier psychoanalytic and behaviorist movements, which it saw as taking unnec-
essarily negative views of human nature. Humanistic
psychology distinguished itself by its address of the whole person and its concern for individual flourishing, sometimes called
"self-actualization."

The roots of humanistic psychology lie in existentialism, a
philosophical movement that privileges subjective experience
as it attends to individuality, consciousness, the self, personal
growth, and freedom. But where existentialist philosophy can
remain an intellectual orientation, humanistic psychology
applies itself to promoting well-being. In short: it's therapy.

Carl Rogers's most significant contribution to the movement
was the person-centered approach. The term "client-centered
therapy" is more commonly used, but in the latter part of
Rogers's career he came to prefer "person-centered approach,"
which he found to be broader in application and more descrip-
tive. Carl Rogers briefly states the central hypothesis of this
approach in his book *A Way of Being*: "Individuals have within
themselves vast resources for self-understanding and for alter-
ing their self-concepts, basic attitudes, and self-directed behavior; these resources can be tapped if a definable climate of
facilitative psychological attitudes can be provided" (p. 115).

Carl Rogers names three conditions for producing such a
growth-promoting climate: genuineness, acceptance, and
empathic understanding. In his essay, "The Foundations of a

Person-Centered Approach," Rogers describes these conditions in a psychotherapeutic context, though they can be applied more broadly.

1. Genuineness refers to the therapist's willingness and ability to be in touch with and open to his or her own feelings and attitudes and to express these to the client.

2. Acceptance, commonly referred to as "unconditional positive regard," describes the therapist's attitude toward the client. The therapist respects the client's feeling, whatever it may be—anger, fear, resentment, self-consciousness, love—and affirms it without judgment.

3. Empathic understanding refers to the therapist's ability to accurately sense the client's feelings and the significance she or he attributes to them and communicate those back to the client.

On the way these conditions lead to psychological growth, Carl Rogers writes: "Briefly, as persons are accepted and prized, they tend to develop a more caring attitude toward themselves. As persons are empathically heard, it becomes possible for them to listen more accurately to the flow of inner experiencings. But as a person understands and prizes self, the self becomes more congruent with the experiencings. The person thus becomes more real, more genuine. These tendencies, the reciprocal of the therapist's attitudes, enable the person to be a more effective growth-enhancer for himself or herself. There is a greater freedom to be the true, whole person." The psychotherapeutic process, when it works, allows an individual to achieve or approach "the goal of life": "to be," in the words of Kierkegaard "that self which one truly is" (p. 110).

If you're thinking ahead, you'll already see some of Fred Rogers's qualities showing through in Carl's ideas, which would not have surprised the psychologist. According to Carl Rogers, the person-centered approach can be implemented broadly. He considered it "a point of view, a philosophy, an approach to life, a way of being, which fits any situation in which *growth*—of a person, a group, or a community—is part of the goal" (*A Way of Being*, p. ix).

As an example of how Carl Rogers's ideas can be applied to various kinds of relationships, let's consider education. In his essay, "Can Learning Encompass both Ideas and Feelings?," he writes, "So if I were to attempt a crude definition of what it means to learn as a whole person, I would say that it involves learning of a *unified* sort, at the cognitive, feeling, and gut levels, with a clear *awareness* of the different aspects of this unified learning" (p. 266).

The teacher in this situation would ideally cultivate all three of Carl Rogers's conditions: genuineness, acceptance, and empathic understanding. His research suggested to him that a teacher who could be with students as him- or herself without presenting a façade was more likely to be effective than one who merely played the part. Acceptance too has particular application to education. Rogers advocates for teachers who care for their students while respecting them as individuals with their own sense of worth. Finally, there's empathic understanding, which must occur on an individual basis: a teacher who is aware of how the learning process seems and feels to each student is more likely to encourage learning in them.

When I think back on the teachers I mentioned at the outset, I see all three of these characteristics in each. By contrast, it's fairly easy to notice the absence of one or more in those less effective teachers I've had. My memory supports what Rogers says is actually the most important condition for learning: the teacher must not only be genuine, accepting, and empathic, but the students must perceive these qualities in the teacher. Such perception is made difficult, according to Rogers, by students' well-founded skepticism that a teacher might possess such qualities. But difficult as it is, a teacher who leads with empathy, Rogers thinks, can get there.

And when they do, the upshot is significant: "To the extent that the teacher creates such a relationship with his class, the student will become a self-initiated learner, more original, more self-disciplined, less anxious and other directed" (*On Becoming a Person*, p. 37).

In other words, the teacher doesn't merely educate in the sense of filling up or, more generously, challenging the student's mind, but more importantly, cultivates the growth and well-being of the whole student. If this sounds to you at all like what you know of Mister Rogers, I think it's no accident.

Rogers, the Teacher

In his essay "Significant Learning: In Therapy and in Education," Carl Rogers applies client-centered therapy to education. Working from the premise that, in contrast to the mere acquisition of facts, educators make a difference for their students, Rogers outlines how genuineness, acceptance, and empathic understanding facilitate such learning. Students who inhabit this kind of learning environment do about as well with factual acquisition as peers in more traditional environments, but outdo the latter group significantly "in personal adjustment, in self-initiated extra-curricular learning, in creativity, in self-responsibility" (p. 292).

If you watch Fred Rogers in the company of children, you'll notice the distinctly Carl Rogerian approach he takes. In fact, if we focus on Carl's three primary criteria for effective learning—genuineness, acceptance, and understanding—we can see Fred not only embodying each on *Mister Rogers' Neighborhood* but explicitly articulating them in his writing, for example, in the book *The World According to Mister Rogers*. Here he is, first, on genuineness: "The greatest gift you ever give is your honest self." Next, on acceptance: "When we love a person, we accept him or her exactly as is: the lovely with the unlovely, the strong along with the fearful, the true mixed in with the facade, and of course, the only way we can do it is by accepting ourselves that way." Finally, on understanding: "When you combine your own intuition with a sensitivity to other people's feelings and moods, you may be close to the origins of valuable human attributes such as generosity, altruism, compassion, sympathy, and empathy." And you can tell *because he is genuine* that this isn't idle talk, but an articulation of values and attitudes that reach to the core of Fred Rogers's being.

I don't mean to suggest that Fred was influenced by Carl. I have no reason to think Fred Rogers ever studied Rogerian psychotherapy. What I am suggesting is that Fred's approach to children and education converged significantly with Carl's theoretical prescriptions.

Fred's direct psychological influence came from Margaret McFarland, with whom he studied at the Arsenal Family and Children's Center in the Friendship neighborhood of Pittsburgh. Arsenal was founded by Benjamin Spock, whose book *The Common Sense Book of Baby and Child Care* was one of the bestselling books of the twentieth century and had an enormous influence on how children were raised in the US. In it, he famously instructed, "Trust yourself. You know more than you think you do."

McFarland, who went on to consult on scripts for *Mister Rogers' Neighborhood* for over thirty years, taught Fred that "attitudes aren't taught, they're caught." This orientation infuses the show. Fred teaches as much by modeling appropriate whole-person behavior as by instruction. Another anecdote from McFarland, which we learn from Maxwell King in *The Good Neighbor,* his biography of Fred Rogers, neatly captures this spirit. When she brought a sculptor in to work with kids, she told him, "I don't want you to teach sculpting. All I want you to do is to love clay in front of the children" (p. 139). If the love of clay can be contagious, so too, Fred understood, could be the love of oneself and the love of one another.

Putting her theory into practice, she taught by example. "By all accounts, McFarland's performance as a teacher was spellbinding. Rather than rely on textbook descriptions of early development, she would bring in a mother and child for fifteen-or-so minutes. Then she would spend the next two and a half hours describing what she had noticed about their interactions" (Sally Ann Flecker, "When Fred Met Margaret," *Pitt Med*, at <www.pittmed.health.pitt.edu/story/when-fred-met-margaret>). Flecker goes on to quote one of McFarland's students, Margaret Mary Kimmel, who also consulted on *Mister Rogers' Neighborhood*, "I learned so much from just watching her watch and describe to the class what was going on between the mother and the baby."

"I like you just the way you are," might be the iconic statement of *Mister Rogers' Neighborhood*. Imagine or remember hearing this message directed to you as a kid. It would be quite natural to take away two things: first, that if Mister Rogers loves you, you must be deserving of love; and, second, that if Mister Rogers can love someone this openly, so could you. Fred Rogers, like Carl Rogers, thought this kind of acceptance (and the self-acceptance it engenders) to be prerequisite for growth. "One of the major goals of education," he said in a speech he delivered at Thiel College, "must be to help students discover a greater awareness of their own unique selves, in order to increase their feelings of personal worth, responsibility, and freedom."

If we can do this we can increase the likelihood of children growing into adults who have healthy core values. This is important to Fred, for whom knowledge and information are good only insofar as they serve healthy values. As he said to the American Academy of Child Psychiatry, "It's easy to convince people that children need to learn the alphabet and numbers. . . . How do we help people to realize that what matters even more than the superimposition of adult symbols is how a person's inner life finally puts together the alphabet and numbers of his outer life? What really matters is whether he uses the alphabet for the declaration of war or the description of a sunrise—his numbers for the final count at Buchenwald or the specifics of a brand-new bridge" (pp. 247–48).

In holding this view, Rogers swam against the cultural current. It's easier to quantify, and analyze information acquisition than personal well-being, genuineness, and compassion. The degree to which he maintained his course against this current is a remarkable demonstration of the power of genuineness. This—the power of being who you are—is one of the abiding lessons of the success of *Mister Rogers' Neighborhood.*

It's impressive that there are people like Mister Rogers out there, who live with such genuineness and treat people (children, most obviously, but not only them) with such dignity. It strains belief that at least one of them ended up on television for more than three decades. Despite the overwhelming evidence to the contrary, Mister Rogers believed that "television has the chance of building a real community out of an entire country." But it only takes one exception to prove the possibility, and, of course, *Mister Rogers' Neighborhood* is that exception. It's simple how he did it, if not at all easy. Rogers spoke directly to his audience, addressing the camera as if it were a person. Every child watching the show feels like Rogers is speaking directly to him or her. It was Rogers's unique combination of intimacy and positive regard for his audience that allowed him his profound impact.

Fred Rogers didn't allow any advertising aimed at children to be associated with his projects. Advertising, in its aim to get something from rather than give something to its audience, is inherently anti–Mister Rogerian and incompatible with doing what's best for children.

The young viewer trusts Rogers in a way he or she doesn't trust every adult, many of whom can be condescending or dismissive of children. Rogers, even through the one-directional medium of television, expresses to kids: I understand you, I respect you, and I like you. That kind of validation releases us, in Carl's terms, from loneliness, and can enable us to be human. We are safe to experience and explore the whole of ourselves. No feeling is off limits to us in Mister Rogers's company. It is the trust he earns from his audience that allows him to explore "difficult" subjects with children. Death, divorce, jealousy, insecurity—kids can handle these things when adults are there to support them and show them how.

In his famous congressional address on behalf of PBS and the Corporation for Public Broadcasting, Rogers articulated quite clearly his primary goal for his show: "I feel that if we in public television can only make it clear that feelings are mentionable and manageable we will have done a great service." In his show and in his personal conduct, Rogers did do this, and it was a great service indeed.

Rogers and Rogers

Both Carl and Fred Rogers had faith in the goodness of human nature. Both men, incidentally, were recognized by people who knew them well as *happy*. Without distinguishing cause and effect, we might note how naturally outlook and experience fit hand in hand.

Such faith (supported by the balance of their research and experience) is a precondition for encouraging people to be fully themselves. Those without such faith must be afraid of relaxing their guard and letting free a self that cannot be trusted. Alan Watts addressed this dilemma precisely in his 1965 lecture "Man in Nature," saying, "Because if you can't trust yourself, can you trust your mistrust of yourself? Is that well-founded? See? If you can't trust yourself, you're *totally* mixed up. You haven't a leg to stand on, you haven't a point of departure for anything."

What if we were to imagine a world in which people treated one another with dignity; a world in which people are secure enough in themselves to be emotionally open; a world in which people are more content with who they are (not *what they do* but *who they are*); a world in which people freely express care; a world in which we treat one another as neighbors?

I, for one, like to imagine such a world. And I think with the influences of Carl and Fred Rogers it's one we can move closer to. What both men encourage us—children and adults alike—to do is continue growing and learning how to like ourselves just the way we are. It sounds so easy. For most of us, it is anything but. Thankfully, good teachers such as Carl and Fred Rogers are out there helping us find the way.

17
A Word from a Man Mister Rogers Ruined

Nicolas Michaud

There are those who truly believe that Mister Rogers and his show did great harm to our country and to our children, particularly our boys. Specifically, they say that Mister Rogers made it impossible for boys to become *men.*

Instead of learning to conquer the world and stand up for themselves, boys learn from Rogers to be submissive and weak. Somewhat famously *Fox and Friends* argued that Mister Rogers made people feel entitled to love, reducing their need to compete and *earn* that love.

I don't know about you, but to me, that sounds insane. It's hard for me to think of any criticisms of Mister Rogers. I feel like I grew up with the man. *Mister Rogers' Neighborhood* was, by far, my favorite TV show as a little boy. Long before there was Elmo or Teletubbies, I was sitting about a foot away from an old thirteen-inch screen (with dials) watching every day. To me, he was the nicest, friendliest, and most caring person I knew—more so than most of the people I actually knew.

So what's there to say bad about the man? And that is where the argument gets interesting. You see, Mister Rogers's care, compassion, and gentleness *is* the criticism. And men like me are examples of the generation this "evil" man supposedly ruined.

It's Such a Good Feeling . . . to Punch People

What I mean is that as men go, I am pretty non-confrontational. I'm not particularly intimidating, and I have no desire to do violence. I might even be (gasp!) a pacifist. Sure, I study martial arts, but I specifically focus on trying to help people not hurt themselves when they try to hurt me. Through my life, I have often been accused of being crazy for forgiving people who hurt me. And I have found that an unwillingness, in our culture, to do harm to those who hurt us is often seen as a weakness. In a world of superheroes who punch, kick, and kill evildoers, we're supposed to stand up against those who would do us harm. And that just doesn't seem to be a value Mister Rogers promotes.

That belief, that strength requires a willingness to hurt others and seek vengeance, became very clear to me when I was a young man. When I was in my late teens, my mother was murdered. When people asked me what I wanted to happen to the man who did it, I told them I wanted him to get help. That answer really upset some people who thought I was wrong for not wanting him to die for it. And the rest said, "Well good for you, but I couldn't do that." But really, I *want* to forgive him and not carry that anger with me. Back then, I reasoned that tremendous harm had already been done to me and my family—*more* harm could only do exactly that . . . *more harm*. Why would I want there to be more suffering in the world just because I was suffering?

I'll be frank. I completely disagree with the idea that Rogers ruined men. Obviously, given that this is how I live my life, I happen to agree that we should be gentle, polite, and caring. However, as I have outed myself as a pretty mild-mannered man, you might think my motive suspect, and that I agree with Rogers only because I am a living, breathing example of the harm Rogers did. So what I'm going to try to do here is outline a cogent argument *in support* of the idea that Mister Rogers was bad for boys, and then, I'll see if I can refute that argument. I am not going to get into deep details about hegemony or patriarchy. Instead, I'm going to try to argue from common sense.

So what arguments are there that Mister Rogers actually did harm to boys through focus on niceness, kindliness, and forgiveness? I can see a few clear arguments:

1. Competition is good, but being "nice" reduces competition and competitive edge.

2. Kindness is easily taken advantage of. Because of that, being kind is unwise as it opens us to being harmed by people who want to use us.

3. Forgiveness is good, but it also removes room for righteous indignation. Sometimes we should be angry because things are wrong!

It's Such a Good Feeling . . . to Know I've Won

So let's consider the first point: competition is good and being nice basically gets in the way. Those familiar with Plato's *Republic* might here think of Thrasymachus in the first book: justice is for suckers! The desire to outdo, acquire, and get ahead is the mark of greatness and strength.

Obviously, in the US, we live in a highly competitive country. In fact, our economy is based on competition (mostly). Also, we believe in competition in sport and games, and many people feel we are losing our edge. Giving every kid on the soccer team participation trophies, for example, seems to undermine the fact that competition teaches a fundamental truth about life— that there are winners and there are losers.

In fact, it seems natural, doesn't it? Survival of the fittest, and all that. And if you don't come out on top, then you come out on bottom. Competition leads to better products and better business. Because we let businesses compete they have to lower their prices. Similarly, competition in sports results in stronger, faster, smarter athletes. So this idea of co-operation that Mister Rogers seems to tout is really not preparing boys for competing in the real world.

The first part of my response is that I think it is a bit unfair to Mister Rogers if we suggest he doesn't believe in competition. Obviously, he has had athletes on his show. And he often touts the importance of hard work and doing our best. Key here, though, is he also believes we should do our *moral* best. In other words, we shouldn't be willing to sacrifice excelling in morality just to get ahead in some other way. If competition leads to immoral action, then how does it really help? So, for example, we shouldn't be willing to do harm to others just to win or get ahead. Competition is good, but not if it costs us *being* good.

Of course, this is just a value judgment on my part. Some people might argue that they would rather have money and "success" than be "moral." There isn't much I can say to rebut that preference, other than reminding us that success is also . defined by us. Some people define success as money and power, but Rogers seems to define success through friendship and love. In fact, in *Life's Journeys According to Mister Rogers*, Rogers says "There are three ways to ultimate success: the first way is to be kind. The second way is to be kind. The third way is to be kind."

For my part, I assume that people want to be successful because they want to be happy. But from what I've seen, it's really hard to be happy when we have little love and are willing to screw over our friends. So perhaps Mister Rogers's way is a more effective way to find success, if by success we mean happiness.

Another note on competition and co-operation . . . These are things that both have their uses at certain points. If we're always competing, we won't achieve our best. Of course, competition can lead to cheaper goods and faster athletes. But when we are a community, a *neighborhood*, one of the best ways to "get ahead" is to work together. Even here in the US it wasn't that long ago when people seemed to feel like they had an obligation to their country and to their community (sometimes even to the world). The idea that we are all in it for ourselves is actually kind of un-American, if you think about how many times Americans have fought for each other and to make things right for the world.

One good example of selfish competition is our interaction with movie theaters. From what I can tell, most people feel like they are in competition with movie theaters. The theaters charge way too much for snacks and we try to sneak in snacks. Interestingly, it is odd that we feel comfortable breaking that rule. I mean, if I had a rule about what things people were allowed to bring into my house for a party, I would expect them to follow it! The funny thing is we all end up worse off because we sneak in snacks. Movie theaters have already been struggling because of services like Netflix. So they make most of their money from concessions. When we sneak food in instead of buying it, that means they make less money, and so ticket prices or concession prices go up. In fact, theaters are starting to go out of business. I think we would all be better off if we worked together. If we didn't sneak in food they would make more money and we could have lower prices. But, when I point that out, people argue that they wouldn't lower their prices, because they just want more money. Which is basically just a way of saying they are in competition with us! But, if we worked together, we could pay less *and* they could make more. And then the idea of a neighborhood makes sense. We are sharing a community and the things that impact the movie theater affect us too.

It's Such a Good Feeling . . . to Keep My Own Damn Money

Well what about the idea that being kind is unwise? People take advantage of kindness, after all. That seems pretty obviously true. I mean, I remember giving money to someone begging for food once, and when I drove away a few minutes later, I saw her walk into a liquor store. Don't we know people take advantage of us? Better to save our money and use it wisely. We might worry about that as a country as well. It isn't uncommon to hear people complain that we give more than the rest of the world and they just take advantage. Maybe we would be better off taking care of ourselves and letting them do the same. But part of Mister Rogers's idea of *neighborhood* is that we're members of a community, and we're all in this together.

In this case, it seems to me to be a question of who we want to be. After all, it is only unwise to be "taken advantage of" if you think you won't be or can't be taken advantage of. People like Mister Rogers are very aware that some people are not honest and are going to take advantage of kindness. Sometimes, if I help the homeless, they are not honest about their situation or what they want the money for. But that doesn't change what I view my obligation to be. I want to be the kind of person who helps. If they take advantage of that help, that's on them, isn't it? But for them to even have a chance to make the right decision, I have to give them that chance.

In other words, I am not a fool if I help others knowing that sometimes they will choose to take advantage of my help. And I don't think Mister Rogers was naive either. The odd thing about morality is that in order to do a right thing it seems that we also have to have the opportunity to do the wrong thing. So if we go into doing kindness for others without the expectation that we will get something out of it or that the other person will do a particular something, we give them a gift. The gift that we give them is the *opportunity* to do right (even if there's also an opportunity to do wrong). So, if anything, it isn't an unwise position, it is a very empowered position, and one that respects freedom. When we are kind, we are giving other people the chance to grow, and a chance to make a choice for their own growth.

It's Such a Good Feeling . . . to Get Even

So what about the final argument? What about the idea that being so forgiving is a weakness? Doesn't our anger provide us with strength? In fact, doesn't anger act as something of a warning emotion? It tells us that something is wrong and should be fixed. Shouldn't we be angry about things like slavery, rape, and murder? Anger isn't necessarily bad. In fact, sometimes it seems right to be angry, like Dr. Martin Luther King, Jr. being angry about segregation.

Here's the thing, I think we would mischaracterize Mister Rogers if we said that he didn't get angry sometimes. He even states, "There are times when explanations, no matter how reasonable, just don't seem to help." And I think we also misunderstand him if we said he didn't think that anger could also be valuable. Rather, we're missing the key idea that there's a difference between being angry and refusing to forgive. Anger is what happens when an offense is committed, forgiveness is what can happen when we reflect on that offense.

When Aristotle spoke about the virtue of mildness (the virtue in relation to anger), he didn't say that the mild person is never disturbed (especially at disturbing things), but he did say that such a person is more ready to pardon than to exact a penalty. When someone needs to "pay back" the offense in order to stop being angry, that is a sign of excessive anger that we should try to avoid.

So it seems we have at least two general cases of forgiveness. I don't want to assume that everyone agrees about the first case—when we forgive because the offense has ended and apologies have been made. We probably should ask, "What is the point of *not* forgiving in that case?" If someone hurts or offends us, and is not doing it anymore and they are sorry and yet we still choose not to forgive, what is the purpose? Generally, it is a kind of self-protection. We don't forgive them because it means that they are kept at a distance and cannot hurt us again. And I would be a crazy person if I suggested that we should let people hurt us again, right?

Well, maybe. Let's look at the second generalization since now they seem pretty similar. What about cases in which an offense persists or may happen again in the future? Don't we have the right to protect ourselves? Well, firstly, I am not going to argue that we shouldn't protect ourselves. And I don't think Mister Rogers would say that we should let people continue to hurt us either. But it is important to remember that Mister Rogers was also a Presbyterian minister, so a Biblical example might help. Let's consider the whole "Turn the Other Cheek" thing . . .

Okay, so you might already know the basics here, but just in case you don't . . . The idea goes like this: Jesus tells his followers at one point that if someone strikes them, not to strike back, but, rather, to turn the other cheek. Now, what I've learned is that this story is pretty misunderstood. On one end, we do seem to just kind of ignore it. We certainly are not a "Turn the other cheek" kind of culture. If someone hurts or offends us, we go and bomb the living daylights out of them.

But, interestingly, the other perspective is a bit mistaken, too. Jesus is not, in my understanding, saying we should just let people hit us all they want. And realizing that means needing to understand Hebrew culture a bit.

Basically, there were two kinds of ways to hit people in Hebrew culture. You could hit someone with the back of your hand or with the palm of your hand. You would backhand people who you considered lower than you, like slaves. And you would strike equals with the palm of your hand. So Jesus's lesson is really pretty brilliant. Imagine that someone backhands you, exposing one side of your face. As long as your cheek is turned in that direction, the person who struck you can continue to backhand you AND demean you. But if you turn the other cheek, then they can't backhand you. They will have to strike you as an equal, if they are going to strike you at all. It was a pretty revolutionary perspective.

The basic problem is this: If someone harms us and we harm them in return, all we are doing is more harm. Maybe it stops them; maybe it doesn't. But let's be honest about vengeance. If someone hits us or harms us, *they do it because they think it is right.* When we get even, to them things are now *uneven.* So it will just cycle. They feel the need to do it again, and when they do, we need to do it to make things "even" again. Eventually, someone probably has to die. So Mister Rogers's way seems to be a way out without saying "it is okay to hurt me."

Remember, too, that Mister Rogers believed that people are special and loved. He wouldn't ever say it is ok for someone to hurt you. He also wouldn't say it is okay for you to hurt them. Rather, he would say that we should respect them and expect them to respect us, like in the turn the other cheek example. When we turn our cheek we're not just adding more violence and disrespecting them in return. We are instead saying, "If you are going to do this, you must respect me as an equal. We are *both* people deserving of respect."

Now, I am not saying that this means that harm will not be done to us if we turn the other cheek. Some people might just go ahead and do it. But I do know this as well. Everyone dies. No one gets to live forever, whether we do good or bad. If someone harms me by choice, they have chosen to do bad. After that, it is up to me to decide how I want to live my life. Nothing I do, no matter what, can stop my death. So even if someone is trying to kill me, even if I kill them, I still die eventually. Maybe not at that moment, but some day. So really, the question is, do I die as someone who has purposefully done harm or die as someone who has chosen to forgive?

The key point here is that we are doing Mister Rogers a disservice if we act as if forgiveness is a weakness. Forgiveness is hard, especially when we know that the harm will or may be done again. We do it, though, not just because forgiveness helps make the world a kinder place, but because it is a way of showing others who *do* harm a better way to be. Again, it is an opportunity, a kind of gift. Every time we forgive someone, we give them the chance to hurt us again but we also give them the chance *not* to hurt us again. So in a sense, we hold their fate in our hands.

Should We Be Neighbors?

Really, the problem I see is that we as a society are in something of a cognitive dissonance with Mister Rogers about our core values. This isn't just about men and who they should be, it is about the values we respect. On the one hand, we do believe people should be nice, kind, and forgiving. We tell our children this all of the time, but we also want to be dominant, powerful, and safe from harm. It's hard to do both. So when people are critical of Mister Rogers because he's encouraging boys to be weak or feminine, we are really criticizing the part of our society and our own psyche that believes that it takes *more* strength to be nice, kind, forgiving people.

The thing I learned from Mister Rogers about being a man, *about being a person,* that I think *Fox and Friends* missed, is that when you teach someone that *they* matter because they are a person, you are teaching them that *all* people matter. Rogers wasn't saying, "You are special and you are the only one who matters." He was saying, "*We* matter. And *we* are deserving of love." The kids who watch him know that. Because they love him too.

He spends so much time showing kids all of the different people who are *also* special. Maybe it makes us a bit less competitive, a bit more vulnerable, and a bit less angry. But, to me at least, it is worth it if it means I can have a friend like Fred.[1]

---

[1] This one's for you, Kat.

18
Lessons from Fred Rogers's Dao

JOHN M. THOMPSON

Fred Rogers is an enigma. A children's television show host for three decades, Rogers never marketed consumer goods, did not hit anyone or brandish a firearm, nor even raise his voice in anger. Instead, he wore sweaters, played with puppets, and chatted with ordinary people.

Often parodied for his gentle persona (see, for example, *Saturday Night Live's* "Mister Robinson's Neighborhood"), Rogers was widely acclaimed, earning dozens of honorary degrees and even the Presidential Medal of Freedom. Years after his death, he remains a beloved figure, as evidenced by *Won't You Be My Neighbor?*, one of the highest grossing movie biographies of all time.

How can we understand this paradox: a huge success who violated almost all our expectations of a stereotypical man? I suggest that the *Zhuangzi* 莊子 ("Master Zhuang"), an ancient Daoist text, provides some clues. Indeed, I claim that this delightful tome helps us see how Rogers demonstrates a genuinely Daoist way for contemporary America.

Words of Warning to the (Not So) Wise

Daoism remains one of the most mysterious philosophical and religious traditions. Some Americans may have heard of Daoism from martial arts movies, Bernard Hoff's whimsical books *The Tao of Pooh* and *The Te of Piglet*,[1] or have seen the "yin-yang symbol" (☯) at some point, but likely have a limited understanding.

---

[1] Since the 1980s, the *pinyin* system of rendering Chinese into the Roman alphabet (Zhuangzi, Dao) has generally replaced the older Wade-Giles system (Chuang-tzu, Tao).

"Daoism" derives from the Chinese term Dao 道 (meaning way or path), which the *Daode jing* 道德經 ("Classic of the Way and its Power"), Daoism's best known text, says cannot be put into words. Yet if we cannot grasp Dao, we can approach it obliquely through images: water, Mother, an uncarved block of wood, a vaporous cloud, a child, a mysterious woman. Such imagery suggests that Dao is the source of all things, vague and impersonal, elusive yet ever present, seemingly weak but powerful. It is the way of Nature itself. Dao contrasts with the assertive ways of humanity. To thrive in Dao is to embrace Nature's rhythms—a mode of life known as *wuwei* 無為 ("non-acting"), an effortless "going with the flow" that transcends our petty perspective.

Dao flows in a movement, variously referred to as *fan* 反; *fu* 復; *gui* 歸, all of which we can translate as "reversal." "Reversal" constantly unsettles, yet by attending to Dao, we can discern its basic oscillation between cosmic poles of *yin* 隱 (dark, cold, female) and *yang* 陽 (light, hot, male). Perpetually moving from *yin* to *yang*, Dao upsets and undermines stasis. Dao is paradox, uniting irreconcilable yet complementary truths. Dao resists attempts at control, poking fun at our efforts to "fix" things. Dao overflows with cosmic humor, prompting us to laugh at ourselves. As the *Daode jing* says, "If they did not laugh at it, it would not be Dao."

Yet while the *Daode jing* is justifiably famous, arguably the *Zhuangzi* is even more Daoist. Attributed to a legendary figure Zhuang Zhou (~369–286 B.C.E.), the *Zhuangzi* shows us that Dao can be found in everyday life. Rather than urge us to get lost in cosmic mystery, Zhuangzi happily wanders through *this* world, drawing out attention to its rich wonders in the midst of the everyday. It's rare to read the *Zhuangzi* without cracking a smile at the basic arbitrariness of the social conventions by which we abide.

From this all-too-brief overview, fans of Rogers may already discern his basic Zhuangzian affinities: notoriously shy, he nonetheless persists despite obstacles and setbacks. Soft-spoken yet insistent, Rogers exudes gentle humor and subtle charisma. And although he is an authority figure, he is loath to tell others what they should or should not do. Of course, I do not claim that Rogers is himself Daoist (he was an ordained Presbyterian minister and never spoke of an interest in Asian spirituality). Instead, I am highlighting Rogers's Daoistic sensibility, arguing that he demonstrates the possibility of finding a way to live meaningfully without chasing wealth and fame, or dismissing other people for being different.

Fred's Dao

We can get a sense of Rogers's Dao by focusing on five inter-twined principles. My choice of five may seem arbitrary, but it is appropriately Daoist, since according to Daoist cosmology, *yin* and *yang* mysteriously combine in various configurations known as the "five phases" (*wu xing* 五行)| that together comprise our world:

Keep It Simple, Stupid!

Simplicity is a prominent theme in Daoism, but such "simplicity" is not a celebration of "meh" so much as an admonition not to bother with trifles. Generally speaking, we do not need flashy distractions from what is more substantive. Getting hooked in by click-bait headlines may offer amusement, but can lead to confusion and frustration in the end. Images such as the "uncarved block" (*pu*樸) remind us that what seems amazing is typically artificial. A showcase garden may appear to be a wondrous display of Mother Nature until we see that the "natural look" came from painting the roses red and spreading green "fertilizer" on newly laid sod. That's not Dao.

Zhuangzi regularly espouses simplicity, often focusing on the ways of ordinary people, some of whom possess extraordinary skill: a hunchback who catches cicadas with a stick pole, a ferryman who guides his boat through treacherous waters, an artist who draws free-hand, as well as others who use a compass or T square. In each case, skill emerges from focusing on the task at hand rather than showing off; simply attending to the situation can have incredible results.

The importance of the everyday shows in a conversation from the *Zhuangzi*:

> Master Dongguo asked Zhuangzi, "This thing called the Way—where does it exist?"
> Zhuangzi said, "There's no place it doesn't exist."
> "Come," said Master Dongguo, "you must be more specific!"
> "It is in the ant."
> "As low a thing as that?"
> "It is in the panic grass."
> "But that's lower still!"
> "It is in the tiles and shards."
> "How can it be so low?"
> "It is in the piss and shit!"

It's hard to get more common than urine and dung, basic—even "gross"—by-products of life, yet Zhuangzi reminds us that this is precisely where Dao always is.

Rogers is never as "earthy" as Zhuangzi in the above passage, but he shares the Daoist's ethos of simplicity. *Mister Rogers' Neighborhood* has a small cast, and never includes animation or special effects. Instead, it features Rogers singing, talking to the camera, and having simple conversations. Yet the show is far from boring. A PBS webpage devoted to Rogers notes that such apparent blandness was intentional:

> Mister Rogers talked in ways children understand, at a pace they could absorb . . . The visually-simple sets and puppets, matching the capabilities of young children, allowed children to use their own imaginations, and encouraged children to create their own playthings and to engage in imaginative play. It all worked: millions of children in three generations have responded with trust and love.

Indeed, the show's incredible influence indicates that the Dao of Rogers has proven "right."

Slow Down, You're Moving Way Too Fast

Ralph Waldo Emerson once advised, "Adopt the pace of nature: her secret is patience." While such words may seem antiquated (at least when we're stuck in traffic), they are rather Daoist. A phrase that Zhuangzi uses for a Daoistic way is *xiaoyaoyou* 逍遥游 ("free and easy wandering"), an effortless sojourning untouched by hurry. It is easy to romanticize such ideals, but Zhuangzi offers this way as an alternative to a life driven largely by artificially imposed goals.

An example of Zhuangzi's "free and easy wandering" is "Cook Ding" (Baoding 庖丁). Praised by Lord Wehui for his grace in butchering an ox, Ding replies, "What I care about is the Way (Dao)," explaining that over the years he has learned just to guide his knife through the natural spaces between the carcass's joints. He adds, "whenever I come to a complicated place, I size up the difficulties, tell myself to watch out and be careful, keep my eyes on what I'm doing, work very slowly, and move the knife with the greatest subtlety, until—flop! the whole thing comes apart like a clod of earth crumbling to the ground." By stepping back to observe, and then slowly proceeding, we join with Dao and accomplish marvelous things.

The admonition *not* to rush also informs Rogers's way. Each episode of his show unfolds at a leisurely pace—something that sets it apart from more commercialized television fare. Rogers himself regarded the fast pace of other children's programs as "bombardment." The fact that the show took place in "real time" had important implications. For instance, in a 1985 episode, Rogers plants a seed and then talks about how it takes time for plants to grow, and that learning to wait is important. He tells us that he used to think that plants would begin to grow right away. "But as I grew, very slowly, I realized that plants grow very slowly too. So little by little, I learned to wait. And waiting is such an important thing to learn to do."

Meanwhile, in the Neighborhod of Make-Believe, X the Owl's cousin, Mary Owl, announces (by means of an "orange-o-gram") that she will be coming to visit him in the neighborhood (episode 1551), but he doesn't know how or when. Like Mister Rogers, X the Owl will have to wait. Such tasks require time and careful attention. They are not glamorous but by doing them in a relaxed manner, we get a sense of life as a series of moment-by-moment events. This is Dao.

Silly Boy, Dao Is for Kids!

Another aspect of Rogers's Dao is his childlike wonder. Typically, episodes of the show feature visits to common places, like Brockett's Bakery or Negri's Music Shop, short movies on how things such as bulldozers operate, or demonstrations of how gadgets like flashlights work. Invariably Rogers exudes sheer joy in such moments, and it is impossible not to feel something similar while watching. In this we are much like Zhuangzi in the memorable scene from his eponymous book where he stops on the bridge over the Hao River to enjoy the happy frolicking of the minnows in the water—much like Rogers's pleasure in feeding *his* fish.

Rogers's sense of wonder has its roots in the fact that his audience was primarily children. This point underscores the connection between Dao and children. The *Daode jing*, attributed to the mysterious Laozi 老子 (a title we can translate as "Old Child") notes that to live according to Dao we must be "like a baby," soft and weak by the world's standards, but dwelling harmoniously with life.

Philosopher Kuang-Ming Wu observes that the closest we normally staid adults come to Dao is by being with children, going on to relate a dream in which a child forces him out of his routine, asking questions and making him explain what he was doing. Wu says of this dream-child, "He seemed to be at home in his ongoing quest; there was nothing uneasy about him.

He was confident, not in himself, but in his questioning, and in my arms in which he questioned. He was at home in me whom he questioned; he was at home without being at home anywhere." Perhaps, Wu suggests, in tarrying with children, we might "dwell in them forever." Perhaps Rogers's ability to come to Dao lies in his ability to be like a child as well.

A key to Rogers's child-like persona is his playfulness. Rogers seems delighted in every episode of his show, but especially when taking us, via Trolley, into Make-Believe. A wondrous counterpart to Rogers's real-life neighborhood, the Neighborhood of Make-Believe is a playground born of his imagination. Inhabited by an array of puppets, including King Friday XIII, Daniel Tiger, and X the Owl, it is the perfect setting for these characters (and viewers) to play out various scenarios. Such literal "child's play" may seem silly, but based on his years of clinical practice, British psychoanalyst D.W. Winnicott (1896–1971) concluded that play is a way, that we never truly outgrow, of actively adjusting to reality. Rogers is an adult perpetually at play, inviting us to play along. Who could resist joining in?

Zhuangzi regularly plays with thoughts and words in ways quite unlike a typical thinker. In one passage he writes:

> I'm going to try speaking some reckless words and I want you to listen to them recklessly. How will that be? The sage leans on the sun and moon, tucks the universe under his arm, merges himself with things, leaves the confusion and muddle as it is, and looks on slaves as exalted. Ordinary men strain and struggle; the sage is stupid and blockish.

We sense that Zhuangzi is playing *us* in such passages but he would likely say it is Dao doing the playing, and that we are all Dao's playthings. Who among us can resist playing along?

Expect the Unexpected

The 1980s television series *Tales of the Unexpected* always began each episode with a rather Daoist line: "A wise man trusts only in lies, believes only in the absurd, and learns to expect the unexpected." Dao does not conform to our likes and desires; the ways of Heaven and Earth are often inexplicable from a human standpoint. Dao always gives us a surprise, typically when we least expect it.

We find many unexpected twists in the *Zhuangzi*, ranging from a miniscule fish transforming into a enormous bird that fills the heavens, to gnarled trees whose incredible longevity stems from being "useless." One striking example of the unexpected is a man nicknamed "Crippled Shu" (Zhili shu 支離疏)) for his deformities ("chin stuck down to his navel, shoulders above his head, pigtail pointing at the sky"). We would expect Shu to lead a horrible life, but Zhuangzi tells us that Shu makes do by performing simple chores (sewing and washing clothes, winnowing grain), is exempt from military service, and even gets free government food during times of famine. It seems "Crippled Shu" is far more fortunate than his "normal" contemporaries.

Similarly, Rogers often does the unexpected. Even in this day of YouTube stars and international video gaming competitions, making a career out of playing with puppets in a make believe world is *not* how most of us would choose to earn our daily ramen. Yet Rogers did it for years. And, unlike most celebrities, Rogers did *not* draw attention to himself; Rogers was the "anti-celebrity." Hosting a long-running television show while eschewing the limelight is truly unexpected in American society.

But this is only one dimension of Rogers's embrace of the unexpected. More importantly is the way that he counters expectations of the stereotypical American man. Rogers exudes an air of caring rather than confrontation, earning him much mockery in some circles as "unmanly." Rogers's way of care, though, did not mean that he shied away from life's harsher realities. Instead, it enabled him to broach disturbing aspects of life that most TV shows avoid. Perhaps the best examples are his public service announcements released after the terrorist attacks of September 11th 2001, where he recalls something he learned from his mother: "Look for the helpers. You will always find people who are helping." The contrast between such sentiments and the angry, self-pitying cries for vengeance that dominated the airwaves at the time is both revealing and sobering. The fact that Rogers's quote asking us to "look for helpers" still circulates on social media in the wake of horrific events is a subtle testament to his insight.

Rogers's "unmanly" way of care helps him challenge common prejudices and attitudes in US society, another rarity, unexpected for a television show. Examples include Rogers bathing his feet in a kiddie pool alongside his African-American friend Officer François Clemmons, or singing "It's You I Like" with Jeff Erlanger, a quadriplegic boy. Such things are small but their effects—the effects of Rogers's Dao—are profound.

Authenticity

In the age of the "curated self," it is increasingly difficult to be ourselves rather than what we think others want us to be. The Who's song "The Real Me" ("Can you see the real me? Can you? Can you?") is even more relevant today than when it was first recorded forty-five years ago. Perhaps this has become a global phenomenon: several years ago in Turkey, I was amused to see shops advertising "genuine fake watches." Are we all "genuine fakes" these days?

The quest for being genuine in the face of pressure to conform has concerned philosophers since the time of Socrates. Twentieth-century thinkers like Martin Heidegger and Jean-Paul Sartre extol authenticity as the key task of human life, contrasting it to our habit of mindlessly adopting routines without taking responsibility for our choices. Even so, "authenticity" has almost become a meaningless "buzzword" now in everyday conversation, or even an excuse for being deliberately offensive.

Zhuangzi also speaks a great deal about authenticity, generally through his depictions of unique, memorable figures. One of them is Rongzi 榮子, a man who rejected conventional standards. As Zhuangzi puts it, the world could praise Rongzi yet it wouldn't cause him to strive for honor, while the world's condemnation wouldn't have brought him to despair. Zhuangzi, though, reserves his highest praise for the *zhenren* 真栄 ("true/ genuine person"), a term for those rare people who embrace Dao's ever-changing movements. A *zhenren* personifies the unfeigned simplicity and spontaneity (*ziran* 自然, "self-so") of Dao. Zhuangzi explains:

> This was the True Man of old: his bearing was lofty and did not crumble; he appeared to lack but accepted nothing; he was dignified in his correctness but not insistent; he was vast in his emptiness but not ostentatious. Mild and cheerful, he seemed to be happy; reluctant, he could not help doing certain things; annoyed, he let it show in his face; relaxed, he rested in his virtue. Tolerant, he seemed to be part of the world; towering alone, he could be checked by nothing; withdrawn, he seemed to prefer to cut himself off; bemused, he forgot what he was going to say.

Later Daoists esteem the *zhenren* more than the *xian* ("immortal") while Chinese Buddhists use *zhenren* as the translation for *arhat* ("worthy"), an enlightened follower of Buddha.

Was Fred Rogers authentic? Perhaps not in the same sense as a *zhenren* but he was authentic in a more relatable sense: he was always himself. Rogers makes a point to behave naturally rather than acting as a character. He once explained, "One of the greatest gifts you can give anybody is the gift of your honest self. I also believe that kids can spot a phony a mile away." Rogers *is* a television performer, but he never fakes it. He is always Mister Rogers, even when he takes us to the Neighborhood of Make-Believe.

Rogers displayed his authenticity in other ways as well. Rogers testified before the US Senate in response to proposed cuts to PBS's budget, arguing that programs such as his that fostered children's intellectual and emotional development fulfilled an essential need in American society. Rogers also was never a corporate sell-out. In the 1980s when Burger King launched an ad campaign featuring "Mr. Rodney" (a parody of Rogers) as its spokesman, Rogers felt that this would confuse children and so held a press conference where he stated that he did not endorse the company's products or their use of his likeness. Suitably chastened, Burger King apologized and discontinued the campaign.

The Way Goes On

I am not arguing that Fred Rogers was an American Daoist. Instead, I am asking us to consider what makes this man so impressive. My study of the *Zhuangzi* prompts me to suggest that we view Rogers as an example of Dao expressed in the life of a man who happily wandered through the late twentieth century and into the hearts and minds of millions of Americans.

Everyone has their favorite story about Rogers. Mine concerns the Lifetime Achievement Award he received at the 1997 Daytime Emmys. After he accepted, Rogers told the audience, "All of us have special ones who have loved us into being. Would you just take, along with me, ten seconds to think of the people who have helped you become who you are. Ten seconds of silence." Looking at his watch, he added, "I'll watch the time." There was laughter at first, but as the silence continued there were shy smiles and nods, and even tears. Not long ago I shamelessly related this story to a group of students at our department reception the day before they were to get their diplomas, with similar results. I leave it to you, dear reader, to draw the moral.

Thanks, Fred, for showing us a way.

19

If Everyone's Special, . . . Is Anyone Special?

GRACE WEHNIAINEN

"You are my friend, you are special," Mister Rogers would sing.

It was a warm affirmation, a reminder to Rogers's young audience that they were important. But the friendly neighbor's critics—few, though they may be—were less convinced. Someone on *Fox & Friends* went so far as to say that Rogers was an "evil, evil man," who "ruined a generation of kids" by telling them they were special without having to work hard. Others have called him a liar, blaming him for everything from a culture of coddling to futile job searches—because if you can't land your dream job, you must not actually be *that* special, right?

Not so fast. Rogers was a smart man—and a good one, too. He never shied away from confronting heavy topics, like death, divorce, war or 9/11. He even deconstructed the myth of Santa Claus for kids who might be scared of a man-in-red who sees them when they're sleeping . . . which, to be fair, is kind of creepy when you think about it (episode 1261). Instead of sugarcoating those serious realities, Rogers handled them in tactful ways that let him connect with his young audience, not condescend to them.

He knew how the world worked, and cared about ensuring that children did, too—so did he really throw that all out the window and choose to mislead them anyway? To make them believe that they should sit back, relax and never lift a finger or aspire toward success?

A Neighborhood for All

While Rogers's critics might have been cynical about his intentions, they got one thing right: he *did* tell kids they were special. A lot. And he meant it every time. As an ordained minister, Rogers's personal philosophy was no doubt shaped, in large part, by Biblical influences—specifically, what the book says about the value of life. 1 Corinthians talks about spiritual gifts, and the way they are bestowed upon each person individually, with no one person's being better (or worse) than another's. "There are different kinds of gifts, but the same Spirit distributes them . . . To each one is given the manifestation of the Spirit for the common good" (1 Corinthians 12: 4–7). For a theology student like Rogers, the message couldn't be clearer: every life has God-given worth, and is important to the world regardless of any accolades one may (or may not) earn along the way.

For Rogers, your specialness is a self-fulfilling prophecy. You *are* special because you were made to be you! And that's a thing that no one else can be. This philosophy isn't totally incompatible with modern definitions of the word "special," though it might be slightly less common. The first definition of the word in Oxford Living Dictionaries, for example, is "better, greater, or otherwise different from what is usual." This definition aligns well with the viewpoint of *Fox and Friends* and other critics— that someone needs to be superior to the rest in order to earn that distinction. The *second* definition, though, matches Rogers's philosophy—and that of his Biblical understanding— a little more closely, defining "special" as "belonging specifically to a particular person or place." That's it.

Much of the Bible revolves around that central philosophical tenet, that life itself is a God-given gift and is, by virtue of that, special. In fact, the idea is laid bare as early as Genesis 1:27: "God created mankind in his own image." If we believe that God is perfect (as a Christian minister like Rogers certainly would), we should believe, too, that anyone created in the image of perfection would be special as a result. Now the Bible talks a lot about deeds, too—the *things* we do, the good and the bad—but not in relation to our being special. We can't be more special, in God's eyes, by getting a promotion at work or even finding the cure to cancer. Those are simply the external manifestations of our internal specialness, the gifts that are given to us at birth. As Rogers sings: "It's you I like / . . . the way down deep inside you / . . . not your toys / they're just beside you."

The Ins and Outs of Being Special

Speaking of external manifestations . . .

It's completely possible that both Rogers and the neighborhood naysayers were right—in their own *special* ways. You can believe that people should work hard and aspire to success while still knowing that they have value without doing any of that. Rogers certainly knew this, and encouraged children to learn new skills. His own success in television is a clear model of hard work. He talked to them about his own interest in learning Greek (episode 1651), and even discussed discipline as a crucial part of learning to play the piano (episode 1491).

The disconnect happens when modern critics apply their own strict interpretation of the word to Rogers's more neighborly take on things. Or, more specifically, when they conflate intrinsic and extrinsic value.

Intrinsic value plays a big role in philosophy, especially when we're talking about morality—good and bad, right and wrong. Things that have intrinsic value are good by themselves, in their simplest form, with no need for qualification, ("x" is good as long as it helps me do "y" . . .) or distinction (only some types of "x" are truly valuable). Sound familiar? Rogers constantly told his viewers that they were special just for being themselves, without qualification. He knew that they had intrinsic value, because they were made with intrinsically good gifts. Extrinsic or instrumental value, on the other hand, refers to the things we can do or make or enjoy along the way. They are still good things! But they don't come from within—rather than being good for their own sake, they are good for the ways they can serve us and our surroundings.

For example, maybe you have a pet dog you love, and see her as intrinsically valuable (an idea with which American philosopher Tom Regan would agree). She has intrinsic value because she is a living animal with an identity—even if all she does is nap! If she makes you laugh, keeps pests away or serves as a seeing-eye dog, those are examples of her instrumental value at work.

Depending on the philosopher you ask, you'll hear varying opinions on what is intrinsically valuable. Hedonism is one school of thought we can look to. It says that pleasure is the one and only intrinsic good. Essentially, it's the meaning of life. Over the years, however, we have seen slightly more nuanced answers to the age-old question, *what's good?* Twentieth-century philosopher William Frankena, for example, agreed that pleasure is intrinsically good—but added many more things, too, offering a comprehensive list that included "life, consciousness . . . happiness . . . mutual affection, love, friendship, cooperation . . . self-expression . . ." These are the things, Rogers reminded us, that we *all* have, regardless of how well we could run a race, ride a bike, sing a song, or do anything else that

might receive recognition from our peers. It's not bad to excel—
remember, Rogers encouraged us to explore our interests!—but
we don't *need* that recognition in order to have value. The lack
of that recognition doesn't nullify our worth.

Rogers expressed this best during his 2002 Dartmouth
College commencement address, where he told graduates, "you
don't ever have to do anything sensational for people to love
you. When I say it's you I like, I'm talking about that part of you
that knows that life is far more than anything you can ever see,
or hear, or touch. That deep part of you, that allows you to stand
for those things without which humankind cannot survive."

Being Your Own Best Neighbor

Rogers told kids they were special every day because he knew
they deserved to hear it every day. But many kids don't hear it
as often as they should, such as, perhaps, children (of parents
like the *Fox & Friends* hosts) who are required to perform in a
certain way in order to have their value affirmed. Mister
Rogers stood in support of these children with his gentle, but
powerful, affirmations.

As well as working the message into regular songs, Mister
Rogers even devoted an entire week of episodes to the idea that
"everybody's special." While looking at his own reflection in the
bathroom mirror, he emphasized that each of us is one-of-a-
kind, explaining what it means to be unique (episode 1686). His
warm, reassuring tone reminded countless young viewers of
their worth. But let's face it—sometimes, we're our own worst
critics. Without regular visits to the Neighborhood of Make-
Believe, how do we embrace our unique character? How do we
come to recognize the special something in ourselves that
Rogers saw all along?

We can start with self-reflection . . . literally. We shouldn't
take it as coincidence that Rogers—as thoughtful as he was—
chose to talk about being unique while standing in front of a
mirror, after all! Even before most viewers were old enough to
know what a "metaphor" was, they could at least understand
that the journey of realizing their own self-worth had to start
by looking within. Now, when you look at yourself in a mirror
you might find things you don't necessarily *love*. But it's pretty
safe to say that Rogers would tell you to look anyway. The physical act of reflection, of examining your teeth, freckles, eyes and
all, can lead you to reflect on the bigger things in life. The
things you care about. The things you're good at—and the
things you want to work on. Perfection, after all, was never

Rogers's goal. He just wanted his audience to take a good look in the mirror, and to realize how special they were.

While Rogers may have come from a theological background, he had a soft spot for antiquity, too. He talked about learning Greek on TV and even referenced sixth-century philosopher Boethius in his Dartmouth commencement address. So maybe it's no surprise that he's such a champion of self-reflection. He learned it from the big guys! The ancient Greek superstars of philosophy urged us to "know thyself," and Socrates said that "the unexamined life is not worth living." By looking at yourself—in a mirror, or even in a pond like Narcissus—you can learn a lot about who you are and what makes you unique.

As you embark on that reflective journey, though, be careful not to shy away from the less-than-perfect stuff. American psychologist Albert Ellis, whose rational emotive behavior therapy (REBT) merged psychotherapy with philosophy, argued that we should strive for self-acceptance over self-esteem. The former, he said, focuses on acknowledging your own worth despite your deeds, good or bad—the latter, though, depends on what you can do and how you earn approval from your peers. It's another case of that good-old intrinsic-extrinsic dilemma, and we can guess pretty confidently what Rogers would have to say about it: *Love yourself first and foremost! You're special without any need for outside praise—that's good, too, but you already have worth just by being you.*

Or, you know, something along those lines.

In *Nicomachean Ethics,* Aristotle made a similar distinction between real self-love and vulgar, or disingenuous, self-love. When you really love yourself, you don't care about amassing wealth or power over others, or even excelling at everything you set out to do. (We're only human, after all.) You just want to better yourself and realize your *own* personal potential, which will in turn help you love your friends, too. This sort of self-love is characterized by a desire to be your best self... with no mention of hating your current self in the process.

What can all this self-love and acceptance do for you? According to Francis De Sales, it might just set you free. The saint, who studied philosophy and humanities before being ordained in 1593, wrote that we should "not be disturbed by our imperfections, because our perfection consists in fighting them. And we cannot fight them unless we see them, nor can we overcome them if we do not come across them." We can almost see Rogers, staring back at the mirror and saying the same thing. Well, maybe he wouldn't say "fight." But the man was a champion for showing kids how special they are, and helping them realize that nothing could take away from that specialness. Naturally, only by deeply knowing ourselves can we realize what makes us truly one-of-a-kind.

Should We Spend to Be Special?

So basically, Rogers wanted us to know how loved we are, as-is. We don't need to do a thing to make ourselves special. It's pretty much a done deal. As adults, we usually take that to mean that we are special without awards or accolades, career breakthroughs or a fashionable home—but while these are all perfectly apt "conditions" we can do without, let's not forget about age along the way! Rogers's target audience was children, after all, and he wanted them to know that they are valid, legitimate people just as they are—even while they're in the single digits.

The only problem? Kids can't spend money, and Rogers's you-are-special (just-for-being-you) mantra goes against a capitalist culture that asks its members what they can do, make, or spend to earn any sort of distinction. Rogers condemned the practice in the 1967 documentary *Creative Person: Fred Rogers*:

> I don't think that anybody can grow unless he really is accepted exactly as he is. 'Cause if somebody's always saying to a child, "You're going to grow up and you're going to be fine—" There's so much of that in this country anyway, that a child is appreciated for what he will be, not for what he is. He will be a great consumer someday. And so, the quicker we can get them to grow up, and the quicker we can get them out of the nest so that they will go out and buy—you know, set up their own home at twelve, maybe—then the better.

Rogers knew that a person had worth *before* buying that house, landing a job, or signing up for her first credit card. Maybe it's no surprise, then, that some of his biggest critics came from traditionally conservative outlets, such as *The Wall Street Journal* or Fox News. Rogers hailed from PBS, public television that didn't require viewers to pay a cent to enjoy. He wasn't exactly a champion of consumerist philosophy. In fact, the mere act of watching Rogers on TV was a self-fulfilling confirmation of your specialness—for no money and just a bit of your time, you were able to learn, laugh and receive one-on-one affirmations from a person who seemed to speak directly to you and what you were feeling.

Rogers's critics had it wrong (fortunately, there aren't *too* many of them to call out here). He didn't want us to be stagnant, to ignore the pursuit of new skills and passions, or to even overlook the places where we had room for improvement. Rogers loved to learn new things! He simply knew that recognizing our self-worth was essential to a strong foundation, one that could weather whatever the world might throw its way. So even if it's been a while since your last trip to the Neighborhood of Make-Believe, revisit the man-in-the-sweater and rediscover what he meant when he said, "you are special." It's tough to find a more important message—whether you're eight, eighty-eight, or somewhere in the big, mixed-up middle.

V

There Are Many Ways to Solve a Problem

20
What Would Mister Rogers Say?

JENNIFER SHAW FISCHER AND BOB FISCHER

Julie Reihs/KUT

It's easy to understand Fred's broad appeal. He was first and foremost a peacemaker, largely staying out of partisan politics. People on both sides of the aisle grew up with him in their living rooms, where he spoke to them directly and deliberately through his program. Throughout the thirty-plus seasons of the *Neighborhood*, he assured us all that he likes us just the way we are; that there is something we can do with the mad that we feel; that there are many ways to say, "I love you."

It's also easy to minimize him. Some have argued that Fred should be left in the playroom, that he has little to say about

177

the crises that wrack our world. Ian Bogost's article in *The Atlantic*, "The Fetishization of Mr. Rogers's 'Look for the Helpers'," (2018) argues that adults should set aside some of Fred's platitudes. Fred once said:

> When I was a boy and I would see scary things in the news, my mother would say to me, "Look for the helpers. You will always find people who are helping."
> <www.fredrogers.org/parents/special-challenges/tragic-events.php>

After the most recent mass shooting or wildfire, you'll find this line being shared on social media. Bogost insists that Mister Rogers was ultimately addressing a young audience; insofar as he was speaking to adults, it was only to advise them as care-givers about addressing painful topics in developmentally appropriate ways. When adults take comfort from it, Bogost argues, the quote creates inaction and apathy. We're supposed to be the helpers—not the ones looking for the helpers—when society is falling apart.

Fair enough: people can misuse Fred's words. But this just shows that we should be discerning, not that Fred has nothing to say to adults as adults. After all, he often spoke to the older set directly:

> The values we care about the deepest, and the movements within society that support those values, command our love. When those things that we care about so deeply become endangered, we become enraged. And what a healthy thing that is! Without it, we would never stand up and speak out for what we believe. (*The World According to Mister Rogers*, p. 35)

However, it seems to us that his advice wasn't—and isn't—just about how to be better individuals. Fred's wisdom applies to national and global problems too. He understood that it's impor-tant to "make goodness attractive" (*Life's Journeys*, p. 136). If we take the time to understand what this means, we'll see how valu-able Fred is—both within and beyond the Neighborhood.

Family Separation

Let's begin in an unlikely spot: the 2018 crisis at the US/Mexico border, where parents and children from immigrating families were being divided. Under Bush and Obama, family separation wasn't a common practice. Families were held in "administra-tive" versus criminal detention, and the focus was on quick deportation. In April 2018, though, Trump's then Attorney General, Jeff Sessions, announced plans to enforce a zero-tolerance policy. This ensured criminal prosecution for all who enter the country illegally. Criminal prosecution means time spent in a federal jail, and people aren't allowed to be with their children there. Hence, family separation.

The stories that emerged were bleak. A son taken from his sleeping mother in the middle of the night. Nursing babies forcibly pulled from their parent's arms. Border Patrol agents telling parents that their children were just going to get a shower, but the kids never returned. Thousands are thought to have been affected, but Homeland Security didn't have an official record of the numbers. Children were transported to various locations for care, but there was no database that specified where everyone was. It became increasingly obvious that there were serious hurdles to reuniting families after their legal issues were resolved.

Many Americans felt moved to advocate for the end of this practice. Rallies were held around the country. One of us—Jennifer—went to a Keep Families Together Rally in Austin. The sign she carried asked the simple question: "What would Mister Rogers say?" To our surprise, the sign struck a chord: over the next several weeks we saw a photo of it popping up on news outlets across the nation. We were glad to see the question out there, but Jennifer still had her qualms: it's a risky thing to suggest that you know what a dead man would say, and more risky still when it's about a politically charged issue. At the same time, the attention was a reminder that Fred's television neighbors, now grown, were still willing to listen.

A Sudden Surgery

Why think we know what Mister Rogers would say? The answer has two parts. The first is related to his biography. One of Fred's most traumatizing life events occurred when his two-year-old son, John, was taken abruptly from him to go into surgery. It was supposed to be a simple outpatient procedure, so the Rogerses didn't know to—or how to—prepare their child. John had been very upset while getting his finger pricked, and he was then being soothed in his father's arms. To Fred's surprise, John was grabbed and taken abruptly, with no explanation. The staff appeared to think this scene was humorous. John screamed for forty-five minutes before being sedated for surgery.

That day had lingering effects on John Rogers and his parents. Psychiatrists working with John attributed that event to

years of fear and accident-prone behavior. He later re-enacted
the surgery for a child psychiatrist at his nursery school. And
Fred had a hard time forgiving himself for his absence in what
was the most frightening time in his son's life. He later created
materials about how to tend to the fears of children in hospitals
<www,neighborhoodarchive.com/publications/children/going_
to_hospital/index.html> and he composed "I like to Be Told" in
1968, which begins like this:

> I like to be told
> When you're going away,
> When you're going to come back,
> And how long you'll stay,
> How long you will stay,
> I like to be told.

Joanne Rogers, Fred's wife, was asked during an interview
what she believed her husband would say to a divided America.
She said: "It would be about the children—the immigrants who
are having their children taken. The children themselves"
<www,youtube.com/watch?v=UKJaOItfRh>. Fred understood
that early trauma has lifelong ramifications. If he was furious
and deeply troubled about his experience, which pales to the
accounts of refugees, it seems eminently plausible that Joanne
is correct: he would have viewed the separation policy as
unnecessary and callous, a form of torture. Fred's repeated plea
to adults in his speeches was:

> Please, think of the children first. If you ever have anything to do with
> their entertainment, their food, their toys, their custody, their day care,
> their health, their education—please listen to the children, learn about
> them, learn from them. Think of the children first. (*The World
> According to Mister Rogers*, p. 168)

Fred the Philosopher

But there is a second, more philosophical reason to think that
this would have been Fred's view, and it's the one that brings
us back to the idea of making goodness attractive. After all, it
isn't exactly shocking that Fred would have been opposed to
separating families at the border. That's why Jennifer's sign
worked: it's obvious what he would say. However, if we reach
that conclusion only because of his work with children, or
because of features of his personal life, then we miss something
crucial about Fred the thinker.

What does it mean to make goodness attractive? To answer this question, we should start by thinking about the gap between our stated and actual values. Lots of us say that it's important to be patient and kind. We think that it's good to be sincere and transparent. We agree that it's important to slow down enough to hear the person who's talking to you, that a person deserves your undivided attention. But when we actually see these virtues in action, our cynicism comes out. The kind person is a pushover. The sincere person is naive. The one who slows down is the one who gets less done.

Fred spent most of his life fighting this kind of cynicism. He appreciated that being a good person isn't just about doing the right thing. It's also about doing the right thing in a way that reveals what's beautiful about acting well. And that's what Fred strived for throughout his life and work. He tried to model a way of being that made goodness attractive—that made people want to have the virtues that he so clearly had.

It was for him, as it is for us, a delicate task. To do it well, you can't just be patient or thoughtful or caring or concerned for justice. You have to be all those things, and you have to balance them in a way that helps people see how these values—which sometimes pull in completely opposite directions—can be integrated and balanced in a way that's lovely.

When we turn our attention to the massive problems that politicians face, such as school shootings, inadequate healthcare, the threat of terrorism, climate change, talking about what's lovely can seem a bit simplistic. And it's true that when we take in the complexities that are associated with each of these issues, it seems plausible that there won't be many beautiful solutions. They will all involve trade-offs that we don't like.

But there are two ways in which Fred's idea is still essential. Most obviously, it tells us what to look for: the goal is to find elegant solutions. Solutions are elegant when they balance our values—and the values of those with whom we disagree—in a way that we all find satisfying. These may be few and far between, but they still serve as an ideal.

Additionally, and crucially, Fred's idea serves as a kind of check on political proposals. At the very least, they shouldn't be ugly. They shouldn't balance our values in grotesque ways, in ways that repulse us when we contemplate them. This brings us back to the crisis at the border.

Admittedly, it's a difficult situation. Very few of us want genuinely open borders, with no restrictions at all on immigration. And if we accept anyone who claims asylum, then everyone will claim it, and we'll have no restrictions at all. So the question isn't whether to have a border or vet asylum-seekers. Instead, the debate is about what counts as humane immigration policy. Moreover, we should recognize that there are legitimate humanitarian concerns created by permissive approaches. If people know that they are more likely to be released into the country if they have children with them, then they may well be more likely to take the risk of bringing their children on an extraordinarily dangerous overland trek—one that may be at least as perilous as whatever they face at home. Furthermore, border agents can have legitimate concerns about people gaming the system: if people know that they are more likely to be released into the country if they have children with them, then there is some risk—however slight—that people will kidnap children in hopes of using them to bypass border security.

Nevertheless, if a policy encourages border agents to lie to parents, telling them that their young children are simply going to the showers to get clean when, in fact, they are going to a separate detention center, we should recoil. If our policies lead us there, then we've chosen the wrong policies; they are too ugly to be the right way to balance all that matters in this context. So there's a corollary to make goodness attractive: don't make your goodness ugly. That is, in the pursuit of things are genuinely good, don't cast your other values aside, lest you end up doing things that are hideous.

Beyond the Neighborhood

All this might seem a bit removed from the quiet streets of the Neighborhood. If so, that's because we've forgotten the scope of Fred's work. He had episodes on warfare, race relations, the environment, and death. In one particularly memorable series of episodes, King Friday comes to believe that his neighbors in Southwood are making bombs, and so he orders his citizens to launch into bomb construction themselves. Tensions escalate and a cold war ensues. Violence is ultimately avoided, but only because spies go to Southwood to see what's really happening. They learn that Southwood is building a bridge, not preparing for an attack. Though King Friday bears a lot of responsibility for the crisis, it's striking that he recognizes the role that his advisors played. He condemns his generals as not being "Generals of peace."

Here too, Fred is trying to suggest a way of making goodness attractive. We live in a world where violence sometimes requires a violent response. But surely not always. So while we can't dismantle the military, we also can't have trigger-happy leaders. In such circumstances, what should we be striving for? Fred's answer is: *Generals of peace.* We should want the military itself to be led by people who value and strive for peace, viewing the use of their own training as a last resort. There is something beautiful about that solution: it doesn't deny the occasional necessity of harm, but it's grounded in the hope that others are never injured.

Similarly, we can see Fred trying to make goodness attractive when we think about his way of responding to the dark aspects of the food system. Fred's vegetarianism wasn't pushy, nor was it particularly principled. He never went vegan, even though all the philosophical arguments for vegetarianism—based on principles like, "Don't cause unnecessary suffering"—will rapidly take you there. Fred wasn't naive: he stopped eating meat because he understood the story behind it, and he sometimes explained his choice by saying that he didn't want to eat anything with a mother. Essentially, though, he stayed vegetarian because he found it so easy. He just didn't miss meat, and he always felt healthier without it.

But "wasn't pushy" is not the same as "didn't try to persuade." He was, for instance, an early investor in *Vegetarian Times*, a magazine devoted to promoting a plant-based diet. And, of course, the Neighborhood never showed people eating meat, in part because he knew eating animals was unsettling to children, but Fred largely wanted to help people imagine the possibility that you could flourish without it.

There is something beautiful about this kind of advocacy; it's perfectly sensitive to the realities of our situation. There are many reasons to condemn intensive animal agriculture: poor animal welfare, greenhouse gas emissions, excessive water use, the creation of antibiotic-resistant bugs. Something has to change. And yet very few consumers are willing to go vegetarian, much less vegan. In such circumstances, making goodness attractive does not look like the set of moral arguments for dietary change, nor does it look like protest in the streets. Instead, it looks like helping people think about what they could eat other than chicken breast. It looks like cultivating our imaginations regarding food.

Fred didn't have the answer to every problem, nor did he pretend to. And we aren't claiming anything so bold on his behalf. We do think, however, the Fred understood something profoundly important about what it means to act well. Whenever we do something, we can point to some reason that favors what we chose. No one says, "I was really just trying to do something terrible."

So, what's the difference between having a reason and actually being virtuous? The answer, we think, is the one Fred suggested: you need to make goodness attractive. Or at the very least, don't make it ugly.

21
Mister Rogers's Lesson for Democracy

MATTHEW USSIA

One of the most striking moments in the wonderful 2018 documentary *Won't You Be My Neighbor?* happens early in the movie when Jun-Lei Li, former director of the Fred Rogers Center, describes the neighborhood from *Mister Rogers' Neighborhood* as a space of conflict.

It's striking because it shatters some personal and popular warm and fuzzy memories of the man in the cardigan. Fred Rogers's gentle nature doesn't seem to lend itself well to conflict. My memories of the show are dominated by his warm voice, the soft tinkling of piano keys, and a land of make-believe where everything works out in the end. Popular recollections of Fred Rogers tend to focus on his general message of kindness and friendship.

Hopefully, more devoted fans of the show will forgive me for my incomplete recollections. After all, Mister Rogers begins the show by coming home, where we are presumably safe, and why would anyone invent a land of make-believe full of conflict when fantasy worlds better lend themselves to visions of hitting the World Seies winning home run? However, as with many things Fred Rogers accomplished as a public figure, he managed to teach in ways his students didn't realize just how much we were all being taught. While some may think *Mister Rogers' Neighborhood* offers only simple lessons on friendship and co-operation, this idea misses something vital to what it means to live in a democracy. This lesson speaks to us in newer and ever more pertinent ways almost two decades after the last episode of the show.

A (Sort of) Beautiful Day in the Neighborhood

My first mistake was thinking the show featured a land of make-believe. It's called "The *Neighborhood* of Make-Believe" and the difference between a fantasy land and a neighborhood makes all the difference. Within landscapes of fantasy the barriers to our success and happiness melt away. Maybe we win the lottery without even buying a ticket, or hit the World Series winning home run. Fantasy has the unique quality to overcome barriers of ability, wealth, time, and even death.

The impulse to "air guitar" our way into our favorite band is not how Fred Rogers used imagination on the show. While he would be the first to tell you, it's fun to pretend, and his background in early-childhood education informed his understanding of the importance of play in a healthy childhood, his Neighborhood of Make-Believe contains a much bigger idea about what it means to live with others. If we think about the citizens of The Neighborhood of Make-Believe this comes into greater focus. There is the pedantic and autocratic King Friday XIII with his stern voice and pompous vocabulary. Then there's Friday's (and sometimes everyone's) arch nemesis the sassy Lady Elaine Fairchilde, the perpetually frightened Henrietta Pussycat, the friendly and inquisitive X the Owl, the infinitely relatable Daniel Striped Tiger, and so many others who most likely would not be friends by choice, yet they manage to live together in spite of their many differences. If you don't believe me, try imagining these characters going out to lunch together. How would they ever manage to pick a restaurant? King Friday would declare they were going to check out the new pizza parlor downtown. Lady Elaine would oppose him on principle. Henrietta would worry about finding parking "meow" once she got there "meow-meow." It would be a mess. However, there would eventually be a building of consensus. Here lies the lesson for people living in a democracy.

Both the documentary *Won't You Be My Neighbor?* and Maxwell King's biography *The Good Neighbor: The Life and Work of Fred Rogers* at length describe how Rogers would use puppets to say what is uncomfortable to say. *The Good Neighbor* features an interview with a child psychologist from Harvard Medical School named Susan Linn who was involved with the show. She explains:

> In Fred's hands, with love and gentleness, the puppets draw forth the
> underside of childhood. By 'underside,' I don't mean the macabre,

warped, or seamy; they tap into the vein of fear, anger, and awkward-ness, and unadulterated self-centeredness that lies beneath the sunny surface of childhood.

Puppets allowed Rogers to explore the unspeakable yet inher-ently human that lies within all of us. In *Won't You Be My Neighbor?*, his sons recall the use of the King Friday voice at the Rogers family dinner table whenever Fred was upset, and *The Good Neighbor* talks about a call a producer received from Daniel Striped Tiger to alleviate her worries about whether she could successfully contribute to the show. Rogers never broke character. In Fred Rogers's own words:

> We deal with the stuff that dreams are made of. And then in the Neighborhood of Make-Believe, we deal with it as if it were a dream. And then when it comes back to me (at the end), we deal with a sim-ple interpretation of the dream . . . Anything can happen in make-believe, and we can talk about anything in reality.

This approach was centered around Rogers's background in early childhood psychology, but it also reveals an important problem in the philosophy of language and communication: how do we speak what is both very real and totally uncomfort-able? What do we do when this information greatly impacts ours or someone else's well-being?

This might be a stranger walking down the street with a piece of tissue-paper stuck to the bottom of their shoe, it might be one of my students hesitant to raise their hand in response to a question because they fear being wrong in front of the whole class, or it could even be a family trauma, which if men-tioned at the dinner table, could turn a relatively pleasant Thanksgiving Day meal into an explosive argument.

Have you ever had to break the news to someone that a loved one has died? There is an emotional and deeply human compo-nent to communication that exists beyond language, and the experience of the emotions I'm describing in these scenarios is where this component inserts itself most noticeably in our lives. It often creates a barrier that can make words very hard to say, yet it is Fred's use of puppets that allows for that language to come out. This is how a children's program could so artfully deal with issues like segregation and political assassination. It's the transition into the Neighborhood of Make-Believe that allows for the sometimes unspeakably unpleasant to come out into the open and be resolved, and this is the lesson Fred Rogers offers us adults living in a twenty-first-century democracy.

Can Jürgen Come Out to Play?

Within the transition between the "real" world of Mister Rogers's home and the Neighborhood of Make-Believe we see a parallel to a very important philosopher from the twentieth century, Jürgen Habermas. Habermas's major contribution to philosophy is the notion of the public sphere. In short, the public sphere is a space where people living in a democracy get together and discuss the problems and issues facing their community. This might seem painfully obvious; of course public debate is part of collective decision making. You might even accuse Habermas or me of a move academics are constantly accused of, which is over-thinking a relatively simple and easily recognizable point. Please bear with me, something vital to our freedom is in play.

Habermas is not only concerned with the existence of these places, but more importantly their meaning, and understanding how the meaning of things impacts how we live our lives is what philosophy is all about.

Habermas and Rogers were born only a little more than a year apart at the end of the 1920s. It can be argued the circumstances of their birth greatly influenced the way both men were concerned about the ways in which individuals living together interacted with one another. The first part of King's biography of Rogers is dedicated to the relative isolation that defined Fred's childhood. He was frequently quite ill, and his parents constantly worried about his wellbeing, restricting his ability to leave his room. His hometown of Latrobe is a relatively small Western Pennsylvania town, and at the time of Fred's birth, the family's business interests employed most of the town. Being the son of almost everyone's dad's boss surely compounded the ways in which the family wealth removed young Fred from the lives of the kids around him.

Habermas was born in Germany in 1929, and in his youth he witnessed first-hand the most spectacular and horrifying failure of democracy, enlightenment, and modernity that hopefully anyone of us will ever have to witness. Fred Rogers also lived through the war years and the years of contentiousness and conflict that followed. Both men were profoundly influenced by advances in child psychology and development that were happening in the middle of the twentieth century. Figures like Erik Erikson and Jean Piaget unpacked the complex developmental stages people grow through.

Habermas used these ideas in his philosophy to explore the evolution of a society's moral and political systems. He believed societies grew in stages much like how Erikson and Piaget defined the lives of children. Fred Rogers used the work of the very same psychologists to create a children's program that is developmentally appropriate to children, and just happens to offer us a lesson about our moral and political system.

Both men chose to think deeply about the *meaning* of the spaces in which we live our lives, and how these spaces both allow our most private selves and our public faces to coexist with others. While the existence of public spaces where individuals hash out decisions might be obvious, for Habermas the meaning of those spaces, how we think of them, and possible threats to their existence is crucial if we are to avoid the human-made disaster he witnessed during his youth. His books *The Structural Transformation of the Public Sphere*, *Legitimation Crisis*, and *Moral Consciousness and Communicative Action* all explore the nuances of this often invisible distinction.

Habermas's theory argues modern life is defined by spaces. We have a private sphere of home. This is a space defined by privacy. I'm sure you are familiar with the phrase "Whatever happens behind closed doors . . ." This is a perfect expression of the private sphere. Within the private sphere we are free from the eyes of others, often allowing ourselves to be vulnerable. We act without concern of what outsiders might think, and it is also the space where many of our physical needs are met in one way or another.

This sounds like a pretty good deal, and why would anyone want to leave? This is where things get tricky. We are all dependent on each other, one way or another. Our very basic human needs we might fulfill in our kitchens, bedrooms, and bathrooms are all dependent on the work of others. Sooner or later we all need a Handyman Negri or a Mr. McFeeley to help us along.

Similarly, we all have to sometimes go out and earn money to pay our rents and mortgages, as well as procure items in the marketplace, even if we are doing so symbolically by shopping online. We also have this concept of other people's privacy. We might be very curious to know what's happening in the house across the street, but to violate the privacy of our neighbors would mean they might feel equally justified in violating our privacy. It is through the work of others and mutually recognized boundaries that these two spheres of life, public and private, are mutually dependent on each other even if they seem very different by nature.

Not only are these two spheres dependent upon each other, but they can also dictate our behavior. We may wish to sit and watch a movie in our underwear while eating nachos; however, the difference between doing so in a theater and our living room is immense. We can easily resent the public when their concerns intrude upon our private lives and desires, and we can just as easily resent others when their private life and desires intrude upon our life in public. After all, we all have our own pet peeves about public behavior. Mine include folks who don't understand that you're supposed to allow those getting off of an elevator to pass before trying to get on.

However, there are much more serious concerns at play when it comes to this balance of public and private. Everyone living in relationship to one another—whether it might be a neighborhood, city, country, or our increasingly globalized planet—faces threats to their security and well-being from time to time. The private sphere is rooted in self-interest, but we need the public sphere in order to secure self-interest. Physical spaces like town hall meetings, coffee shops, and yes, even a Trolley can be a place where individuals meet and debate the collective concerns of the day. We can see this in the "theme weeks" that dominated *Mister Rogers' Neighborhood* after 1979, where subjects like death and divorce were dealt with openly and honestly.

King Friday the XIII and the Temptation to "Reply All"

Habermas is not only concerned that the public sphere exists, but that any democratic society is both aware it exists and it has a clear concept of that space, its workings, and its boundaries. He's also particularly concerned about the fate of the public sphere when there is a threat to a society, because without a healthy public sphere, we cease to live in a democracy.

A perfect example of when the public sphere of mutual interest and concern falls apart in reaction to a threat is during the first week of the first season of *Mister Rogers' Neighborhood*. The cantankerous Lady Elaine Fairchilde has re-arranged the Neighborhood of Make-Believe and put the Friday administration into crisis mode. Citizens of the Neighborhood are frightened and confused by this sudden turn of events. Everyone, including Trolley, must present their name, rank, and serial number upon entering the neighborhood. A barbed-wire wall goes up around the castle, and King Friday's new mantra is "Down with the Changes! Down with the Changes!" Henrietta Pussycat is afraid of violence, and one of the saddest moments of the first week is when Chef Brockett is humiliated by the increasingly authoritarian

Friday after Brockett attempts to present a cake as a gesture of kindness and goodwill.

Those of us who remember the aftermath of 9/11 might see a bit of a historical parallel. Fear has a powerful capacity to tempt us to retreat from others and secure any space where we might encounter strangers. The "new normal" of increased security is as symbolic as it is a physical product of fear and vulnerability. Rogers, in an afterward to a book called *The Power of the Powerless,* reminds us we should, "wonder if there isn't a part of each of us which feels powerless and in need of unconditional acceptance." The question is not whether we are vulnerable, but what we do in response.

It's quite easy to get cynical about the freedom and opinions of others. French philosopher Jean-Paul Sartre responded to the same pressures and tragedies of the twentieth century by concluding, "Hell is other people," and in the era of twenty-four-hour cable news and social media punditry (and a work week where my calendar says I have five hour-plus long faculty meetings on top of the deadline for this chapter), it's hard sometimes not to agree with Sartre. Imagine what it would be like to be on a work-related email chain with King Friday. Could he possibly resist clicking the "Reply all" button to declare to anyone and everyone exactly what's on his mind? But to heed Sartre's siren call is to ignore the thing that Rogers and Habermas can teach us about living with others.

In both *Mister Rogers' Neighborhood* and the philosophy of Jürgen Habermas not only must we have a space to work out our thoughts and feelings with others, but we must be able to imagine ourselves within those spaces. This is what the jump to the Neighborhood of Make-Believe symbolizes so very well. In that first episode of *Mister Rogers' Neighborhood,* we learn not only about the chaos of Lady Elaine Fairchilde's doings in the Neighborhood of Make-Believe but also the changes to Mister Rogers's house. Under this very Habermasian system, an event occurs, and we are all invited to a space where we're able to work through the next steps of how we respond and move forward.

Oh, Won't You Be . . .

At the end of the first week of *Mister Rogers' Neighborhood*, King Friday is overwhelmed by messages of peace and love from his subjects, and the Neighborhood of Make-Believe once again embraces the values of an open society. If only our politics were so easy. Likewise, while a fantasy of hitting the

World Series winning home run is nice, how many of us hold in our hearts a much deeper fantasy that we could somehow get though this life without hurting anyone, ever? The difference is, of course, that Joe Carter did hit such a home run for the 1993 Blue Jays, but such a life is impossible. The question is, What do we do with ourselves if we want to live in peace with others?

Both Habermas and Rogers were highly skeptical about the rise of media culture. Habermas concluded that TV debates were a poor substitute that threatened to hijack the actual public sphere, leaving citizens silenced and helpless as media figures do the talking for them. Fred Rogers expressed his reservations about the fast-paced nature of *Sesame Street* privately, but was not at all reserved in how he felt about other popular children's programming that centered around slapstick humor, fighting, and the selling of merchandise. Rogers used television in a way very different than most. The Neighborhood of Make-Believe is the type of space where diversity meets and it is reasonable to work through the very uncomfortable thoughts and feelings that arise during the course of our lives.

Rogers and Habermas are ever more relevant to us as our lives become increasingly privatized. I'm writing these words at a time when the way in which folks seem to be glued to their phones is a common concern. Think about the possible relevance of these words in a near-future where virtual reality is mainstream, offering all of us the possibility of a fully-immersive waking fantasy where we can tune out the needs and opinions of others. Minister turned environmental activist Bill McKibben once wrote about hearing an executive of a home builder's association speak during the height of the McMansion craze and declare, "We call this the ultimate home for families who don't want anything to do with one another!" Where once the family was a refuge, we could see this quote as evidence of an increasingly shrinking public imagination, putting even the folks in our private sphere out of reach.

As Habermas argues, when the public sphere is overtaken by media, or consumerism, or by power-hungry individuals acting maliciously, the public can feel disconnected, powerless, and chronically angry. Remember this the next time you find yourself enraged by someone posting a clip from your least-favorite twenty-four-hour news channel on social media. These are strange times where we're publicly rewarded by sharing our deepest thoughts with something we keep in our pants pocket.

All is not lost however, there is a friendly and familiar model we can all explore. Fred Rogers wanted to help children transition from the private spaces of home and into the world. His transitions to and from the Neighborhood of Make-Believe and the frequent guests on his show is a manifestation of this hope. We might have thoughts and feelings that are less than kind towards others. We might want to run away from difficult circumstances and choices.

Fred Rogers gives us a model for working through all of this. His show about a space where conflicts are resolved is a vital lesson for anyone living in a democracy. It's been sitting right there in a lot of our childhoods. If we allow ourselves to re-imagine it, we can learn from it.

22

Won't You Be My Comrade?

CHRISTOPHER M. INNES

Mister Rogers was one of the kindest and most caring individuals you'd ever like to have as your neighbor. And it's his particular caring disposition that stands out to us most of all; there's no question of his willingness to come to our aid in times of need, and to help us solve our problems. But what sorts of problems does Mister Rogers aim to help? What do we need Mister Rogers for?

I suggest his kind of caring is an ideal kind, that doesn't touch upon our problems at a material level. For example, in any given episode, Mister Rogers's featured story might be to do with the family, how to get on with friends at school, or even how to cope with your parents getting divorced. He cares, but as much as his care helps us emotionally to deal with such problems, it's powerless to do anything about our material conditions.

This is not Mister Rogers's fault. He's concerned with neighborhood problems as well as big world problems including the Gulf War or the 9/11 terrorist attacks and wants to help lessen the "psychic terrors" in the minds of kids, but perhaps his concern is too detached.

Maybe that's because he's on TV and this sort of contact is not really possible. Even so, a viewpoint of caring, which only exists in a make-believe neighborhood and not in an actual neighborhood, might suggest that his care for others is nothing more than a meaningless and shallow expression. We don't want this to be said of Mister Rogers, though. And, after all, we don't want to criticize Rogers for something that's not his purpose.

Rogers has made an honest attempt to put this care into action within his own community. The worry is that Mister

Rogers's television neighbors might believe that his care can improve their practical circumstances, when it can't. Is Mister Rogers's neighborhood expression of care too detached from the actual lives of his viewers to be significant?

It's Always a Beautiful Day in the (Idealized) Neighborhood

We're going to ask our friend Mister Marx what he would think of Mister Rogers's effort to help children. Karl Marx (1818–1883) developed a way of thinking called historical materialism, which is famously critical of Georg Hegel's (1770–1831) historical idealism.

In Mister Marx's *Critique of Hegel's Philosophy of Right*, it looks like Mister Hegel understands care for others in much the same way that we'll try to understand Mister Rogers's care for his neighbors. Any disagreement is seen in a largely idealized way, where a certain problem is theoretically understood, a theoretical solution to the problem is put forward, and its solution is put into action.

All this reasoning is done with little contact with the material world. In an idealized way, Mister Rogers makes it clear that personal, social and political problems are solved by reason. Divorce was seen by Mister Hegel as a natural part of the social world where individuals get married for love and when that love is no longer there, then they can't stay married. This is straightforward and clear, and similar to the way Mister Rogers thinks about problems.

Marx's materialist viewpoint will lead us to say that the real reason people marry is not because of this unclear human emotion called love. The real reason is to do with money. To get married is to be financially secure. Love has little to do with why couples are getting married and staying together.

It's Always a More Beautiful Day in the Material Neighborhood

Marx thinks Hegel's viewpoint is like a storybook. An individual is seen as an ideal individual, as a thing that needs certain things, and their lot in life is seen in ideal terms. But the truth of the matter is that the individual's talents and ability are being used to make money for someone else. In the Marxist historical conception of capitalism, Mister Rogers's greeting of "Won't you be my neighbor?" is a qustion the individual is asked only in an idealized way. It's imagined that such a neighbor exists and is able to be friends with you. The disconnected individual has no real link with others. Accordingly, Mister Rogers's connection with others is only possible as an ideal; it's not real in a down-to-earth material way, which is like when someone says they are sorry. They are being genuine, but the apology is not materially effective. For an apology to be effective, the individual needs to feel the harm done to the other.

Mister Rogers encouraged individualism and community, as did Marx, but Marx noticed that both are given only symbolic representation in capitalism; there is no real representation. While capitalism is said to be grounded within the political ideal of liberalism that values individual rights, Marx thought that individuals, in a capitalist system, are really sucked in, chewed-up and then spat-out with no care for self-esteem or being a true member of the community. Rights are an ideal that is only afforded by the ruling class.

We see this in the Make-Believe discussion of war, in the weekly theme on conflict. There's talk about war as not being nice and that their neighborhood has never had a war, which to us, sounds too good to be true (episode 1521). Prince Tuesday sorrowfully points out that to the victor goes the spoils. War in our modern-day real world is the highest form of capitalist conflict. Capitalism is where individuals are *alienated* through exploitation—which is to say that they are not true members of the community. Such a conception of exploitation, like that of an act of war, is side-tracked in the Neighborhood of Make-Believe with wishful thinking and polite conversation.

Marx wrote to his friend Arnold Ruge, saying that his Young-Hegelian friends should "show less vague reasoning, fine phrases, conceited self-admiration, and more precision, more detail on concrete circumstances, and more knowledge of the subject," which we might also say of Mister Rogers's puppets. There is conflict, and the Young Hegelians, like the puppets, are not getting to the heart of the problem.

This point is also well expressed when Marx says justice is an ideal. He does this by discussing the process known as the *material dialectic*. In the real neighborhood, one class of people fights against another class to bring about actual change. The capitalist class exploits the working class. The workers resent the exploitation and will eventually revolt against those who own the businesses and control the institutions.

There's a loss of community brought about by capitalism needing liberalism to stress the need for individual rights which were not allowed under an oppressive monarch. King Friday XIII, the imperial monarch of the Neighborhood of

Make-Believe, is much like King George III. King Friday XIII often expresses silly sentiments and is at times not taken very seriously by others in the Neighborhood just as the American loyalists made fun of King George III for his silliness. The stress for individual rights is a symbolic gesture for something that didn't exist under the monarchy, which is more like a sentiment than a real force of liberty. Such documents as the Declaration of Independence or the Bill of Rights might be decent gestures that preach individual integrity, but they are nonetheless only gestures. The weight of material oppression needs more than gestures to liberate individuals from their burden.

Could We Instead See Mister Rogers More Like Mister Marx?

Are we being too unreasonable with Mister Rogers? He has a strong sense of decency, which Mister Marx might say is a cover-up for the exploitation of children when they grow up. But this might be seen instead as a more down-to-Earth concern for the care of these kids and for them as workers when they grow up. His idealist way of thinking and his anachronistic outlook can perhaps be seen as part a bygone paternalist expression. This is where we see everything cared for in its correct place: with work and leisure clearly viewed as different, the workers happily doing their work, and the disadvantaged are looked after with kindness.

Mister Rogers has a strong sense of care. With the sermon about "family" or about being "brave," we see that Mister Rogers is aware of the perils of modern life. Our Marxist viewpoint of him might be too skeptical about his possible detachment from economic material causation.

We can still see the problem that in *Mister Rogers' Neighborhood*, things are seen as symbols about what should happen. Mister Rogers shares a paddling pool with Officer Clemmons in 1969 and later in 1993 (Mister Rogers Talks about Love) suggesting equal rights for black Americans. This is like a storybook. According to Marx, any form of equality should be seen in material, historical and economic terms. This is why Marx brings in the material humanist Ludwig Feuerbach (1804–1872).

Mister Feuerbach's materialism is Marx's cavalry called to rescue Mister Hegel's historical view of change from its inaccessible idealist heights. This allows Marx to appreciate social and political action happening in the actual neighborhood. This is a harsher neighborhood. It's the neighborhood of class conflict with all the related ills such as race conflict, inequality, and the poor treatment of the handicapped.

We see the courageous boy Jeff Erlanger show Mister Rogers how his electric wheelchair works. Jeff was certainly inspired by Mister Rogers, but we might doubt whether the inspiration had such material effect in the real neighborhood. We're reminded of this in Eddie Murphy's 1983 SNL spoof *Mister Robinson's Neighborhood* showing rough city life in materialist terms of theft, slums, poverty, and inequality. Did Mister Rogers notice this rougher neighborhood?

Was Mister Rogers a Radical Social and Political Pioneer?

Let's look at Mister Rogers's understanding of his neighborhood. Fred Rogers was the son of an industrial brick-making and iron forge family. His father was company director of McFeely Brickmaking factories in and around Latrobe in Pennsylvania. Fred lived within the constant presence of industrial turmoil. The McFeely Brick Co. might not have had any serious industrial disputes, but there were plenty nearby, such as the Ambridge Strike of 1937, one of many that the young Fred experienced. It undoubtedly would have been a daily consideration for this aspiring thinker.

Again, we notice that Mister Rogers's TV show reflects what could be seen as a view of class struggle, with Mister McFeely as the mailman who is always saying "speedy delivery." Mister McFeely is always making a delivery. He's not on strike, but he's usually very rushed. When, in certain episodes, Mister Rogers shows videos on how things are made, we don't just see the production process; we see the worker as central with their self-esteem emphasized. In the making of suitcases (episode 1600), Mister Rogers remarks of a worker putting the lining into a suitcase, that "she knows her work." We might say that Mister Rogers succeeded where all Marxist theoreticians and union leaders have failed. Mister Rogers understands the worker alienation and exploitation, though in understated terms.

Marx also analyzed the worker's role in his major work *Capital* (1867). It's highlighted by Marx that in the pre-capitalist guild system, the guild worker would make the pin by himself with the help of an apprentice. The job gives the worker pride. With the industrial introduction of division of labor, the work of making the pin is now broken down into more than forty tasks. The worker becomes alienated from the product of their labor, and their belonging to the community is sacrificed for the purpose of making profit.

On Mister Rogers's visit to Sesame Street, he confides in Big Bird that individuals don't like losers. Big Bird has just won a race against Mr. Snuffleupagus and he is worried that his friend will think that they are no longer friends. Mister Rogers's reasoning is that Big Bird should let Snuffleupagus know that they are still friends. We might not be so hopeful that under capitalism the winner will be so appreciative of the loser. Like the working class being the loser, the winning upper class are not likely to treat them so gracefully. Everybody wants to be a full individual, by being productive and equally creative. We see that Mister Rogers includes the least advantaged, but does he do so in a materially effective way?

He is progressive, that's for sure! He's an enlightened conservative and maybe even a liberal, which might well sum-up Fred Rogers's political outlook. At any rate, Mister Rogers works in a world of imagination. Mister Rogers might go to a suitcase factory, where individuals are seen as important, where they have integrity, not to be used as a means to others' greed.

We must not forget that Mister Rogers's investigation is done in the realm of imagination. The viewpoint that individuals have rights is just as imaginary in the ideal world. Capitalism only allows rights for the class in charge. As we see in much of liberal discussion, Mister Rogers is prescribing a view of rights and an agreement (social contract) that respects others' rights. He is not proposing a critique. We need to ask if capitalism allows everyone to have rights.

Mister Rogers putting on his cardigan in the opening of each episode is a nice ritual, but it's a ritual that puts in order one part of human conduct and another; work and leisure are not the same, just as workers and bosses are different. Decency isn't held in doubt, where individuals are portrayed as independent of the industrial machine. As Marx said in *Capital*, the material world ties individuals inseparably to the work, where "the worker is an appendage to the machine." This is to say that Mister Rogers is using a "bourgeois rights based ideology." Fred Rogers might be seen as a *bourgeois socialist*.

Marx wrote in the *Communist Manifesto* that the *bourgeois socialist* only demands reform and has only a slim idea of radical change. It might be progressive, but it's not liberating. And we can say that there is an imaginary sense of freedom that's betrayed once the show's finished. It's again betrayed once the child grows up and gets a job. The magical process of the trolley and puppets are a strange ideological trick that keeps us from overthrowing the capitalist system.

Mister Rogers's solution is a demand for democratic inclusion. As we've seen, such idealism doesn't work. We admire Mister Rogers's ridicule of the monarch, King Friday XIII. This is a sign of progress. Progress is a nonstop direct historical charge to ultimate human freedom. The problem is that there is no end of the line station called *capitalism*. Historical determinism sees the monarchy as an evolutionary stepping stone to capitalism. Democracy is introduced and Mister Rogers vividly illustrates that King Friday XIII needs democracy to keep on reigning but democracy does not need the monarchy to keep on representing individuals. Progress is seen in Mister Rogers's neighborhood when the monarchy is mocked, and Marx's notion of historical change will ask why Mister Rogers has stopped at democracy.

In one of the episodes on work, Ellen Paterson and Beaver O'Day, from Paterson's Pipes, explains to King Friday that $3,000 is needed to fix the water pipelines in the neighborhood (episode 1529). This means that the money set aside to build King Friday's swimming pool needs to be used to fix the pipes. King Friday and Lady Aberlin happily agree to the pool not being built. King Friday's declaration "even kings can't have everything they want," implies a lack of class consciousness. Ellen would not be able to expect such compromise, and in the real world of kings and queens who deceive and take away the dreams of their subjects, her suggestion would be met with contempt. Monarchies in the real world would have the king's subjects (of the neighborhood) pay vast sums in taxes to pay for the new pipes, while King Friday still gets his swimming pool.

The acceptance of the need for equality, fairness, and justice is done as a great progressive leap forward, but it's a continuous direct set of leaps. History does not stop at capitalism, democracy and liberalism; this is where the ideals are expressed but only in socialism leading to a shift to communism do we see freedom truly put into action in the nitty-gritty neighborhood.

As with Marx, Mister Rogers sees capitalism as a theater performance. With Marx the theatre play has the rejection of Hegel's idealism as the main performance. This is when it's stressed that the neighborhood isn't to be seen in ideal terms. The neighborhood is a political theater where the stress and strain of economic life is played out to an inquisitive audience. Economic interests are fought out in the material world. The ruling capitalist class exploit the working class, and bicker amongst themselves about how the workers should be exploited. This is the real neighborhood. We're not sure whether Mister Rogers's neighborhood is so real.

Is Mister Rogers the Kids' Comrade?

Fred Rogers has described the area between the TV and the child as "holy ground." We're not sure whether Mister Rogers is part of a dominant political force, and we might like to see him more as an innocent neighbor used by capitalism to con the kids into thinking that capitalism is fair. Not all institutions are reducible to economic interests, maybe. At any rate, questions need to be asked. Mister Hegel's and Mister Rogers's viewpoints are imaginative and admirable but are at the same time too simple.

Marx thinks that love can only be possible with a shift from an idealist love to a materialist love of your neighbor. This is to say that instead of making sentiments, Mister Rogers should get out into the neighborhood. This will allow substantial gestures, and not the hollow sermonizing of liberalism influenced by Dr. Benjamin Spock. The neighborhood is in the realm of *metaphysical materialism* which is to say that all we do is the result of material happenings and not because of story-like fiction of the idealists.

We might have to admit that Marx would admire Mister Rogers more than he would admire Mister Hegel. Mister Hegel's neighborhood is never visited because it does not exist outside of the minds of its creators. But, at least Mister Rogers's neighborhood is visited, albeit in the Neighborhood of Make-Believe, and short field-trips to factories and offices in VHS video recordings, where drawing, music, and tapestry can be appreciated by all social classes. We might have to accept that certain aspects of the Marxist critique see some aspects of Mister Rogers's progressive liberalism as acceptable. Mister Rogers's concern about "throwing a pie in someone's face" as demeaning is a humanist sentiment that Marx would have taken seriously.

But, we essentially might think that the kids are being duped. The magic of the Trolley and the charm of the puppets conspire to convince kids that they'll have to accept a life of exploitation by the ruling class when they grow up. We can be generous to Mister Rogers and suggest that being aware of our emotions will lessen the harm of alienation which is much worse than not knowing our feelings at all. This will lessen the burden of exploitation. As we said at the beginning, we don't want to find Fred Rogers guilty of taking part in the exploitation of children as they grow up. But, then again, this is a Marxist critique and it's often quite relentless.

Maybe we might see Mister Rogers as the man of our times who stood up and provided a clear view of freedom that was possible in this time in history. However, his good intention will not have the desired effect in the material world. There was not much more that he could have done. We might still call Fred Rogers a *bourgeois socialist*, but he did fulfill an important role.

23
The Neighborhood Is Us

TRIP MCCROSSIN

"Love is at the root of everything," Mister Rogers urges, with characteristic optimism, in Morgan Neville's *Won't You Be My Neighbor?*, "all learning, all parenting, all relationships, love or the lack of it." In this light, he continues, "what we see and hear on the screen is part of who we become," loving or otherwise. "Television has the chance," in this additional light, we hear him ponder a bit further on, "to make a real community out of an entire country."

Mister Rogers "had a singular vision of kindness and love," Tom Junod we hear, journalist and friend, acknowledge. "But a question that I think of a lot," he worries in turn, "is whether his attempt to influence America succeeded or not."

It did.

Before Pittsburgh (Way)

"Back in the 1950s, there was a school of people at the University of Pittsburgh looking at early-childhood education," we learn early on from Max King, Mister Rogers's biographer, "Dr. Benjamin Spock was part of it [*Baby and Child Care* pictured], Berry Brazelton, the famous pediatrician was a part of it [*To Listen to a Child*], Eric Erikson, the extraordinary psychologist, was a part of it [*Childhood and Society*], and Fred's part of that group."

Back further still, way further, in the 1760s, there's another person looking at childhood education with whom Mister Rogers forms a kind of group: Jean-Jacques Rousseau, and the story he tells of young Émile's radical upbringing. *Mister Rogers' Neighborhood* and Rousseau's *Émile, or On Education* are similar in their methodologies, as Mister Rogers and Rousseau are in their motivations.

Being an ordained Presbyterian minister, whose ministry was *Mister Rogers' Neighborhood*, Mister Rogers would naturally have struggled with the Old Testament's parable of Job, (who, as a test of faith and reason, suffered horribly even while incomparably virtuous) and so with the philosophical problem for which Job is the conventional touchstone, which is the problem of evil. The story of Job's unfathomable suffering is set against his unparalleled righteousness, as a test of his reason and faith. And so the philosophical problem for which Job is the conventional touchstone is the problem of evil. Susan Neiman nicely describes it as the perniciously difficult to satisfy "need to find order within those appearances so unbearable that they threaten reason's ability to go on," as when proverbially bad things happen to good people, and good things to bad people. *Mister Rogers' Neighborhood* begins with the recognition that bad things (including bad television) happen to good kids.

His ministry's medium being *television*, and so his congregation as multi-denominational as we can imagine, he would just as naturally have struggled with the problem of evil in *both* of its modern formulations, as Neiman explains. Midway through the Enlightenment, the problem evolved from its primarily theological version—human reason straining, in the above "find order" spirit, to reconcile conspicuous human suffering with faith in divine wisdom, power, and benevolence, which either makes or allows it to happen—to include also a more *secular* version. Here, while it no longer arises in response to suffering's ostensibly divine origin, reason strains similarly nonetheless. In both versions, we worry that the strain may be sufficient to call into question reason's *ability* to make the order it so fervently desires.

And his ministry's intent being *political* in the broadest sense, finally, its hope nothing short of society's rehabilitation, he would again naturally have favored Rousseau's response to the problem of evil over Voltaire's response. Rousseau insists, as Neiman writes, that "morality demands that we make evil intelligible," but for Voltaire, "morality demands that we don't."

Mister Rogers' Neighborhood begins not only with the idea that bad things happen to good kids. It begins just as importantly with the idea that education and parenting, if properly understood and conducted, can mitigate the ill effects. This allows happier and more loving kids to emerge, and in turn, happier and more loving grown-ups, and eventually a society that suffers the problem of evil less acutely. This is clearly cut far more from Rousseau's mold than Voltaire's. And while Junod's worry—that Mister Rogers may in the end have influenced our era less successfully than he hoped—arises all the more as a result, it's in this that he, and we, may find consolation.

Émile in the Neighborhood

Rousseau brings Émile to life for us in response to Voltaire's Candide, the central figure in *Candide, or Optimism*, which had appeared four years earlier. It reflects publicly the withering contempt he'd expressed in correspondence for Rousseau's *Discourse on the Origin and Foundations of Inequality*, which appeared as many years before *Candide*.

Candide, as Voltaire tells his story, is unceremoniously expelled in his late teens from previously idyllic circumstances, and prey then to seemingly endless misfortunes. He's nonetheless consoled by his former tutor, Dr. Pangloss, who while similarly expelled and preyed upon, remains nevertheless optimistic. The good doctor reasons that a divinely-made world must surely be "the best of all possible worlds," to which our sufferings contribute just as surely as our joys. Candide eventually tires of Pangloss's optimism, however, finding greater consolation elsewhere. "To involve oneself in public affairs," he learns from a Turkish farmer tending a small plot on the outskirts of Constantinople, "is to perish at times miserably and deservedly." But simply working the land instead, as he does with his family, "distances from us three great evils: boredom, vice, and need." Suitably inspired, Candide and his ersatz family follow suit on a "small plot" of their own, but with a twist. "Let us work," they resolve, but "without reasoning," Candide adds, "as the only way to make life sufferable."

Émile, on the other hand, as Rousseau tells *his* story, is also tutored through his late teens, but tutored differently, in pursuit of a different "way to make life sufferable." To wait until adulthood to heed the Turk's warning, Rousseau believes, and Mister Rogers would surely agree, is to wait *far* too long. Such affairs are part of the world he'd bemoaned in the *Discourse*, beset by all manner of evil, as a result of humanity's long history of imprudent development. The key to a sufferable life is not to work "without reasoning," he thought, but to work *on* our reasoning, using it to make long flourishing evil *newly* intelligible.

Working *on* our reasoning, Rousseau thought, was the key to a sufferable life, rather than *without* it, as Candide proposes to Pangloss. It's the business of helping reason to make long flourishing evil *newly* intelligible, as Lady Aberlin helps Daniel

Striped Tiger to do, in the segment of the Assassination Special included in *Won't You Be My Neighbor?* At its most intelligible, Rousseau proposed, we recognize such evil as resulting from unwittingly promoting our natural instinct to *preserve and promote ourselves*, little by little across the ages, at the expense our equally natural instinct to *act compassionately toward others*.

To recognize the imbalance is to yearn to redress it, as again Mister Rogers would surely agree. This we could do, Rousseau proposed in his *Discourse on Political Economy*, by adopting a two-pronged strategy for a new kind of social contract based in the idea of a binding "general will" among us. We seek along one prong, to make laws as they ought to be, in order to protect us from the effects of our corruption (assuming we remain as corrupt as we are). We seek along the other prong, to make *us* as *we* ought to be, through an idealized system of educating children from infancy (assuming our laws remain as ineffectual as they are).

Unlike Rousseau, however, who understood that the two prongs were equally essential, Mister Rogers pursued just the one—to leave laws as they are, while making us as we ought to be, by allowing our younger selves to feel loved just as we are. But given that his project was nothing short of society's rehabilitation, even while it was flanked by illusion-shattering assassinations and large-scale political terrorism, was pursuing just the one prong enough?

It was.

Coat and Tie

"When President Kennedy, Dr. King, and Senator Kennedy were assassinated," Mister Rogers recalled to the National Symposium on Children and Television, in October 1971, "I felt that I had to speak to the families of our country about grief." The vehicle was *Mister Rogers' Neighborhood*, of course, as reflected in what came to be known as the "Assassination Special," which aired on June 7th 1968, in prime time, two days after Senator Kennedy's assassination, and only a few months into the show's first season. While not routinely viewable in its entirety, we are fortunate to have a nicely detailed description of it from Adam Nedeff, and a healthy portion of the third of its three excursions to the Neighborhood of Make-Believe in *Won't You Be My Neighbor?*

The special's structure is unusual, geared to allow him to speak not just to children, but to *families*. It begins in the usual way in the usual place, with a chat with him in his television house, but, as Nedeff reports, what follows is unusual in a number of ways. The beginning is preceded, for example, by no program title. We're simply all of a sudden there. Similarly, the special's three excursions to the Neighborhood of Make-Believe aren't initiated in the usual way, via the Neighborhood Trolley. Again, we're simply all of a sudden there. Perhaps most surprising, to anyone who'd watched the show even once before, Mister Rogers is uncharacteristically ill at ease, and equally uncharacteristically dressed in coat and tie, instead of his trademark cardigan, signaling that this and subsequent chats on this particular evening were to be with parents.

Many years later, he would appear again on television in a time of national crisis, again in coat and tie. In a tragic coda to the thirty-three-year run of *Mister Rogers' Neighborhood*, from February 19th 1968, through August 31st 2001, striving to change the world for the better by helping generations of kids to feel loved *just the way they are*, on September 11th 2001, the world all of a sudden appeared to have changed not only not for the better, but for the worse. He appeared in a public service announcement shortly afterward, and once again on the occasion of the one-year anniversary, appealing in each instance to grown-ups.

"When the horror of 9/11 really hit him," Margy Whitmer tells us, toward the end of *Won't You Be My Neighbor?*, describing his frame of mind during the production of the first announcement, "it was a real eye-opener." "He was realizing that it was just so big," she continues, that "it's always going to be an ongoing struggle to overcome evil." "I just don't know," she tells us he worried ultimately, "what good these are going to do." Still, he persisted. "Especially in our world today," he implored, visibly shaken, "we are all called to be *tikkun olam—repairers of creation*." "Thank you for whatever you do," he continues, "wherever you are, to bring joy and light and hope and faith and pardon and love, to your neighbor and to yourself," subtly emphasizing "pardon," and assuming optimistically that gratitude was due in the first place.

Less than a year later, in the second announcement, he's visibly more at ease. "It happens so often," he begins, that "I walk down the street and someone twenty or thirty or forty years old will come up to me and say, 'You *are* Mr. Rogers, aren't you?', and then they tell me about growing up with the Neighborhood, and how they're passing on to the children they know what they found to be important in our television work." Confessing then to being "just so proud of all of you who have grown up with us," he connects the earlier anxiety with a familiar theme. "I know how tough it is some days to look with hope and confidence on the months and years ahead," he continued, "but I would like to tell you what I often told you when you were much younger: *I like you just the way you are*." "I'm so

grateful to you for helping the children in your life," he concluded, "to express their feelings in ways that will bring heal-
ing in many different neighborhoods."

He was surely relieved that the world hadn't ended, literally
or figuratively. Also likely, he saw confirmed once again what his
mom famously told him as a child. "When I was a boy and I would
hear about something scary," as he tells the story toward the end
of *Won't You Be My Neighbor?*, "my mother would tell us, 'Always
look for people who are helping. You'll always find somebody
who's trying to help'." Likely there was something else, though, in
addition. Mister Rogers was always playing the long game.

The Castle in the Background

"Anything could happen in [the Neighborhood of] Make-
Believe," Bill Isler delights, in *Won't You Be My Neighbor?*, but
"Make-Believe wasn't real," which is why Mister Rogers "never
appeared in Make-Believe." In the post-9/11 public service
announcements, however, he's speaking to us against the background of one of its central landmarks, none other than King
Friday XIII's castle, with a bit of the Great Oak Tree, where
Henrietta Pussycat and X the Owl lived, also visible in the
frame. The departure, while subtle, is nonetheless provocative.

He's effectively bringing *into* "our world today," with all of
its troubles, a world in which *all* things are imaginable, in particular being safe from them. In merging the two realms in this
way, for grown-ups now, he's proposing that Make-Believe *is*
real, after all, and that creation *can* be repaired, perhaps even
improved, if only we have faith—spiritual, if that's the sort we
have, but otherwise just regular-old, garden-variety faith *in
one another*. The sort, in other words, that *kids* have.

The choice of background can't be lost on us either. Other
locales in the Neighborhood of Make-Believe would likely have
been just as reminiscent—the Great Oak Tree, for example, as the
primary background, or the Grandfather Clock with No Hands,
where Daniel Striped Tiger lived, which doesn't appear at all.
Instead, it's King Friday XIII's castle, and not only that, but neither the King, "one of the few remaining 'benevolent despots'," nor
his queen, Sarah Saturday, appear to be any longer in residence.

Won't You Be My Neighbor? begins with fascinating footage
borrowed from Judy Robins's *Lessons from Mister Rogers'
Neighborhood*, of him sitting at the piano, in 1967, describing a
novel way of thinking about helping kids to negotiate the "different themes in life." "One of my main jobs," he begins, is "to help
children through some of the difficult modulations of life." It's

"easy, for instance, to go from C to F," he continues, playing the modulation on the piano, but "to go from F to F-sharp, you've got to weave through all sorts of things, and it seems to me if you've got somebody to help you as you weave . . ." He trails off at this point, worried that he's being "too philosophical," "trying to combine things that can't be combined," even though the idea to him "makes sense." The idea being simply that if you've "someone to help you as you weave" through them, otherwise daunting modulations won't be so daunting after all, won't be as prone to failure, with all that failure may entail, not so much in the musical life of an expert pianist, but the emotional life of a child, *and* of the adult they'll eventually become.

Some modulations are daunting for individuals, some more broadly. And some modulations take just a little while to master, while others take longer. Some in particular take thirty-four years, and involve a considerable swath of an "entire country." What else can account for Mister Rogers being more at ease in the second public service announcement than in the first, or in the Assassination Special for that matter, all those years earlier? Perhaps just this: the realization that he was proud not only of "all [*those*] who have grown up with us," but "of *all of you* who have grown up with us," that the *all of you* are now legion, and that he was speaking directly *to them*, urging *them* on.

Television had "the chance of making a real community out of an entire country," and Mister Rogers realized that chance, at least in part. He helped it to make a real and growing community within an entire country. And what of the final modulation? What else but, with King Friday XIII's castle conspicuously in the background, weaving through all sorts of things in order to transition from separating imagination from reality, to *incorporating* imagination *into* reality.

And with King Friday XIII's castle conspicuously in the background, but the King himself nowhere in sight, to transition from being ruled by a despot, benevolent or otherwise, to whatever better arrangement infusing imagination into the world will naturally afford us—as long as love is at the root of it.[1]

---

[1] I'm ever grateful to Susan Neiman, for my fascination with, understanding of, and commitment to the problem of evil. To Marina Sitrin, who grew up with *Mister Rogers' Neighborhood*, and whose perspective on the world helped me, as always, to see something more than I was seeing on my own. To my mom and dad, who made choices that meant that I unfortunately didn't, wishing that I could talk to them about what I've learned from it as an adult, this is dedicated to them. To my spring 2019 "The Problem of Evil in Philosophy and Popular Culture" folks, for their patience and assistance. Finally, to the volume's editors for their patience and assistance, far above and beyond the call.

24
Fred Rogers and the Ethics of Care

A.G. HOLDIER

When *Mister Rogers' Neighborhood* went off the air, it capped a run of nearly nine hundred episodes spanning more than forty-five years. At the fiftieth anniversary of Fred Rogers's brainchild, tributes include everything from a movie starring Tom Hanks to an honorary postage stamp. After a decade of gun violence, natural disasters, disease outbreaks, and political acrimony, memorials to a man known primarily for loving others offer refreshment from an often-stressful news cycle.

Such inspiration is a fitting legacy for Rogers who spent his career encouraging his audience with his natural sense of the universe's moral foundations, couched not in terms of a formulaic calculation or some complicated rationalistic principle, but in the simple desire to care for others.

When called to his own fight, over congressional funding for PBS in 1969, Rogers argued, "We've got to have more of this neighborhood expression of care. And this is what I give. I give an expression of care every day." Although it's unlikely that Fred Rogers was familiar with the philosophical literature on the nature of "care" (much of which would not even be written for another fifteen years or more!), his desire to demonstrate it writ large in practical ways places him comfortably within the quarter that philosophers and psychologists like Nel Noddings and Carol Gilligan would later outline in the 1980s and after.

Care Ethics

Rather than prioritizing matters of justice or retribution, care ethics approaches moral questions as if they are, first and foremost, imperatives to nurture the well-being of other individuals. Initially born out of feminist critiques of standard psychological models in the mid-to-late twentieth century, care ethics has since grown into a full-fledged moral theory of its own and is often contrasted with rights-based views insofar as it prioritizes relationships between individuals instead of dispassionate universal rules.

Although some moral theories are grounded in a kind of abstract formula for determining proper actions in various situations, it's difficult to treat care ethics in this way, given its inextricability from particular, embodied practices aimed to benefit others in particular contexts—what's good to do for Neighbor Aber, for example, will likely differ from what's good for Chef Brockett or Handyman Negri. What consistently grounds care ethics is, instead, a concern for the extended narrative of an agent's relationship with the people around her.

The Heinz Dilemma

Imagine that Henrietta Pussycat and X the Owl are arguing about whether or not a man should be blamed for robbing a pharmacy to obtain expensive medicine he cannot afford for his sick wife. If X the Owl takes a justice-based approach to the situation, he will likely focus on the value of the ill wife's life to assert that her utility will be maximized if the man breaks the law to extend her life or that the universal duty to preserve life supersedes other concerns—both of these rationales would find plenty of defenders, under names like "utilitarianism" and "deontology."

Henrietta Pussycat, however, might pause to consider not only the question of robbing the pharmacy, but the later ramifications of such a choice—would the man then go to prison, leaving his ill wife all alone? How could such a circumstance possibly be ethical? Instead, Henrietta might recommend seeking a different solution entirely, relying on the strength of the couple's relationship with the pharmacy owner and that owner's own caring nature to work out a deal beneficial to all.

This bit of make-believe is based on a famous thought experiment called the "Heinz Dilemma," used by psychologist Lawrence Kohlberg in the 1950s to develop his model of moral development stages. According to Kohlberg, all humans progress through six basic stages of growth in moral processing abilities as we mature into full-grown adults; initially, small children act in certain approved ways primarily to avoid punishment coming upon themselves, but (eventually) mature humans act on the basis of universal principles or rules.

Carol Gilligan, a student of Kohlberg, pointed out that this framework assumes from the start that *principles* are the desired form of moral maturation—if the paradigm is shifted to instead target rich relationships with those around us (regardless of what universal principles might necessarily be violated in order to maintain those relationships), then every stage of the process will likewise shift.

Although Gilligan initially used gender as one variable to raise the issue of factors that Kohlberg had overlooked, she strongly denied that care ethics has any essential connection to gender-based considerations. X the Owl could just as easily be imagined to focus on the narratival relationship of the individuals as Henrietta Pussycat might argue for justice-based concerns.

What's more important is that the theme of "care" is fundamentally emphasized, a concern defined by Joan Tronto as consisting of four key features: 1. attentiveness, 2. responsibility, 3. competence, and 4, responsiveness. If Daniel Tiger has been mugged and King Friday passes by him in the royal carriage, in order to show him "care," Friday must 1. recognize Daniel's need, 2. take it upon himself to assist Daniel, 3. actually be able to assist Daniel successfully (either by rendering direct aid or by bringing him somewhere that can), and finally 4. performing 1–3 in a manner that is constantly sensitive to Daniel's fluctuating needs and desires.

The care King Friday could offer to Daniel Tiger in this case is different not only from the care that Friday might be able to offer Edgar Cooke if he were in that same situation (since Edgar's needs would invariably differ from Daniel's), but it's also different from the care that King Friday could offer Daniel Tiger if he finds Daniel in a similar state the following week. Care is heavily dependent on the context of the situation in question. It has been labeled as a virtue, a disposition, and a value (or set of values), often by defenders of various justice-based systems aiming to claim and subsume care-ethics underneath certain theoretical umbrellas. But care, understood by care-ethicists, is inarguably connected with certain practices aimed to benefit others. So, whatever else it may be, genuine care cannot simply be described in the abstract, but must be instantiated in order to obtain. No matter how caring I consider myself to be, it's essentially just make-believe unless I actually demonstrate that care with my actions towards others.

This other-oriented ethical perspective, even in the face of social rules or conventional wisdom, was repeatedly evidenced by Mister Rogers both on and off-screen. His television program broke barriers, famously casting African-American actor

François Clemmons as a police officer only four months after Martin Luther King Jr. was assassinated.

When the United States was still remembering protests at racially-segregated public pools, Rogers welcomed Clemmons to the program by inviting him to share a small pool of water wherein they could both cool their feet. At the height of the Cold War, Rogers invited Tatiana Vedeneeva, the host of a Soviet children's show onto his program, commenting on air how nice it was "that people can understand one another even in different tongues"—the guest could only communicate with Rogers via an interpreter (episode 1589).

Even one of Rogers's most well-known dictums—that he likes you "just the way you are"—is a powerful affirmation of the importance of relationally caring for others. This expression of care that Rogers promotes is not the output of an ethical formula, but simply for the sake of, in Rogers's words, helping "realize how rare and valuable each one of us really is, that each of us has something that no one else has—or ever will have—something inside that is unique to all time. It's our job to encourage each other to discover that uniqueness and to provide ways of developing its expression."

Animal Care

By all accounts, Mister Rogers's gentle attitude is more than just a character he plays on television (as the crew of *Candid Camera* discovered when he laughingly took their attempted televised prank in his stride). In his personal life, Rogers equally emphasized this concern to care for others around him and not, notably, only human others. Although he did not often discuss it publicly, Rogers's vegetarianism grew from his desire to "be a vehicle for God, to spread his message of love and peace" to all creatures, regardless of species—something that led him to repeatedly claim, "I don't want to eat anything that has a mother." And although Fred Rogers might well have blushed at the "sexual politics of meat," he could have had many agreeable conversations with thinkers like Carol Adams, the feminist-vegan advocate, activist, and writer who first started arguing for a connection between animal abuse and human mistreatment (particularly injustice towards women) in the 1970s.

For Adams, any act of meat-eating is connected to a depersonalizing process of turning a living being into a faceless cut of meat. Calling this facet the "absent referent," Adams argued that this process destroys humanity's relationship with non-human animals and advocated a vegetarian lifestyle as a solution to maintain interspecies relations of care. There does indeed seem to be an important semantic difference between calling an object on my plate a juicy sirloin steak instead of a piece of Harriet E. Cow's primal loin. Not all care ethicists agree that our ethical obligation of care extends to all (or any) nonhuman creatures, but it's not hard to see the perspective of those who do.

Self-Care

In addition to caring for other people and other animals, care ethics can also help to ground caring for oneself. Like care ethics as a whole, self-care has its roots initially in various feminist and other resistance movements of the 1960s: when sickness was demonstrated to adversely affect marginalized communities, taking care of yourself became a political activity. Since then, an industry of skills and commodities has arisen to support a wide variety of initiatives that aim to tend to one's own well-being. Particularly as psychologists have learned more about the damaging effects of common features of daily life in the twenty-first century (ranging from the prevalence of noisy interruptions to increased exposure to lit screens to the constant burden of war), the appreciation for pausing to intentionally prioritize one's own mental and physical health has become ever more recognized.

In light of this, consider the benediction Mister Rogers would offer at the end of each episode of his show: "You always make each day a special day. You know how: by just your being you. There's only one person in the whole world like you, and that's you yourself. And people can like you just the way you are! I'll be back next time. Bye-bye!" Never one to shy away from the value of self-affirmation and a demonstration of love—even love mediated by a television screen—Fred Rogers happily offered half-hour doses of soothing warmth that consistently underscored his message that everyone deserves to be cared for.

The Neighborhood Expression of Care

Altogether, the memory of Mister Rogers and his make-believe neighborhood, as well as the ethical lessons demonstrated therein, perhaps endures, in part, because he never tried to present ethics as a matter of dilemmas to solve or calculations to run, but simply as a series of embodied choices made by and about real people. Fred Rogers may well be one of the only celebrities to authentically model an ethics of care and, consequently, may be one of the only celebrities to deserve the attention that, even now, he continues to get.

To put it another way: we like him, just the way he is—and we might even like ourselves a bit more if we were more like him.

References

Adams, Carol J. 1990. *The Sexual Politics of Meat: A Feminist-Vegetarian Critical Theory*. Bloomsbury.

Aristotle. 1984. Metaphysics. In *The Complete Works of Aristotle*. Princeton University Press.

———. 1984. Nicomachean Ethics. In *The Complete Works of Aristotle*. Princeton University Press.

Bandura, Albert. 2003. Observational Learning. In John Byrne, ed., *Learning and Memory*. Second edition. Macmillan.

Buber, Martin. 1965 [1947]. *Between Man and Man*. Macmillan.

———. 1970 [1923]. *I and Thou*. Scribner Classics.

———. 1958 [1945]. *Moses: The Revelation and the Covenant*. Harper.

Collins, Mark, and Margaret Mary Kimmel, eds. 1996. *Mister Rogers' Neighborhood: Children, Television, and Fred Rogers*. University of Pittsburgh Press.

Eaton, Marcia Mueldar. 1999 [1987]. *Basic Issues in Aesthetics*. Waveland.

Estabrooks, G.H. 1929. Mysterious Mesmerism. *The North American Review* 227:4 (April).

Ezra, Elizabeth. 2017. *The Cinema of Things: Globalization and the Posthuman Object*. Bloomsbury.

Eugene T. Gendlin. 1997 [1962]. *Experiencing and the Creation of Meaning: A Philosophical and Psychological Approach to the Subjective*. Northwestern University Press.

———. 2007 [1978] *Focusing*. Bantam, 2007.

Frankena, William K. 1973. *Ethics*. Pearson.

Gilligan, Carol. 1982. *In a Different Voice: Psychological Theory and Women's Development*. Harvard University Press.

Gross, Kenneth. 2009. The Madness of Puppets. *The Hopkins Review* 2:2.

Habermas, Jürgen. 1962. *The Structural Transformation of the Public Sphere: An Inquiry into a Category of Bourgeois Society.* MIT Press.

———. 1968. *Legitimation Crisis.* Beacon.

———. 1990. *Moral Consciousness and Communicative Action.* MIT Press.

Hadot, Pierre. 2011 [1981]. *Philosophy as a Way of Life: Spiritual Exercises from Socrates to Foucault.* Blackwell.

Hamann, Johann Georg. 2007. *Writings on Philosophy and Language.* Cambridge University Press.

Haraway, Donna. 1991. *Simians, Cyborgs, and Women: The Reinvention of Nature.* Routledge.

Heidegger, Martin. 2008 [1928]. *Being and Time.* Harper Perennial.

Hoff, Benjamin. 1983. *The Tao of Pooh.* Penguin.

———. 1993. *The Te of Piglet.* Penguin.

Holub, Robert C. 1991. *Jürgen Habermas: Critic in the Public Sphere.* Routledge.

Horton, Donald, and R. Richard Wohl. 1956. Mass Communication and Para-Social Interaction: Observations on Intimacy at a Distance. *Psychiatry* 19:3.

Jackson, Thomas. 2001. The Art and Craft of "Gently Socratic" Inquiry. In Arthur Costa, ed., *Developing Minds: A Resource Book for Teaching Thinking.* Association for Supervision and Curriculum.

James, William. 1988. *William James: Writings 1902–1910.* Library of America.

Kant, Immanuel. 1993 [1785]. *Grounding for the Metaphysics of Morals.* Hackett.

King, Maxwell. 2018. *The Good Neighbor: The Life and Work of Fred Rogers.* Abrams.

Latour, Bruno. 1999. *Pandora's Hope: Essays on the Reality of Science Studies.* Harvard University Press.

Linn, Susan. 1996. With an Open Hand: Puppetry on Mister Roger's Neighborhood. In *Mister Roger's Neighborhood: Children, Television, and Fred Rogers.* University of Pittsburgh Press.

Long, Michael. 2015. *Peaceful Neighbor: Discovering the Countercultural Mister Rogers.* Westminster John Knox Press.

Marx, Karl. 1974 [1875]. Critique of the Gotha Program. In *The First International and After.* Penguin.

———. 1981 [1867]. *Capital.* Volumes 1–3. Penguin.

Marx, Karl, and Frederick Engels. 1992 [1848]. *The Communist Manifesto.* Oxford University Press.

McCarthy, Thomas. 1994. *The Critical Theory of Jürgen Habermas.* MIT Press.

McKibben, Bill. 2007. *Deep Economy: The Wealth of Communities and the Durable Future.* Holt.

McLellan, David, ed. 2000. *Karl Marx: Selected Writings*. Oxford University Press.

Montessori, Maria. 1992. *Education and Peace*. ANC-Clio.

Morton, Timothy. 2017. *Humankind: In Solidarity with Nonhuman People*. Verso.

Nelson, Victoria. 2001. *The Secret Life of Puppets*. Harvard University Press.

Neville, Morgan. 2018. *Won't You Be My Neighbor?* Directed by Morgan Neville. Focus Features. Film.

Nygren, Edward John. 1970. Rubens Peale's Experiments with Mesmerism. *Proceedings of the American Philosophical Society* 114:2 (April).

Parssinen. Terry M. 1997. Mesmeric Performers. *Victorian Studies* (Autumn).

Peirce, C.S. 1998. *The Essential Peirce*. Volume 2. Indiana University Press.

Plato, 2014. *Theaetetus*. Oxford University Press.

———. 1997. Meno. In *Plato: Complete Works*. Hackett.

———. 1997. Symposium. In *Plato: Complete Works*. Hackett.

———. 2005. *Republic*. Hackett.

Pocetto, Alexander T. 2008. Self-Acceptance Not Self-Esteem as a Basic Principle of Salesian Pedagogy. *Indian Journal of Spirituality* 21:3.

Pomeroy, Leon. 2012. What Is the Value of a Human Being? *Psychology Today* (November 14th). <www.psychologytoday.com/us/blog/beyond-good-and-evil/201211/what-is-the-value-human-being.>

Public Broadcasting Service (PBS). 2018. Parents: Mister Rogers' Neighborhood: The Method Behind the Magic. <www.pbs.org/parents/rogers/the-method-behind-the-magic>.

PBS Kids. 2017. 1969 Senate Hearing. YouTube <www.youtube.com/watch?v=J9uLI-o2yqQ&t=350s>.

Rogers, Carl. 1957. The Necessary and Sufficient Conditions of Therapeutic Personality Change. *Journal of Consulting Psychology* 21:2.

———. 1980. *A Way of Being*. Houghton Mifflin.

———. 1995 [1956]. *On Becoming a Person: A Therapist's View of Psychotherapy*. Houghton Mifflin.

Rogers, Fred. 1975. *Mister Rogers' Neighborhood: Everyone Is Special* (A Tell-a-Tale Book). Western Publishing Company.

———. 1988. Afterword. In Christopher De Vinick, *The Power of the Powerless*. Doubleday.

———. 1995. *You Are Special: Words of Wisdom for All Ages from a Beloved Neighbor*. Penguin.

———. 1996. *Dear Mister Rogers: Does It Ever Rain in Your Neighborhood?: Letters to Mister Rogers*. Penguin.

————. 2002. Dartmouth College Commencement Address. Speech, Hanover, NH. *Dartmouth News*. <news.dartmouth.edu/news/2018/03/revisiting-fred-rogers-2002-commencement-address>

————. 2003. *The World According to Mister Rogers: Important Things to Remember*. Hyperion.

————. 2005. *Life's Journeys According to Mister Rogers*. Hyperion.

Santayana, George. 1968. *The Birth of Reason and Other Essays*. Columbia University Press.

Scheler, Max. 1973 [1913]. *Formalism in Ethics and Non-Formal Ethics of Values*. Northwestern University Press.

————. 1992 [1915]. Ordo Amoris. In *Selected Philosophical Essays*. Northwestern University Press.

Winnicott, Douglas. 1953. Transitional Objects and Transitional Phenomena: A Study of the First Not-Me Possession. *International Journal of Psycho-Analysis* 34:2.

Wu, Kuang-Ming. 1990. *The Butterfly as Companion: Meditations on the First Three Chapters of the Chuang Tzu*. SUNY Press.

Zimmerman, Michael J., and Ben Bradley. Intrinsic vs. Extrinsic Value. *Stanford Encyclopedia of Philosophy*. <plato.stanford.edu/entries/value-intrinsic-extrinsic/>.

Zhuangzi. 2013 [1968]. *The Complete Works of Zhuangzi*. Columbia University Press.

Good Neighbors

SYDNEY BALL is a student at Saint Vincent College in Latrobe, Pennsylvania. Hailing from Rochester, New York, Sydney is a Pre-Med Biology major/English minor with aspirations of a medical career in gastroenterology. However, human guts aren't the only thing she's interested in. As a member of the esteemed Fred Rogers Scholar Society at Saint Vincent, she also enjoys digging through the guts of Fred Rogers's work and legacy. Beyond the classroom, Sydney is a successful college golfer with several wins and nine Presidential Athletic Conference awards. Her Airedale Terrier, Hershey, is not only an avid Rogers fan, but also shares his love of sneakers.

STEVE BEIN, aka Chip, is Associate Professor of Philosophy at the University of Dayton. He's a fan of both philosophy and Philosophy. He does the former as a regular contributor to books on pop culture and philosophy, on topics ranging from *Blade Runner* to Wonder Woman. He does the latter in books and articles on Asian and comparative philosophy, mostly about Zen Buddhism and the ethics of compassion. He's also a sci-fi and fantasy novelist, and his short stories make occasional appearances in Philosophy and Science Fiction courses. *Mister Rogers' Neighborhood* entranced Steve from a very young age, and to tell the truth he never quite left the Neighborhood of Make-Believe.

FERNANDO GABRIEL PAGNONI BERNS grew up fascinated by how Mister Rogers was able to complete a wardrobe change during his opening song. As an adult, he works as Professor at the Universidad de Buenos Aires (UBA)—Facultad de Filosofía y Letras in Argentina— where he teaches courses on international horror movies. He has written chapters in *Reading Richard Matheson: A Critical Survey* (edited by Cheyenne Mathews) and *Gender and Environment in Science Fiction*, among others.

DAVID BOERSEMA is retired emeritus Distinguished University Professor of Philosophy at Pacific University (in Forest Grove, Oregon) where he taught for more than three decades. He also served as director of the Pacific University Center for Peace and Spirituality. He is past president of Concerned Philosophers for Peace. Among his publications are *Philosophy of Art: Aesthetic Theory and Practice* and *Spiritual and Political Dimensions of Nonviolence and Peace*, co-edited with Katy Gray Brown. As a doting and devoted dad to Helen the cat, he is often heard around the house speaking glowingly of Henrietta Pussycat and Daniel Striped Tiger.

MARLENE CLARK teaches in the Division of Interdisciplinary studies at the City College of New York. Her courses include literature, art, film, history, and philosophy as a way of showing the world from many different perspectives. She is delighted to be a part of a volume of essays essentially a tribute to a man who still helps people, big and small, to "get enough quiet."

ELIZABETH F. COOKE is Professor of Philosophy at Creighton University in Omaha, Nebraska, where she teaches and writes in Philosophy of Science, Philosophy of Social Science, and American Philosophy, especially the philosophy of Charles Peirce. She's the author of *Peirce's Pragmatic Theory of Inquiry: Fallibilism and Indeterminacy* (2006) and various essays on pragmatism. Recent publications include "Peirce on Musement: The Limits of Purpose and the Importance of Noticing," in *European Journal of Pragmatism and American Philosophy* (2018), and "Mulder's Metaphysics," in *The X-Files and Philosophy: The Truth Is In Here* (2017). After completing her PhD in Philosophy, Elizabeth Cooke bought a one-way ticket on the Trolley deep into the World of Make-Believe to inhabit a permanent realm of pretend and play, where she presently rules as philosopher queen in her castle, apparently with no intention of ever returning.

BOB FISCHER teaches philosophy at Texas State University. He's the author of a number of books, including *The Ethics of Eating Animals* (2019) and *Animal Ethics: A Contemporary Introduction* (forthcoming). He's the editor of a handful of others, and has published essays on animal ethics, moral psychology, and the epistemology of modality. His trolley tattoo is among his favorites.

JENNIFER SHAW FISCHER spends her professional energies on elementary education and literacy. While she eagerly watched *Mr. Rogers' Neighborhood* as a child, it wasn't until her son, Jeremiah, was born that she became truly smitten by Fred's message. She and her husband, Bob, named their second son, Frederick, in his honor. Her nostalgic tendencies draw her to antique shops, and one of her favorite finds was a signed copy of one of Fred's books.

JACOB GRAHAM is an Associate Professor of Philosophy at Bridgewater College in Bridgewater, Virginia. He co-edited *True Detective and Philosophy* with Tom Sparrow, has written two articles for the *Internet Encyclopedia of Philosophy*, and has a forthcoming chapter on the usefulness of philosophy to be included in a volume edited by Diego Bubbio and Jeff Malpas. Jacob once wondered whether the trolleys in his small town in the Shenandoah Valley might take him to hold court with King Friday XIII. He has been proven incorrect, as usual.

JONATHAN HEAPS is a PhD Candidate in Religious Studies at Marquette University. He works on questions in philosophy that have significance for Roman Catholic theology. He lives and teaches in Austin, Texas. He tries to be good about restricting screen time for his pre-school-age children, but really they can watch as much *Mister Rogers' Neighborhood* and *Daniel Tiger's Neighborhood* as they want.

A.G. HOLDIER is a graduate student in the Philosophy department of the University of Arkansas, studying animal cognition and the philosophy of language, as well as an Ethics Instructor for Colorado Technical University. Along with his wife and three young daughters (Ellie, Audrey, and Tessa), he lives in his own Neighborhood of Make-Believe (and is certainly no stranger to Daniel Tiger).

CHRISTOPHER M. INNES gained much wisdom and knowledge from watching Mister Rogers with his children. He got his PhD from Goldsmiths College, University of London. This is where many TV personalities such as Julian Clary, Sam Taylor Wood, Kalki Koechlin, Amelia Warner, and Goldierocks got their degrees. He has keen interest in literature, TV, movies, and all manner of popular culture that holds in its exquisite grasp a wistful elegant view of philosophical ideas, notions and problems. He now teaches philosophy at Boise State University in Idaho.

Like King Friday and Queen Sara, who rule over the Neighborhood of Make-Believe, JASON KING AND SARA LINDEY pretend to preside over the neighborhood of Saint Vincent College. Sara Lindey is an English professor there; she teaches widely in American literature and her previous publications examine the representation of children in nineteenth-century America. Jason is a Theology professor at Saint Vincent College. He does work on marriage, family, and children. Jason and Sara's book on environmentalism in *Mister Rogers' Neighborhood* is forthcoming. They each have appointments as Fred

Rogers Faculty Fellows with the Fred Rogers Center at Saint Vincent College.

HOON J. LEE is Visiting Assistant Professor of Philosophy at Purdue University Northwest. His work focuses on moral philosophy and the history of philosophy, with a specialty in the eighteenth century and Enlightenment studies. His book *The Biblical Accommodation Debate* examines the intersection of biblical exegesis and philosophy during the Enlightenment. His current project is a study on the appropriation of Socrates by Johann Georg Hamann and Søren Kierkegaard.

DANIEL LEONARD is a doctoral student in English at Boston University, where he previously earned an MFA in creative writing. He also holds an MA in Philosophy from the University of Leuven. Daniel once purchased Fred Rogers's book *You Are Special* on a whim at a Mennonite book sale—complete with parked horses and buggies—without noticing until he got home that it was signed by the cardigan-carrying caretaker himself! During part of his childhood, Daniel regularly wore a pinned-on tiger tail, which was striped.

BENJAMIN LUKEY, a.k.a. Dr. Ben, is Associate Director of the University of Hawaii at Manoa Uehiro Academy for Philosophy and Ethics in Education. Thankfully, he doesn't have to say the full title all that often. He started doing philosophy with children (p4c) back in 2001 and hasn't stopped. While he occasionally writes about p4c, comparative philosophy, or philosophy of disability, he's usually busy doing philosophy with students and teachers in Hawaii's public schools. There he's able to frequently experience the wonder and imagination of inquisitive minds that so often inspired Fred Rogers.

TRIP MCCROSSIN teaches in the Philosophy Department at Rutgers University, where he works on, among other things, the nature, history, and legacy of the Enlightenment. Fielding students' concerns, he occasionally wants very much to channel Henrietta Pussycat: meow, meow, meow, meow, meow . . .

NATHANIEL J. MCDONALD is a civil rights and education lawyer in Cleveland, Ohio. He is a graduate of Kenyon College, and has a teacher's diploma from the International Center for Montessori Studies in Bergamo, Italy. A former public defender, Nate has also been a teacher, a principal, a consultant, and a parent at Montessori schools, and currently serves as the vice president of the board of Stonebrook Montessori, a public Montessori school.

JAMES MCLACHLAN's neighborhood is the philosophy and religion department at Western Carolina University in the mountains of North Carolina. He goes to a neighborhood of make-believe several times each week, where, with a group of friends, they try to learn about the world's religions and ideas of how we all might just get along.

NICOLAS MICHAUD grew up watching Mister Rogers. To this day, the theme song reminds Nick to try to be a better person and a good neighbor to everyone. He believes in Mister Rogers's message and is glad to be your neighbor! He has edited *Frankenstein and Philosophy: The Shocking Truth* (2013) and *Adventure Time and Philosophy: The Handbook for Heroes* (2015), and is currently working on a book about how Star Trek can help us live our lives.

ERIC J. MOHR is fortunate to teach philosophy in the neighborhood of Saint Vincent College, located in Mister Rogers's hometown of Latrobe, Pennsylvania, and site of the Fred Rogers Center. He also lives in the east end of Pittsburgh, with his wife and co-editor, Holly, and three children, near Fred Rogers's former Squirrel Hill home. He has published articles on phenomenology and ethics, in particular, the philosophy of Max Scheler. Like Mister Rogers, he tries to help people understand their personal uniqueness, though in very different ways.

HOLLY K. MOHR serves as Director of Religious Education at a Catholic parish in Pittsburgh. She strives to embody the spirit of Mister Rogers through evolving spaces where children and adults can understand their dignity, their role in building up a peaceful and just world, and the wonder inherent in creation. Having taught philosophy for several years before entering ministry work, she is continually delighted to discover the overlap between the two, helping people discover meaning and live with more intention. She is honored to partner with Eric Mohr, both on this work, and the work of life.

LEILANI MUELLER teaches competitive drama and British literature to high-school students. Her philosophy comes via osmosis from both her philosopher husband and lots of attention paid to Plato and Aquinas. She would love to live in Mister Rogers's Neighborhood, because she believes that every day is a "neighborly day for a beauty."

NATHAN MUELLER is a doctoral student in philosophy at Baylor University. His research interests center on issues in social epistemology and philosophy of education. If he visited the neighborhood you might find him wondering if the "neighborhood," considered as an entity in its own right, has beliefs, or find him sitting down for a chat with Mister Rogers about both the end and the means of education.

SCOTT F. PARKER is the author of *A Way Home: Oregon Essays* and *Being on the Oregon Coast* (forthcoming) among other books. He is also the editor of *Coffee—Philosophy for Everyone: Grounds for Debate* (with Mike W. Austin), *Conversations with Ken Kesey*, and *Conversations with Joan Didion*. You can find him watching *Mister Rogers' Neighborhood* with his son in Bozeman, Montana, where he also teaches writing at Montana State University. His students will tell you, if he learned nothing else from Mister Rogers, he at least learned how to pair sweaters and sneakers.

FRANK SCALAMBRINO has written six books, authored over fifty professional peer-reviewed publications, and taught over one hundred university-level courses, including graduate-level courses in philosophy and psychology. He is a graduate of Kenyon College and Duquesne University. Before teaching, he worked in mental health counseling, psychiatric emergency rooms, and trauma settings, and founded a Community Mental Health Suicide Prevention Respite Unit and Clinical Intervention Center in Ohio.

JOHN M. THOMPSON regularly spends time in the Neighborhood of Make-Believe with his wife and daughters, goofy dog, and two ornery kitties. In the "grown-up world" (where he usually doesn't wear sweaters or sneakers) he is a professor of Philosophy and Religion at Christopher Newport University. Even so, John still sings to himself and often overhears students and colleagues referring to him as "special."

MATTHEW USSIA is a Teaching Assistant Professor of English at Duquesne University in Pittsburgh. He has been reading freshman composition essays long enough that he no longer remembers what it was like to read anything for fun. Dr. Ussia has presented at several national conferences and has other publications in the works. He co-edited *The Dreamers Anthology* of creative works that celebrate the legacy of Martin Luther King, Jr. and Anne Frank. He has an alter-ego named Theremonster who performs doom metal on a theremin. Writing this essay re-kindled memories of a time when watching *Mister Rogers' Neighborhood* was the most peaceful part of his day. He considers himself an X the Owl type, but folks who have spent too much time with him think he's more like a King Friday XIII, without the charm.

GRACE WEHNIAINEN recently graduated with a Motion Pictures degree from the University of Miami, where her professors sparked her passion for media studies. She grew up watching Mister Rogers and wrote about his message to "look for the helpers" in a piece for the school newspaper, *The Miami Hurricane*. Today, she enjoys writing about film and TV, and hopes to follow Rogers in his commitment to changing media for the better—even though her sweater collection is nowhere nearly as impressive! Blame the South Florida heat.

Index

Index of Episodes